Schrader on Schrader
& Other Writings

REVISED EDITION

Schrader on Schrader

& Other Writings

Revised edition

Edited by
Kevin Jackson

faber and faber

Schrader on Schrader & Other Writings first published in 1990
by Faber and Faber Limited
The Bindery, 51 Hatton Garden,
London ECIN 8HN
This revised edition first published in 2004
Published in the United States by Faber and Faber Inc.
an affiliate of Farrar, Straus and Giroux LLC, New York

Printed by CPI Group (UK) Ltd, Croydon CR0 4YY

Paul Schrader and Kevin Jackson are hereby identified as authors of
this work in accordance with Section 77 of the Copyright, Designs
and Patents Act 1988

A CIP record for this book
is available from the British Library

ISBN 978–0–571–22176–9

FSC
www.fsc.org
MIX
Paper | Supporting
responsible forestry
FSC® C013604

Printed and bound in the UK on FSC® certified paper in line with our continuing
commitment to ethical business practices, sustainability and the environment.
For further information see faber.co.uk/environmental-policy

Contents

List of Illustrations

Acknowledgements

The principal debt is, of course, to Paul Schrader himself. The interviews comprising this revised edition were recorded at intervals between 1989 and the present, very often when Schrader was at work on the films under discussion, and under these trying circumstances the thoughtfulness and coherence of his responses were all the more striking.

Thanks for assistance, editorial, practical and otherwise – are also due to Simona Benzakein, Bernardo Bertolucci, Walter Donohue, Dr Glyn and Mrs Evie Johnson, Richard Kelly, Tony Mosher, Roger Parsons, Linda Reisman, Liz Rigbey, Jane Robertson, Thomas Sutcliffe and David Thompson.

Stills and other photographs appear by courtesy of Paul Schrader and BFI Stills, Posters and Designs, as well as Artificial Eye, BFI Distribution, Columbia Pictures, Erre Productions, Entertainment Films, Rank Film Distributors (UK), Warner Brothers and Weintraub Screen Entertainment. The portrait of Charles and Ray Eames is reproduced by permission of the British Architectural Library, RIBA.

A note on the editor

Kevin Jackson has wide experience of television and radio as producer, writer and presenter. He was associate arts editor of the *Independent* and is a freelance writer, broadcaster and lecturer.

His publications include *Invisible Forms: Curiosities of Literature*, *The Language of Cinema*, *The Verbals: Conversations with Iain Sinclair*, *Letters of Introduction*, and as editor, *The Humphrey Jennings Film Reader* and *The Oxford Book of Money*. He has also edited editions of the *Revolutionary Sonnets* of Anthony Burgess and the *Anatomy of Melancholy* by Robert Burton.

Introduction to the Revised Edition

Morocco, November 2002. After twenty years or so away from studio film-making, Paul Schrader is, quite suddenly and unexpectedly, in charge of a big-budget (rumour has it, about $45 million), high-profile production: *Exorcist: The Beginning*. Long since used to cutting corners, making his independent films quickly, light-footedly and modestly, Schrader once again has the chance to paint on a big canvas. By far the biggest canvas of his career, in fact, since the latest addition to the *Exorcist* canon is a period film on a grand scale – a prequel to the events portrayed in the previous three, modern-day films, set partly in Holland towards the end of World War Two, but mainly in the heart of Kenya a couple of years later, as British rule of the territory begins to falter.

Since Kenya itself proved to be an unsuitable location, and the government of Morocco offers generous incentives to visitors from Hollywood, the Kenyan scenes are being shot in a replica village here, freshly built by the production design team inside the walls of a rambling industrial compound, about half an hour's drive from the northern suburbs of Marrakesh. Just a few miles further north still, amongst the weird, other-worldly rock formations of the desert, bustling teams of local workmen are busy building a full-scale artificial mountain face (polystyrene, but utterly convincing even from a few inches away) which, as shooting proceeds, will gradually be excavated by diggers to reveal layer upon layer of ancient chapels . . . and still more ancient evils. A gaping pit near the foot of the fake mountain yields up a (polystyrene) statue of St Michael pinning down the Dragon. The Dragon's face will be all too familiar to anyone who has gone through William Friedkin's original *The Exorcist* using the frame-advance button. The Dutch scenes – which portray a moral dilemma in the vein of *Sophie's Choice* – will be shot on sound stages in Rome.

This chapter of the *Exorcist* legend features Stellan Skarsgard, the most eminent Swedish actor of his generation, in the role of Father Lankaster Merrin, previously taken by Max Von Sydow, the most eminent Swedish actor of the preceding generation. Skarsgard's fellow players include the polyglot French actress Clara Bellar, as a Jewish missionary doctor who somehow survived the Nazi extermination camps, and Gabriel Mann, as the youthful Father Francis, whose faith has yet to receive the crushing blow which has made Merrin abandon the Church to lose himself in archaeology.

Until 'Quiet!' is called and filming starts, though, it's not always easy for the visitor to pick out the costumed leading players from the hundreds of other people milling around inside the phoney village. There are dozens of extras here, most of the light-skinned ones dressed as British soldiers (though few of them speak more than a word or two of English), most of the dark-skinned ones dressed in traditional tribal costume (though quite a lot of them are Londoners through-and-through, and have needed dialect coaching for their African-accented dialogue). There are countless technicians, caterers, assistant directors, animal wranglers, animals – camels, dogs, a frighteningly vicious hyena – drivers, gofers, military advisers, tutors and chaperones for the child actors: all the standard members of a big cinematic army and its camp-followers. The great Italian cinematographer Vittorio Storaro, the only man within miles wearing a tie, strides around the compound in an elegant light-weight suit, co-ordinating his personal lighting team with the air of a world-class conductor leading his orchestra through a Mahler symphony.

And at the centre of it all, chain-smoking but otherwise looking remarkably calm despite the serious shooting delays caused by unseasonal rain, is a stocky man dressed in polo shirt, shorts and baseball cap: Schrader himself. Just a few months earlier, Schrader had not the faintest idea that such a lavish production was about to fall into his hands. (The process by which it happened is fully explained in the interviews which follow.) By pleasing co-incidence, it was in the first edition of *Schrader on Schrader* (p.167, to be exact) that the director expressed his opinion that the original *Exorcist* film contained the greatest metaphor in the history of the cinema – God and the Devil locked in a single room, fighting over the soul of a young girl. That declaration of interest seems to have played no part in landing Schrader this job; but Schrader's unforeseen passage from offering critical observations on the supernatural franchise to directing its latest avatar gives this revised and updated edition an agreeable sense of symmetry.

*

Schrader on Schrader was first published in 1990, and covered his unique, tripartite career as critic, screenwriter and director up to the shooting of *The Comfort of Strangers* in the late months of 1989. (The Venetian apartment in which the four main characters danced through their deadly seduction rites was built on a sound stage just outside Rome; to our collective wonder, we spent one evening glued to CNN as the Berlin Wall fell.) In the thirteen years between that shoot and the post-production of *Exorcist: The Beginning* in the summer of 2003, Schrader has written many more screenplays, both unproduced and produced – most notably *Bringing Out The Dead* for Martin Scorsese – and has directed another half-dozen films: *Light Sleeper, Witch Hunt, Touch, Affliction, Forever Mine,* and *Auto Focus.* Though the discussions of these films later in this book are intended to be comprehensible and, with luck, interesting even to readers who have never seen them, and the extended filmography includes plot synopses, a fingernail résumé of those films and their commercial and critical fates will probably be useful at this point.

Light Sleeper, starring Willem Dafoe as a middle-aged drug dealer anxious to find a way out of his dangerous career, was intended by Schrader as the third episode of a series of character studies, depicting an existential loner in his twenties (Travis Bickle in *Taxi Driver*), his thirties (Julian Kay in *American Gigolo*) and his forties. He has since written, and hopes soon to direct, *The Walker*, which revisits this lonely archetype in his fifties, and discovers him to be a wealthy, gay escort of politicians' wives in Washington, DC. *Light Sleeper* split critics between those who think that it may be Schrader's best film, or at any rate an outstanding achievement by any standards, and those who found the film's violent denouement and final prison sequence at once too genre-based and too similar to the Bresson-inspired conclusion of *American Gigolo.*

Witch Hunt came to Schrader from the producer Gale Ann Hurd, at a time when he was frustrated at his inability to make other films he had written, and was therefore relieved to have a ready-made project just waiting to be shot. Financed by and shown on HBO, the film was a sequel of sorts to a well-received earlier HBO feature, *Cast a Deadly Spell*, which combined elements of 1940s film noir pastiche and the murky supernatural horrors of the strange American writer H.P. Lovecraft. *Witch Hunt* jumps forward to the 1950s, and amusingly transforms the McCarthyite witch hunt for Communist infiltrators in the movie industry into a much more literal kind of pursuit of witches and warlocks. As we discover in the Populuxe opening sequence, sorcery has become a potent if disreputable tool in the hands of Hollywood; actors rely on spells and amulets to retain their star quality, and curses destroy the weak and the unwary. Schrader's lightest film by far, it went straight to video in the UK and has seldom been seen, let alone discussed – a shame, since it has (pun almost unintended) charm as well as wit, and shows a deftness of comic touch that might not have been predicted from his more intense dramas.

Touch, again, combines elements of the supernatural with comedy of various registers, from social satire to fantasy to downright slapstick (hence the portly presence of Tom Arnold). Adapted and updated from one of Elmore Leonard's earliest urban novels, it sketches the sordid but often incompetent media circus which develops around a handsome young faith-healer and stigmatic (Skeet Ulrich.) The excellent cast includes Bridget Fonda – sexy and touching as the stigmatic's eventual girl-friend – and Christopher Walken, and the film as a whole has a sprightly, upbeat tone, but did not find much of an audience.

Affliction, discussed at considerable length below, is an adaptation of Russell Banks' highly respected novel about a profoundly troubled and potentially murderous local sheriff (Nick Nolte) and his tangled relationship with a violently abusive father (James Coburn) and distant younger brother (Willem Dafoe). The film earned unexpected Oscar nominations for Nolte and Coburn, and the Academy Award itself for Coburn. It was a considerable critical success, and may well come to be seen as Schrader's masterpiece.

Forever Mine, a project Schrader had been trying to make for well over a decade, is a romantic fable set in the early 1970s and the late 1980s, about a poor, love-smitten young suitor (Joseph Fiennes) who is shot and left for dead by his lover's rich gangster boyfriend, but returns, transformed, many years later to claim both her and his bloody revenge. A troubled project, it never went on theatrical release in the United States. Finally, Schrader made *Auto Focus*, a sly, inventive and deadpan comedy of self-deception which follows the life of a minor television star, Bob Crane (Hogan of *Hogan's Heroes*) as he drifts from prosperity into nonentity and the ever-diminishing pleasures of narcissistic, home-made porn movies. Cool in both the emotional and the demotic senses of the adjective, *Auto Focus* was, again, very well received by many reviewers.

How does this mixed track record stand up to that of the years between *Blue Collar* (1978) and *The Comfort of Strangers* (1990)?

Pretty well by most criteria, I would argue; and astonishingly well in the light of both a dramatically changing film industry and Schrader's own changing circumstances. In the earlier version of this introduction, one of the suggestions I made was that the peculiar fascination of Schrader's work as a director might be seen to derive from a fruitful and highly unusual tension between his different preoccupations: emotional, intellectual, pragmatic. His early screenplays, both for others and for himself, tended to be driven by ferocious emotional need. Think of *Taxi Driver* as the starting point and the template for these works: a film of rage, loneliness, bewilderment, and an aching need for redemption, whether through normal human love or some terrifying act of purgation. To different degrees, the other Schrader protagonists all participated in those pains and hungers – the unreflective ones (Jake La Motta, say) like wounded brutes, the reflective ones (Yukio Mishima, say) with a tragically precise awareness of their own doomed condition.

Harnessed to this fierce emotional dynamo was a degree of intellectual ambition without peer in the commercial cinema. One of Schrader's most potent mental escape-routes from the privations of his childhood among the religious fundamentalists of Grand Rapids, Michigan was his discovery, late in his teens, of the classic European (and Japanese) art cinema – the highly personal works of Bergman, Bresson, Cocteau, Dreyer, Godard. He went on from these austere masters to a more thoroughgoing acquaintance with cinema history, but that select group of visionaries provided him with his compass points, his deep sense of how the cinema could function as a means of artistic expression, and even – see his precocious critical work *Transcendental Style in Film: Ozu, Bresson, Dreyer* – as a vessel for Ultimate Truth.

Crucially, Schrader did not go on to work in the protected zone of the art cinema, and would probably not have wanted to, even had the modes of aristocratic or state patronage enjoyed by many of the older Europeans been open to him. Like the missionaries who had been held up to Calvinist schoolboys as heroic exemplars in his childhood, he wanted to go preaching in the marketplace, and bring his visions to the masses rather than to a coterie of like-minded intellectuals. (Nor was he immune to the lures of material success; such indifference is the prerogative of saints.) It was a quixotic ambition, and a dangerous one for a man who does not relish compromise. Torn in this way, a director might easily end up either watering down challenging material to the point where it becomes denatured, even bland; or, alternatively, producing superficially commercial matter which proves so spiky and rebarbative that the mass audience is repelled. What is truly remarkable about Schrader's early career is not that he sometimes erred in one direction or the other, but that he so often achieved the type of work that could delight the drifting Friday night multiplex-goer and the fastidious *cinephile* alike.

Schrader has maintained these same drives and ambitions in the years since *The Comfort of Strangers*, but his work has also modulated in response both to his own personal development and to the state of the art and the market. To put it simply, he has matured. Note his remark, later in these interviews (p. 226), about a difficulty he had with *Bringing Out The Dead* – he thought that the lead role should be played by an actor in his twenties, since this was the story of a kind of spiritual collapse that only a young man suffers. When he wrote his earliest work, he was still within hailing distance of the emotional intensities of adolescence; it is no coincidence that, every year, new generations of pained boys (not so many girls) discover and are enthralled by *Taxi Driver*.

Like any intelligent man with a difficult past, Schrader still has his share of private demons to wrestle with, but he is, obviously, no longer entirely plausible as an angry, marginal loner: today, he is a man of internationally recognised accomplishment, a contented husband and father of two teenage children, a hard-working and well-paid professional. (And spiritually, he has found himself more at home of late with the urbane and intellectual-friendly Episcopalian church – crudely put, Anglicanism without the Monarchy – than with the hellfire mentality of his upbringing.) Inevitably, his ruling preoccupations have changed, though not necessarily mellowed; again, it is no coincidence that his three most critically acclaimed pieces of the last thirteen years, *Light Sleeper*, *Affliction* and *Auto Focus*, all deal with different versions of the kinds of pain or dislocation or bewilderment that may hit men in their forties and fifties.

Yet these are films which have been produced at a time when the mainstream cinema has gone chasing ever more rabidly after the youth market – which brings us to the second great change of the last decade and a half. Schrader himself, as these interviews show, is somewhat sceptical about the sort of Jeremiad which howls that the cinema has never been more cretinous. He is alert to, and keenly interested in, what the new technologies of the moving image will bring to audio-visual narrative, and what rising generations of film-makers will produce with their digital cameras and internet distribution deals. Sure, he says, it's a bad time for cinema; but then, most times have been bad.

This refusal to give in to the standard middle-aged lament about the worthlessness of the times and the morals is admirable; and Schrader's refusal to live in the past is one of the qualities that have kept his artistic arteries from hardening. (As we have spent more time in each other's company over the years, I have often been struck by the youthfulness of Schrader's appetite for cultural and scientific phenomena: he reads new books, listens to new music, and travels and debates with the avid energy of a wealthy graduate student. Like many interesting people, he is interested in just about everything.) He is, surely, quite right to insist that reports of cinema's death rattle, not long after its first centenary, are mostly silly. Quite apart from the vitality and variety of work coming from Asia, parts of the former Soviet Union, Iran and other nations of the Third World, the American independent cinema has produced countless surprises, shocks and joys in the past decade and a half, and even some big-budget productions have shown a fair share of originality, heart and beauty.

Still, Schrader would also concede that it is important that the last word of this debate should not go to Pollyanna. Granted: there was certainly plenty of dross about in the wonder years of the 1970s, when Schrader and Scorsese and Coppola and Spielberg and Milius and Altman and Rafelson and dozens of others brought wholly new themes and styles and tones to the mainstream American cinema. Even so, a balance has shifted, and the characteristic Hollywood product of today is as formulaic, as compromised, as toothless and as numb to human feeling as it has ever been. Cinema-goers now in their forties are faced with the curious experience of seeing the shared reading matter of their old school playgrounds being reincarnated as monstrously expensive summer movie attractions: *Spider-Man*, *X-Men*, *Daredevil*, *The Hulk* . . .

Only those with vested interests would want to deny that this is a different environment. Different for good, or for ill? In some measure, the answer has to be a matter of generational experience. For those with a comic book or music video sensibility, we are living in a true Golden Age. For those brought up on a more mixed diet of classic Hollywood and the art traditions of Europe and Japan, not to mention other art forms, there has seldom been less incentive to venture away from a quiet evening with a book. Hence, it seems to me, the wholly unanticipated and largely unwitting switch of emphasis between the interviews which filled the first edition and those which now supplement and complete it. Though it still seemed pertinent enough to talk about ideas and styles, metaphors and shooting methods, the very nature of the stories Schrader had to tell about his working life (project X was delayed for three, or five, or thirteen years; project Y was scuppered by an actor; project Z was dropped at the last minute when funding dropped out . . .) meant that there had to be a much stronger and more sustained attention to financial realities. Put very briefly, the new interviews show just how hard it is to make a Paul Schrader film in the era of *Charlie's Angels: Full Throttle*.

Nil desperandum, though: this addendum to the first *Schrader on Schrader* is not an extended whine, but the fascinating story of how, with enough tenacity and strategic thinking (and the odd stroke of luck), an artist with a set of wholly unfashionable preoccupations can still continue to operate and, at times, to add triumphantly to an already distinguished body of work. For example, there is nothing else in American cinema quite like *Affliction*: deeply rooted in specifically North American experience, but as unremittingly raw and bleak and emotionally wrenching as a Dostoyevsky novel; and as gracefully deceptive in form as a fiction by Nabokov. And *Affliction* is still just a few years old; who knows what other surprises Schrader will bring us in the next thirteen years, in the wake of his *Exorcist* adventure . . . ?

At that point, the first draft of this introduction should have stopped. But events have overtaken the writing, and in a way that is only too painfully apt to the discussion. In August 2003, Schrader e-mailed me to say that the head of Morgan Creek had watched the first completed cut of *Exorcist: The Beginning*, and – even though Schrader's film is painstakingly faithful to the shooting script – waxed outraged at the fact that it was not enough of a genre horror movie. He tried to fire Schrader, but discovered that the DGA would not let him. He asked Schrader to quit, but Schrader refused. Finally, on September 15, 2003, it was duly announced to the media that Paul Schrader and Morgan Creek had parted company on the film due to 'creative differences'. Once again, the industry had showed just how hard it can make life for Paul Schrader.

Kevin Jackson
September 2003

CHAPTER I

Background: The Road from Grand Rapids

KEVIN JACKSON: *Critics have made a great deal of your strict Calvinist upbringing in Grand Rapids, Michigan, but the exact details have tended to be hazy. For example, what nationality were your parents and grandparents?*

PAUL SCHRADER: My grandparents on my mother's side came over from Friesland. My father's background is much less clear. His own father was German, which is why it's a German name, and he came down from Canada. But the community in which I grew up was Dutch. My father came into this community when he married my mother and she converted him.

When I was very young my grandparents would still speak Dutch and there were still Dutch services in the afternoons, though they gave that up some time in my boyhood. When I went to Amsterdam a few years ago I had a real *frisson*, because I was riding a bus and behind me there was a mother chastising her little boy, and though I don't understand Dutch the intonations brought back a flood of memory.

My mother's family settled about half an hour away from Grand Rapids, and they got all this swamp land virtually for free. Because they were Dutch they knew what to do with it: they dyked it up and became celery farmers. There were so many Dutch families in Grand Rapids that when they split the class up alphabetically the halfway mark would usually fall somewhere between the Vans and the Van Ders. If you were just a Van, like a Van Anderson, you were still in the first half of the alphabet.

KJ: *There's a joking reference to that in* Hardcore, *and it sounds as if the view of Grand Rapids in that film is close to life.*
PS: The montage of churches at the beginning is made up of Reformed churches I knew, and I worked in that factory and so on. It's pretty close.

KJ: *And was your father a businessman like Jake VanDorn in* Hardcore?
PS: Yes. He worked for a pipeline company that maintained the pipes that

ran from Canada through to Ohio, so he was not in the farm business, unlike my mother's side of the family.

KJ: *Did that make you a little more middle class than some of your schoolmates?*
PS: Yes. Grand Rapids is a town that's about a third Polish Catholic and a third Dutch Calvinist and the other third sort of mediates the town and runs it. The Polish always lived on the north and west sides and the Dutch on the south and east, but we always lived in the Polish area because it was closer to where my mother's relatives all lived.

My church had a very strong educational background, but not a very enlightened one, particularly when it came to the arts. They didn't really have much sense of visual arts; they were still very Cromwellian in that way. Of my ninth-grade graduating class, only one other student went on to college, and he went in as a minister. The kids I hung around with when I was growing up were more manual labour and farm oriented than our family was.

KJ: *Does that account in part for your sympathy for uneducated working-class characters in films like* Blue Collar?
PS: *Blue Collar* comes right out of that background. Grand Rapids was a furniture-manufacturing town, but it was also one of the satellites of the auto industry in Detroit – Grand Rapids made the ashtrays and windshields and stuff.

KJ: *Were you always an academically gifted child?*
PS: I wasn't the brightest, but I was one of the more original, with that kind of creative intellect that's always scheming and putting things together. As a kid I was one of those door-to-door capitalist types: I was always selling things, and when I was thirteen or fourteen I started my own little store to sell flowers. That kind of community is very oriented to business success, and of course it's a precept of that type of Calvinism that God rewards his own with wealth, so that material success and religious success go hand in hand. Of course, that's also ensured by having a closed economic system – you don't buy from Catholics, you only buy from each other.

KJ: *Did your creativity manifest itself in any way other than through being an entrepreneur? Did you write from an early age, for example?*
PF: No. It wasn't encouraged very much. I do remember that from very early on I wanted to be a minister. I had a surfeit of religious education –

not only church on Sunday, but chapel every day in school, religious classes in school, Calvinist Cadet Corps instead of the Boy Scouts, and all the youth groups were run by the Church.

All the way through high school I never had any real contact with people outside our Church. There were people on the block, but my mother disapproved of us going into their houses too much. It was television that started to break that down. When television arrived they tried to keep it out, and I think rightly, because they saw it as a threat to the ideologically pure community we had, which was the same reason we couldn't see movies. But what they found was that the kids would be going down the block to watch television, and we'd be sitting there in the neighbours' house surrounded by statues of Mary and watching *Howdy Doody*. At which point they sort of gave up and said, 'Well, if we have TV in our own homes at least we can control what they see.'

One of the reasons for my interest in becoming a missionary was that I was named after my mother's two favourite biblical characters, Paul and Joseph – Paul, this evangelical misfit who transforms the world by crossing it on foot, and Joseph, who is maligned by his brothers and goes off and becomes a prince in Egypt. So they were very grandiose fantasies, and during the long, boring church services I used just to sit and read about them in the Bible because they were so fascinating. I had a very strong fixation on St Paul; in fact I was more interested in Paul than in Christ. In some ways what we believe today is Paulinism. Christ is like Socrates: a mysterious figure we only know about through Plato, just as we only know about Christ through Paul. Paul had his hands in all the Gospels. There's good reason to believe he wrote Luke and he supervised the rewriting of the others.

And Paul's martyrdom always interested me more than Christ's. If there was one passage I read and reread, it was the last letter to Timothy and Paul's farewell: 'I fought the good fight'. So whether or not it was because my name was Paul, this is what I really wanted to do. I wanted to go into a city and stand on a stone and start to talk, just the way Harry Dean Stanton does in *The Last Temptation of Christ*, bringing the good news and then getting stoned for it. Of course, martyrdom was always part of the appeal.

KJ: *Was the Bible also the main influence on you when you started to write?*
PS: Well, we read the Bible every day and we read sequentially, so that nothing was omitted. We read all the begats – there would be a week of sitting around the table listening to your father reading 'So-and-so begat so-and-so' – but there would also be fascinating things. Those Bible stories

1 Schrader's name saint: Harry Dean Stanton as Paul in *The Last Temptation of Christ* (1988).

are such potent stories, and, yes, they continue to leave a mark on the things I write.

The other big source of images and fantasies at the time came from the religious songs we sang at school. Imagine a bunch of grade-school kids all standing around singing 'This world is not my home' – it's very peculiar. And there's the rich blood imagery of it all. Another song I remember very vividly is 'There is a fount drawn from Emanuel's veins' – that is a very potent image: a fountain of blood coming out of Jesus's arms. Christianity really is a blood cult and a death cult; as much as they say otherwise and talk about the God of Love, it really does focus on the Passion and the bleeding, and those are the images that hit a child.

KJ: *What about your non-religious reading at the time?*
PS: All the usual staples: Hemingway, Stephen Crane, Mark Twain, Ring Lardner. I think the first real big book I read was *Les Misérables*; it's certainly the first one I remember reading. Apart from the Bible, the most influential book of my adolescence was an illustrated edition of *Pilgrim's Progress*, the Slough of Despond, the Golden City and all that.

KJ: *But you had no idea of an artistic vocation?*
PS: Not at all, not at all. But I was always an English major, as was my brother Leonard, who was three years older; I think that we were both spurred on by the same teacher. In ninth grade we had a woman who had a very vibrant attitude towards literature, and though it doesn't sound like much today, I remember her standing on her chair in front of the class reading Lady Macbeth's soliloquy and I found that just stunning; the idea that there was another world out there apart from the religious one. Up to then all my escapist fantasies had been couched in religious contexts, but that showed me that there was a way of escape to another world.

KJ: *Was it at this time that the cinema also showed you a means of escaping? There's a much-repeated story about your sneaking off to see your first film at the age of seventeen or so.*
PS: Well, we had TV at home by this time, and on the *Mickey Mouse Club* they always advertised the new Disney films, so a friend and I went off after school and took a bus downtown and sneaked into the theatre. We saw *The Absent-Minded Professor* and I was very unimpressed by it. But then one summer I was staying with some relatives down in Indiana who were a little less strict than my family, and my aunt just said, 'Oh, why don't you kids all go see a movie?' I was amazed. So we went to the local theatre and

saw *Wild in the Country*, with Elvis Presley and Tuesday Weld . . . and then I realized why my mother didn't want me to see movies.

KJ: *So the moment of revelation came with* Wild in the Country?
PS: Yes, and then my mother started allowing me to see one or two other films. She allowed me to see *Spartacus*, which I wanted to see desperately, not only because of the romantic boy's aspect but because of the martyr-dom.

KJ: *And did you conceive the ambition of becoming a film-maker at this time?*
PS: No, no – that was just not something that anyone we knew did. It was just not in the realm of possibility.

KJ: *So when did you start to feel the first stirrings of rebellion against your background?*
PS: I think the first stirrings were to do with blacks, because it was a racist kind of background; our Church was the same as the one in South Africa. There was one particular episode which my mother used to mention – she blamed everything that happened to me and everything I did afterwards on this one event.

I really wanted to get out of Grand Rapids and see something of the world, so I hit on the idea of going to military school for the summer. I bugged my parents for years to let me go, and finally they gave in and sent me for the summer to a school in Virginia, on the border of North Carolina, called Hargrave Military Academy. When I got there I found that I was the only one who was there of his own volition: the rest of them were basically the miscreant children of the rich who were sent off by their parents. Everything came very much to the fore that summer, which I recall very vividly.

We had a Jewish boy on our floor who was relentlessly hazed. Now I hadn't even met a Jew before; I had no idea why he was being hazed, and so I took his side. And at the same time Martin Luther King was marching just about ten miles away across the border – this was in a segregationalist area where the whole town was divided by a line. The Commandant of our school offered to arm the students to protect the town, whereupon the Governor slapped a curfew on the whole school, but I snuck out and watched the marches and saw all the people being arrested.

To show my disquiet about all this, I made a kind of protest in my civics class. This was taught by the wife of the Commandant, who routinely referred to the Supreme Court as the 'Nine black-robed Satans', so I did my

2 Tuesday Weld and Elvis Presley in *Wild in the Country*, directed by Philip Dunne in 1961.

term paper on the book *Black Like Me*, which was about the experiences of a white writer who posed as a black in the South. And of course I got back the paper marked with a D or something and with 'This is not true' written all across it. Clearly the perversity of doing something which flew in the face of that institution was a flowering of a lot of latent rebelliousness on my part, and when I got out of Hargrave and went back to Grand Rapids one of the first things I did that fall was to write a short story about the bullying of a Jewish student.

As I say, my mother always believed that I was never the same after that, and I think she was probably right. All of a sudden there was that little change of environment which let me see the world, and for the first time in my life I was surrounded by kids who were basically non-believers.

KJ: *Did that rebelliousness continue to express itself creatively, or did it take other forms?*

PS: Well, I continued to write. Possibly one other form it took had to do with my going to Calvin College. Calvin was still part college and part seminary; it had begun as a seminary and had spun off a liberal-arts curriculum. In order to graduate you had to major in theology and then you could major in another subject. When I first went to Calvin I was still planning to be a minister, but that changed when I read a biography of Clarence Darrow, the great defender of the little man, a great liberal lawyer. And so the fantasy changed from being an evangelical preacher to being an evangelical social force, a defender of the poor, and that again came out of my summer at Hargrave. So by the time I was in college I was heading towards being a lawyer, but that changed when I took a course in public speaking and realized that I was not comfortable in that role. The fantasy didn't work because I wasn't any good at it. So then I moved on to writing, which was another way of being evangelical without having to be a public figure.

The other thing that happened when I went to college was that I fell in with a crowd of kids from New Jersey, who although they were from our Church were far more liberal, and they were already big drinkers. All my rebelliousness blossomed in their company, and I spent most of that first year just drinking and doing pranks. I was a very prudish kid in a very prudish environment, so the main reason for my bad behaviour was sexual displacement, just being too shy to get in the dating game and too inhibited to feel comfortable with any sexual life at all. It all exploded in this kind of vandalism and eventually I was thrown out of the dorms because I set my desk on fire.

KJ: *Was this high spirits or a mark of desperation?*

PS: I was having a good time. I remember very vividly the first time I got drunk, which was with these kids at Calvin, and I remember feeling an extraordinary sense of freedom and saying, 'Oh, I don't have to feel like this – there's another way to feel. I don't have to be a prisoner in my own body – there's another me and alcohol has flooded it out.' Eventually creative work slipped right into that same slot.

So that time was just a kind of explosion, just violating and doing everything wrong that I could, and finally it came to the point where I got thrown out of college. My father got me back in by – I suspect – donating some money. Then my brother pulled me aside and said, 'You know, you're not the only person who feels like this. There's a lot of other kids here who have the same attitude, and we all work at the newspaper.' So even though my brother didn't really want to let me in, because I was his kid brother, he brought me around to the newspaper office and I started hanging out with that crowd. And then I became involved in essentially the same type of vandalism, except that now the vandalism was confined to the world of ideas, and the primary form of vandalism was to do with movies. The best way to call down the wrath of the institution was to press that movie button, because we were not supposed to write about movies in the school paper; and so I got involved in movies as a means of revolt.

What happened was that there was a little cinema in town that was going broke, and in desperation they started running art films. They ran all the early Bergman films because the kids from Calvin would come and see them, partly because the sensibility was the same, that northern Protestant sensibility, but partly because there was a great sense of revolt, and little by little the battle was won. The following year the students ran a review of the next Bergman film and the authorities didn't have the paper shut down; then some students set up a film club and started showing movies off campus, and of course the paper would then run a review of the movies they were going to show.

KJ: *So you started to run the film club as well as write?*

PS: Yes, in my sophomore and junior years. Because the film club was off campus the college had some problems with it, so they agreed to let it be on campus, though not officially sanctioned, so that they could keep an eye on the films that were being shown. So I got in there and started programming more and more controversial films, and not only would we have a review of the film in the *Chimes* (the college newspaper), often written by myself, but I would get some of the more liberal members of the faculty, particularly the theology faculty, to have a seminar afterwards. The

Reverend So-and-so and a professor from the sociology department would sit behind a table and discuss the film, and the more controversial the film the more powerhouse religious people I would talk into participating. By the time I showed *Viridiana*, which was the straw that broke the camel's back,[1] I had a number of ministers up there; besides which, the events were becoming extremely popular and we would fill up an auditorium for 500 people.

All this time, much of the money from the screenings was going into my pockets and the pockets of my friends, because there was no official organization, and so finally the college saw that they were going to have to have some kind of control over the society and they asked me to write a constitution for it. So I wrote a constitution which they accepted on condition I had nothing to do with running it. Over the years in which the film club had been semi-legal, the selection of films was very intense: *Ordet* and *Marienbad* and *Nazarin*,[2] all idea films; but as soon as it became legalized and part of the non-curriculum agenda at the college, the entertainment forces took over and the films became progressively less adventurous. Today they just show pap films.

KJ: *And you were writing about films all this time?*
PS: Well, writing reviews was how I broke into the newspaper circle before I had any power, but by the end of my junior year I had this reputation for being trouble and it had become obvious that I had moved the locus of my troublemaking into the arts.

I said, 'Well, you won't let me run the film council so I'll run the newspaper instead,' but in order to run the newspaper you had to be elected, and they wouldn't let me be in the election because of my record. At the time I was going with a girl whom I subsequently married, who was a straight-A student, and so I said to her, 'You run the paper. They'll let you run it because they don't think you'll cause any trouble, and I'll be the associate editor,' and sure enough they let her run it, and by the time the next semester rolled around she was as radicalized as I was.

I remember having a meeting with the staff of the paper that spring – the spring of 1968 – and saying, 'The way things are going in the country right now, if we don't get the paper shut down we haven't done our job.' But the trick was not to get the paper shut down until the very end of the school year. The previous fall there was a big march on Washington, and we used school funds to send a bus off on the march – this is from a very conservative student body, a body that had voted for Goldwater. So they went off and came back with this big picture of the Calvin flag out in front of the Pentagon with all the other marchers, and there was a big headline in the paper saying 'Chimes Remonstrates War at Pentagon'. The college authorities found out that the school had bankrolled the protest, but they didn't throw us out, and that spring I was starting to get a little worried that they wouldn't throw us out: the people who ran the discipline committee were hip to what I was up to and saw that what we really wanted to do was make them look like fuddy-duddies, and that to throw us out would be playing into our hands.

But then, finally, an occasion did arise that we were able to get them on. Dick Gregory was going to speak on campus, but he was disinvited by the college President because of his liberal views, so we wrote this up but still didn't get fired. The next week we said, 'This is it – everything we've got,' and ran a big front-page editorial attacking the President, demanding a public apology and insinuating that the whole thing had been racially motivated and basically just ridiculing the college authorities and throwing down the gauntlet. That doesn't sound like much today, but in that context they were furious, so they shut us down and in the last month of college we started a second newspaper called *Spectacle*, which I was editor of. I think we managed to bring out three issues before the end of the year.

It's funny – a few months ago I got a Calvin alumni magazine which had a big write-up of the great *Chimes* protest twenty years on, but in fact the *Chimes* protest was about twenty students out of a student body of about 4,000 just making as much fucking trouble as they could.

KJ: *When you describe yourself as 'radicalized', was that in any coherent political sense or was it just vandalism by other means?*
PS: It's difficult to separate the hard politics from the fashion politics. The *Chimes* office looked like an outpost of China Books, with posters of Ho Chi Minh and Mao Tse-tung. It looked out over the ground floor of the campus, and it didn't really matter as much whether or not we believed it all as that we knew it would drive them crazy.

But then I became involved in the anti-war movement and carried it on when I went to UCLA and got involved in protests there. My politics were very much on the Left: pro-Vietcong, pro-Civil Rights. There was a period of two or three years when the fringe Left and the middle Left met, and then as soon as the war was over they went their separate ways. The war held these divergent forces together and as soon as the war was over, then for a lot of people the battle was over.

KJ: *What else did you do at college apart from run the newspaper and stir up trouble? Did you continue to study hard?*
PS: Yes, I was a damn good student, though I remember making a decision

3 Schrader (*right*) as a student journalist at Calvin College.

whether or not to be an A student, and I ended up as an A-minus/B-plus student, because I deliberately took a number of courses in subjects I knew I wouldn't get As in, like music and German lit. I had enough presence of mind to know that I was there for an education, not to get As, and I was a real student in a real student's school. We had to take six hours of Calvin's *Institutes* alone, and courses in contemporary theology – Martin Buber, Heidegger and all that – and you really had to know your stuff, you couldn't weasel around it.

KJ: *When did you realize that your interest in films was becoming more than a matter of intellectual vandalism?*
PS: By the time I was in my sophomore year I had moved away from the minister fantasy and the lawyer fantasy and now saw myself as a writer, a journalist and social critic. Then when I ran the film club I started reading about all these films, but with the exception of the ones I hired there was no way of seeing any of them. So one summer, the summer of 1967, I came up here to New York City and took three courses in film at Columbia just to educate myself. I also took a job, but I got fired from it.

This business, the film business, is the only one I've ever been able to hold a job in. I've been fired from every other job I ever had. I even got fired from my father's company.

KJ: *For insubordination?*
PS: Basically. Sooner or later a guy always comes up to you and says 'Do this,' and you say 'No, I've got a better idea,' and he says 'I don't care about your better idea,' and you say 'Well, I don't care about yours.' And the next thing you know you're out of a job. So I realized that whatever living I was going to make would have to be in the freelance field, and that there had to be a way to outwit the system and make a living by being my own boss. In business if you come up with a good product you can be your own boss, so the problem was to find the same thing in the arts.

So I came up to Columbia and took these courses, and after class I would go out drinking until three or four in the morning with fellow students. One night I was sitting there talking about Pauline Kael's *I Lost It at the Movies*, which had just come out, and saying how much I liked it, and one of the other people sitting there said, 'Well, let's go and see Pauline.' It turned out that this was a guy named Paul Warshow, who was the son of the critic Robert Warshow. Pauline had liked his father, who was dead, and had taken Paul under her wing, so we went over to her place on West End and talked to her. I hadn't seen many films, but I was full of ideas and I still must have had this notion of becoming a minister in the Church. The

4 Student radical: Schrader at an anti-Vietnam war rally.

first night I was there the conversation just went on all night long, with real arguments – I liked the films she didn't like and vice versa – and I ended up sleeping on her couch. The next morning as I left she said to me, 'You don't want to be a minister – you want to be a film critic.'

I went over there a number of times that summer, and when I left to go back to Grand Rapids Pauline said to me that I should leave Calvin right away and go to UCLA, where she had a friend, Colin Young – who's now at the National Film School in Britain – and she thought she could get me in. But I only had one year to go at Calvin and I wanted to run the newspaper, so I went back. But I kept in touch with her throughout the year and sent her all my articles.

One of them was about her, and I'm sort of chagrined about it now because it's so wrong-headed, but I believed it at the time, and it won a contest and was published in a book of the winners. It was called 'Matthew Arnold in L.A.'. I think the reason I wrote it was that my favourite course in college was Victorian lit. I wrote my thesis on post-'Kubla Khan' Coleridge, concentrating on his sermons. I loved John Henry Newman and Pater and that whole group, and I guess between loving what Matthew Arnold had done and loving what Pauline was doing I had to find some way to compare them. The truth was, of course, that they were totally different.

In my last spring at Calvin I wrote to Pauline and said, 'You were right – I want to go to UCLA,' and even though I had no training and theoretically UCLA was a hard school to get into, Colin Young just took Pauline's word for it and let me in. So in the fall of 1968 I came to California and entered UCLA film school.

Notes

1 Luis Buñuel's *Viridiana* (1961) stars Sylvia Pinal as an idealistic young nun whose charitable actions meet with cruel ingratitude. Calvin College was not alone in being offended by the film (and particularly by its finale, a blasphemous parody of the Last Supper): it was banned in the director's native Spain as soon as it was released.
2 Carl Dreyer's *Ordet* (*The Word*) (1954); Alain Resnais's *L'Année Dernière à Marienbad* (*Last Year in Marienbad*) (1961); Luis Buñuel's *Nazarin* (1958).

CHAPTER 2

The Critic: *L.A. Free Press* to *Transcendental Style*

JACKSON: *Shortly after you arrived at UCLA you began to write film criticism professionally. How did that come about?*

SCHRADER: Well, that was sort of ironic. I was working part time, delivering for Chicken Delight, which is a take-out place, and I was making about $20 a week. A professor at UCLA who was a friend of Pauline's told me that the *L.A. Free Press* were looking for an above-ground critic – there would be two critics every week, an underground movie critic and a critic for the conventional theatrical things. So I submitted a long review of *Faces*[1] to them and they liked it and hired me, and they were also paying me $20 a week! I said, well, this is great! I get to see free movies, I get to write about them, and I get the same amount of money as for delivering chicken. It couldn't be better!

Looking back on those publications is a little strange, because I'm clearly the most conservative writer on the whole magazine. But what happened next was that I went to them and said, 'You're paying me $20 a week for this article. If you will let me have a block, a heading, with my name on it, which will be printed every week, I'll give you your $20 back.' They said, 'That's fair,' and so they printed this box that said 'Movies: Paul Schrader'. I wanted it so that people would remember my name rather than just being another by-line, and I still run into people today who say, 'Oh, I remember your stuff in the *Free Press*,' and of course they don't really remember the reviews, they remember that little black box.

KJ: *Did you feel constrained to write in some approximation of an underground house style, or did you write as you saw fit?*

PS: I got fired over that very issue. It happened in 1969, over *Easy Rider*. I hadn't been getting much pressure from anyone at the *Free Press* and all of a sudden this movie came along and I realized that it was going to be a big film in the underground. I got to the screening and Peter Fonda was sitting next to me, Tommy Smothers was on the other side and Dennis Hopper was sitting behind me. Nothing like this had ever happened to me before. So I saw the movie and I hated it and I went back to my editor and said,

'Look, this is going to be a big underground film and a big *Free Press* film and I hate it, so I would like you to run side-by-side reviews, one by me and one in favour, because I don't think you're going to be comfortable attacking this film – it's just not politically correct for you.'

But the editor said, 'No, we are the *Free Press*. We are free and you are our critic. You write your review.' So I wrote this extremely long review – it's actually one of the better pieces I've done – and lo and behold I was fired.

The editor backed me but the publisher was furious. The staff demanded a meeting to discuss why the *Free Press* had panned *Easy Rider*, and the editor stood up against the staff and against the publisher, and the upshot was that we were both fired. The dispute became a kind of *cause célèbre* – Diana Trilling wrote an article in the *Atlantic* about *Easy Rider* and used the fight over my article as indicative of the hypocrisy of the Left.

KJ: *But you went on soon afterwards to found your own magazine, didn't you?*
PS: It was an already existing magazine called *Cinema*, and I weaseled my way into the editorship. When I took it over it was a sort of vanity magazine, owned by a fellow who had a clothing store in Beverly Hills and a restaurant and a disco called the Daisy Disco. If you were a member of the Daisy your films got written about in *Cinema* and there were big glossy pictures of all his friends in it. I talked him into letting me take it over and to placate him I kept the glossy format, but then I wrote serious articles and did them in little 8-point type because he didn't ever read the copy. As long as there were big glossy pictures he was happy.

KJ: *Your ambitions at this time were entirely focused on being a film critic?*
PS: That's how it seemed at the time, though I now have reason to doubt it. I did an interview with Don Pennebaker for the *Free Press* around the time of *Monterey Pop*, and I really believed at the time that all I ever wanted to do was be a critic, and I'd said that to people for years. Then, a few years ago, I ran into Pennebaker at a festival and I said, 'You may not know this, but I did an interview with you once,' and he said, 'I remember it clearly.' And the reason he remembered it was that he had gone back to his motel room after the interview and the first thing he had said to his girlfriend was, 'Well, there's a guy who won't be a critic long.' My memory of it was just the opposite, but obviously it wasn't true.

KJ: *What were you hoping to achieve through your criticism?*
PS: What people don't understand any more is that around that time, in the

late sixties, criticism was a form of the Movement. Society was going to have to change at every level and we had to carry the message of Godard and Resnais, we had to go to the barricades, and film criticism was revolutionary. This all came to a head in 1968 when the film-makers and film critics shut down the Cannes Film Festival.[2]

So you're talking about a time when film criticism was evangelical in tone. We were all opposed to the staid old critics who just sat in judgement rather than becoming involved, which is why Pauline was so influential: she was a populist, intent on changing people's perceptions, educating them, enlightening them and getting the right people to theatres to see the right films – promoting a film like Godard's *Masculine/Feminine*, for example. Today criticism has lost that edge and become much more a kind of consumer profession.

KJ: *Godard is an obvious case of someone who followed the path from criticism into directing; was he a role model or hero for you at the time?*
PS: *Masculine/Feminine* was the film that really turned me around and seemed to be everything a film could be. It was personal and political and original and sexy; it was a film of my generation, the children of Marx and Coca-Cola, it was our film. *Breathless* really wasn't our film so much, and when *La Chinoise*[3] came along it was a barricades film. You had to take sides: you were either for *La Chinoise* or against it and I was for it.

My course at UCLA was a film-criticism course and didn't involve much practical work, but you did have to make one student film, an 8 mm film, and mine owed a lot to Godard and to *La Chinoise*. It was a Maoist film, a film about student revolutionaries taking over a TV station and broadcasting propaganda. I used a French student as my leading actor, and he was always reading extracts from the Little Red Book and holding it up.

At this time both the students and the faculty had a say in who would be chosen to go ahead to the film-making part of the curriculum, because only a limited number of students could use those resources, and I was not voted ahead: I was put in a limbo category and told to do a second film. I was furious, because I felt that the films that had been voted in were not very good. One of them was a documentary about MacArthur Park, cut to the pop song of the same name, and they had a cake melting in the rain and stuff; whereas although mine was very ragged it was chock-a-block with ideas. So I took that as a signal that I was not to be a film-maker and just went ahead with critical studies.

KJ: *Apart from Pauline Kael, which critics were you reading at the time?*
PS: *Cahiers du Cinéma*[4] was being published in English at that time at

Andrew Sarris's instigation, so I was reading that, and I was reading *Film Quarterly* and *Film Comment*. It's strange: I have a library of all my film books and magazines, and they all end abruptly round about the end of 1972. Up to then I have pretty much everything: all the issues of *Cahiers*, all the issues of *Positif*, all the issues of *Sight and Sound*, all sorts of rare things like every issue of *Sequence*. I read everything at that time, because I saw this as my chosen profession.

Then one day you say, 'I'm no longer that'; you stop reading the books and magazines, and it's amazing how quickly everything just cuts off. Now it's almost impossible for me to read a book about film. Occasionally, about once a year, a book does come up that actually is enlightening, like the one about the Jews in Hollywood or Kazan's autobiography, but I almost never read a traditional book about film.

KJ: *Were you conscious of standing in a particular relation to earlier American film critics?*
PS: I was aware of it, and I was a big promoter of certain traditions. One of the things I tried to do at *Cinema* was to promote Parker Tyler, whom I felt was a major critic who had been segregated into a gay slot and not really appreciated for his insights into what he called 'the pansexuality of cinema', as opposed to the bisexuality of cinema . . . I was very influenced by his work.

KJ: *Was your critical bias more in the direction of considering movies as a cultural phenomenon, or were you interested in close readings of texts?*
PS: The initial intent was to try to emulate Pauline, with a liberal use of the first person plural, which she still uses to this very day: 'We like movies because of X, Y and Z'; and you read this and sort of agree with it and afterwards you think, 'Well, wait a second, is that really why *I* like movies?' But she's very persuasive and I found myself writing in the same fashion: 'People go to movies because they want to identify with certain kinds of characters,' and so on. It's really just imposing yourself on the reader and saying that because I feel this way, you also feel this way. But then I came under other influences, particularly that of a man called Jim Kitses from the British magazine *Screen*, and Pauline's philosophy ran head-on against the *Screen* philosophy.

KJ: *This would be the pre-structuralist* Screen, *presumably?*
PS: Yes, this was the pre-*Young Mr Lincoln* phase,[5] before they printed that seminal analysis of the film that really changed and redefined their whole direction. This was very Leavisite; Leavis was worshipped. So when

Jim started influencing me – this was a person with whom I was talking about films five days a week and more; obviously you're not attracted to that extent unless there's some basis – what he was doing, in effect, was calling me back to my theological training.

Our Church was big on exegesis of the text: you had a biblical passage and you went back to the Greek or the Aramaic and you exegeted the passage word by word and tried to decide exactly what the biblical writer was saying. The text itself is held as sacred; if there's an error or a flaw, it can only be the interpreter's because the text is written by God Himself through the agency of human hands.

Having been raised with that sort of notion, the *Screen* philosophy fitted right in and it was, of course, diametrically opposed to Pauline's view, which was that we as viewers are equal participants in the experience of a film and that how we perceive it has just as much validity as its intrinsic qualities. If we perceive a film in a certain way, then that must be inherent in the text and it's not a fault or misperception, so we should study our perceptions as much as we study the text. Now I feel that both schools are equally valid.

KJ: *Another aspect of Leavisism is an insistence on traditions, on a canon of agreed value. Did you subscribe to any such canon at the time?*
PS: Well, Sarris had laid out the Bible for the American cinema and had created a pantheon that was pretty much adhered to. One could diverge from Sarris now and then, but basically it was accepted as primary and superseded Pauline's taste. The general feeling was that Sarris's assessments were accurate, but that Pauline's perceptions were more to the point – if you wanted to read about how you *feel* about movies, you read Pauline.

KJ: *Presumably the greater part of your studies at UCLA, though, was devoted simply to seeing films?*
PS: Yes. When I came to UCLA I had a lot of opinions about film but not a great deal of information. I just hadn't seen that many movies. So I devoted my first two years in LA to seeing films, plain and simple. I was living in a house with four or five other students and they all had active social and sexual lives and I had none. All I did was see films and keep a log. At the end of the first year I went through the log and found that I'd been seeing twenty or twenty-five films a week, scuttling back and forth to all the various film societies and educating myself in my future profession of critic. As soon as I had cleaned up the European cinema, which was my first love, I got on to the American cinema, the Sarris canon, and cleaned

that up. Then I got into silent cinema and educated myself in everyone from Griffith to Clarence Brown, and I covered thirties and forties comedies, but I still know today more or less where I stopped: I stopped just short of musicals. Even today my knowledge of musicals is rather thin, and I didn't care much for spectacle, so my knowledge of that is thin.

It was a very peculiar education. I am truly an exception in the gamut of Hollywood film-makers, of film-makers period, because every one of them is informed by this kind of eclectic adolescent taste where they were weaned on spectacles and boys' adventures and musicals, and they hold these films near and dear to their hearts. Where for Steven Spielberg *Gunga Din* is still alive and for Scorsese Minnelli is alive, they're not alive for me, and they never were in an adolescent context.

I went through the history of films in a brutally analytical way in terms of what interested me, and would say, 'OK, now I've cleaned up Hawks, Ford and Walsh and Sturges, maybe it's time to move further down the Sarris pantheon.' So I find myself alone among my colleagues in not having childhood memories of movies to fall back on. My childhood memories revolve around theological discussions at the kitchen table, around religious proselytizing. There are no movie memories, period.

The enormous advantage of this fact is that it sets me absolutely apart. As I was breaking into movies I never felt that I was in competition with anyone, because I knew that whatever I was going to do I was the only one that was going to do it. It just didn't matter to me how successful my friends were because I wasn't making their kind of movies and they weren't making mine. I never felt that internecine rivalry because, say, Walter Hill would go off and make his John Ford film whereas I would go off and make my Grand Rapids film. That's the upside.

The downside is an intellectual's perception of mass entertainment as opposed to a child's. I looked at films which I enjoyed, which I even loved, but I have no concept of seeing them with an adolescent sensibility. It's different with rock and roll because I remember hearing that as a kid, even though it was forbidden. But movies don't have those emotional associations for me, and the truth is that that's a rather damning curse. When Pauline Kael writes of me, as she did, that *Patty Hearst* is the work of a brilliant film-maker who lacks the ability to make the audience feel, it's something I hate to hear and I certainly don't want to agree with it, but to the extent to which it is true it comes from the fact that I'm a film-maker who never learned to feel about film during his formative years.

KJ: *Which were the films, though, that you came to feel passionately about as an adult, during this period of gorging yourself on twenty-five movies a week?*

PS: My college years had been very much informed by Bergman and that kind of hyper-intellectual cinema, but when I got to LA I fell in love with Ford and Renoir, the great humanist directors, though at the same time I fell in love with Bresson too. I also realized that Hitchcock was a great film-maker, and that *Vertigo* and *The Searchers* were two of the greatest films ever made.

I met Renoir in 1969. There was a local man, Joel Reisner, who had a radio show and he sort of became my patron. He called me up when I was writing criticism and said, 'I like what you write. Would you come over to my house?' He was a gay Jewish guy – he's dead now – who was a friend of artists; he knew Huxley and Fritz Lang as well as Renoir, and he sort of took me under his wing and introduced me to that circle.

We would go up to Renoir's house almost every Saturday, and Renoir was fascinated with me. He was intrigued as to why this bright, intelligent critic loved Bresson more than he loved Renoir, and we would always talk about that. The truth was that I loved Renoir very much. The three most impressive film-makers I ever met were Renoir and Rossellini and Peckinpah, all of whom are very humanistic people – even Sam. I just sat at Renoir's knee that summer and he really turned me around on a lot of things. I still think to this day that *The Rules of the Game* is the quintessential movie, and that if you had to select just one movie to represent all of the cinema, all that it can be, then that is the movie you must choose because it is the nonpareil, humanistically, politically, cinematically. That is *the* great film.

KJ: *When did you meet Rossellini?*

PS: That happened after I had graduated from UCLA in 1970 and become a Fellow at the AFI, the American Film Institute. I graduated from UCLA under circumstances as peculiar as I got in, which was that I'd been writing around a lot and working for the *Free Press* and saw my career as a critic moving forward and my time as a student coming to an end.

So I went to Colin Young and said that there really wasn't any reason for me to continue at UCLA but that I wanted my degree, and I was arrogant enough to say that I thought they would want me as an alumnus. He said, 'How much do you have left to do?', and I told him that I had a language exam to take, six hours of courses and a Master's thesis to present. He knew that I had already begun work on my book *Transcendental Style*, so he said, 'OK, submit all the criticism you've written and we'll call that your six hours; submit the first part of your book and we'll call that your

5 Young academic: Schrader, fellow of the American Film Institute, in 1971.

thesis; just take your language exam and we'll give you your degree.' So I did, and went to the AFI.

The AFI was then in its first year of existence and it was really a sort of country-club organization. There were only, I think, eleven Fellows and twenty support faculty, and I was the only critical Fellow, which is to say that I was the whole critical faculty, and I was given three professors and a screening schedule of my own.

The AFI had a lot of visiting speakers, and one day Rossellini came and I went to speak to him after his lecture. He was still *persona non grata* around Hollywood because of the Ingrid Bergman scandal. When you first saw him you wondered, 'How could Ingrid Bergman have forsaken her career for this man?'; but when he opened his mouth it was as if you were in a small room and he had suddenly thrown open all the windows and made you realize how big the world outside was. You fall in love with people like that, and you realize in an instant why Ingrid Bergman had fallen for him, because physical attractiveness pales very quickly when set beside a kind of spiritual attraction where someone is actually making your world bigger and better.

Rossellini is almost alone among film-makers in having been at the forefront of three totally different and original film styles. When neo-realism came along he was in the forefront of that; then came the European spiritual idea films and he was at the forefront of that; and then that cool sort of documentary style came in and he was at the forefront of that too. He had the kind of restless imagination that the moment he touched anything he made it bigger.

KJ: *You've written about the last of those three styles in your article about* La Prise de Pouvoir par Louis XIV.[6]
PS: That was the one I could be evangelical about, because people just didn't understand how brilliant it was; they weren't understanding what was going on. They were keeping Rossellini in this little box and he didn't want to be in that box; he wanted to turn television into an art.

But neither Rossellini nor Renoir was the biggest influence on me at the time. The greatest influence, and the reason I think I was able to become a film-maker, was Charles Eames, the architect.

In 1970, Eames came to give one of the AFI's talks. I heard him and thought that this was something extraordinary, and decided that I would do an article about him. But even then the notion of an article was something of a guise because I sensed that here was this person who was standing by a door and that if I approached him he would open that door for me.

6 Charles Eames and his wife Ray in 1976.

So I went and interviewed him, and the interview became more and more protracted because I didn't want to leave the workshop. He had this huge warehouse workshop down in Venice where on any given day he would be making furniture, making films, making slide-shows, making toys . . . it was a truly Renaissance environment.

KJ: *Was it particularly the films which caught your imagination, or Eames's whole practice?*
PS: Well, I had been raised in an environment that believed that ideas were the province of language, and that if you had something to say you used words to say it, and that if you wanted to speak of beauty or of spirituality you used words. This is what Calvin had used, this is what Luther had used, this is what Knox had used. What Charles taught me, and taught me with great patience and diligence, was that an image or an object can also be an idea.

So, for example, you have the word 'wineglass', a nine-letter linguistic concept, and you have this object, a wineglass, which is related to the word by a semantic code but which is not the same idea. And if you have a different wineglass then you have a different idea again, and again; and only when you appreciate that those ideas have just as much validity as the word 'wineglass' will you be visually literate.

Eames taught me that there is a visual logic in life and that to be a poet, or a poet of ideas (which is what I called my piece), doesn't mean you have to use language. I was like Paul on the road to Damascus when I heard this. I had always believed that people who thought visually were inferior thinkers, and that painting was essentially an illustration of ideas, which is how it was taught at Calvin, rather than an idea in its own right. Whenever any truly powerful idea hits you it overwhelms you, and that just knocked me out and I was changed permanently.

Today, occasionally, when I talk with students I grow impatient with their questions and with the repetitious things they're saying. Whenever that happens I remember Charles and think, 'Jesus, here was a man telling me what to him must have been the most prosaic and mundane truth imaginable, being a designer and architect, and yet he took the time to explain it to me patiently and make me understand it. If he could take that time, as busy and important as he was, then who am I to think I'm too superior to pass on that kind of simple information to the next person?'

KJ: *Was his patience with you just a sign of his personal generosity, or do you think he saw you as a kind of protégé?*
PS: When I look back on my life and think of the various people who have

befriended me, whether it be Pauline or Charles or whoever, obviously they saw in me a hungry, thirsty sensibility that wanted what they had to give very badly, and if you're a decent person then you realize that this is what you are put on this earth to do. It's one thing to try to tell people things they don't want to know, but when someone appears before you who is, as the Bible says, hungering and thirsting after righteousness, then you have to give it to them.

Another thing that Eames told me had a tremendous impact, though now it may seem prosaic. I was asking him how he designed a chair and he said, 'Well, the first thing I did was to call everyone on my staff in and measure their asses, because human physiology is always changing and I want to know what the idea of an ass is.' Then he said to me, 'You like to think you're different. In fact you really do think that you are something different to me; in fact you think you are something special, but you are not – you are wedded to me; you are more like me and always will be more like me than a tree will be, and you have to accept that.'

That may be a cliché, but I guess that simple truth fed into all my religious training about how we are all equal in the sight of God. I had been in LA watching films which exalted idiosyncrasy and the cult of personality and here comes this man who says that the cult of personality is transient, that we are in fact all alike and that if you don't understand how we are alike then you won't get anything done. That thought, together with the thought that images are ideas, overturned my world.

KJ: *That last point sounds reminiscent of some of the arguments in* Transcendental Style, *favouring universality of means as against idiosyncrasy of personality.*
PS: Yes, a lot of *Transcendental Style* was written after my time with Charles.

KJ: *How did the idea for that book come about?*
PS: I found myself in a unique position. I had been involved with a lot of people at Calvin who were interested in movies but were very ignorant about them and had no idea what made them good. Then I came out to UCLA and got involved with a lot of people who talked about spirituality in film and had absolutely no idea what they were talking about; they'd had no religious education.

So I came up with this idea for *Transcendental Style*, which was published in 1972, and I realized that I was too young to write it but that there was nobody else out there who was going to write it, and that if I didn't write it now I never would, because it meant a year without pay. So one of the reasons the references are so guarded is that I just felt I was too young and had to cover myself. The book just goes, A said this, B said this, C said this and now I, D, am saying this. If I wrote it today I think I would make it much less scholarly.

The book had three strong personal influences: Eames; a philosophy professor I had at Calvin, Nicholas Waltersdorf; and Jim Kitses, who, as I say, weaned me off Pauline's influence and on to F. R. Leavis's textual criticism.

KJ: Transcendental Style *gives the impression of being the work of someone who is still a believer.*
PS: But a believer in spirituality, not a believer in any sectarian notion of God. I was no longer a member of my Church or a believer in its doctrines.

KJ: *When had you lost your faith? Was it sudden and traumatic, or gradual?*
PS: It was gradual. Maybe it began to hit me after I came back from military school that summer, but basically I had to keep my mouth shut about it until I was twenty-one. What hit me was that religions of that nature are really social institutions, not spiritual institutions, and that spirituality was just an occasional adjunct of its social and economic functions. I just felt that I didn't really belong in this club any more.

KJ: *Though at first sight the book seems like an auteurist study of Ozu, Bresson and Dreyer, in fact it is interested in different ideas – ideas that go against what must have been the conventional grain at the time.*
PS: Yes, and that was fine with me. I had a streak that made me deeply enjoy all my schisms with Pauline just as I deeply enjoyed talking to Renoir about why Bresson was a greater director than he was. It's a measure of the greatness of the man that I was invited back week after week, though I think he was also glad to have someone around the house who hadn't just come to kiss the ring.

KJ: *It's also a book that showed you'd been studying avant-garde films by the likes of Warhol and Michael Snow, and that you had a certain amount of sympathy and regard for them.*
PS: Very much so, because those were films from the cinema of denial, of sparse means. The whole of the *Transcendental Style* hypothesis is that if you reduce your sensual awareness rigorously and for long enough, the inner need will explode and it will be pure because it will not have been siphoned off by easy or exploitative identifications; it will have been

refined and compressed to its true identity, what Calvin called the *sensus divinitatus*, the divine sense.

Calvin was a brutal intellectual, an intellectual *par excellence*, and the goal of all his work was to reduce the window of faith to as small an aperture as possible. We can define and understand the whole world, and all we have to leave is this tiny hole for faith to enter in by. But of course the more you define the world and the tinier the aperture, then the more blinding the light of faith becomes in its brilliance. *Transcendental Style* uses the same argument: strip away conventional emotional associations and then you're left with this tiny little pinpoint that hits you at the end and freezes you into stasis.

One of the things that I've tried to do in my films – and I shouldn't say this because it's exactly what people criticize me for – is to try to have an emotionally blinding moment, like Mishima's suicide; or like the end of *American Gigolo*, where this spiritual essence suddenly pops out of the flimsy lounge lizard; or like the moment in *Light of Day* when the girl is reconciled with her mother, where, despite all her toughness, she can't deny any more that there is something which transcends you, and that the more you suppress it the more it's going to knock you on your ass.

This is very hard to do, and one of the problems I've run into is that it doesn't really work in the commercial cinema because in order to get these blinding moments you have to deny so much, and if you do too much denial then you're out of the commercial cinema. So what I've tried to do is a little bit of both. I've mitigated the denial, but then of course the blinding moments don't stand out so much.

KJ: *Did you ever consider the option of working outside the commercial cinema, as an underground film-maker?*
PS: No, because I have the evangelical impulse, which is the need to go out and preach to as many people as possible and to reach all of them. I also know that the true way to reach them is via a method that is uncommercial. But when you are working in a mass medium you have to accept the restrictions of a mass audience, which means millions of people, because to make a movie you need to deal with a minimum of two or three million units. Also, I'm a firm believer in the Christian notion of stewardship: if people give you money then it is up to you to have a coherent vision of how to return that money. It may not happen, but on every film I'm involved in I want all the people who invested to get their money back.

I used to have enormous sympathy for Godard when his films were engaged, but for the last twenty years he's been talking to an empty room, and what sense is there in that? I'm sure he would say, 'It's important that I keep talking and I don't care that no one is listening,' but I can't go along with that. I think that if you're working in this medium you've got to make sure people are listening.

On the other hand, I do have a sort of rainbow notion of communication, which is to do with the levels of information which can be communicated to different numbers of people. Say you have a professor who has 100 per cent intensity of communication with his ten students. One of the students goes off and writes a book which has only a tenth of that information but a thousand people read it. Now a film-maker comes along and delivers only a tenth of that book, but he delivers it to ten million people. Well, I believe that there's a sense in which the value of all those levels of communication can be seen as equal, that the professor who teaches the few and the popularizer who teaches the many are equally valuable.

My problem as an artist is that I see myself some way down that spectrum. I see myself as a popularizer, but in fact I remain a purist. But I'm not the equal of a Freud or a Marx, and I don't want to talk to just a few people. So part of the reason I put that Bressonian ending on to *American Gigolo* was a kind of outrageous perversity, saying, 'I can make this fashion-conscious, hip Hollywood movie and at the end claim that it's really pure'; and in *Cat People* I could make this horror movie and say it was really about Dante and Beatrice.

That, I suspect, is what makes my movies of interest. I also suspect that it's what makes them problematical in terms of the commercial cinema. An old friend of mine says to me that my problem is that I go too far, that right at the end I always have to take that one step too far. Well, what that one step is is an attempt to make it all really redemptive, to say, 'This looks commercial and ordinary but it's not; it's really spiritual and extraordinary.'

KJ: *Was it the desire to address a wider audience that finally led you away from writing criticism?*
PS: What happened was this. At the time I was a member of a group of young critics who were all influenced by Pauline and we jokingly called ourselves the Paulettes – Roger Ebert, David Denby, Paul Warshow, Gary Arnold at the *Washington Post* and others. We were all across the country and we were in constant contact with Pauline – you were on the phone to her every week, and sent her everything you wrote and when the word came down from New York you toed the line. She would say, 'There's this terrific new film called *Bonnie and Clyde*. It's been misunderstood and it's not getting a fair shake. We have to go out and beat the drums for it.' Nine

times out of ten she was dead right about it, and if you just followed what she said you were more likely to be on the mark than off it.

All the time she would get phone calls from major publications saying, 'We're about to have an opening for a critic on *Newsweek* or whatever – who would you recommend?' And the unstated understanding was that if you remained in the Pauline camp you would eventually be placed in one of these jobs and then work your way up the system.

I remember my break with Pauline because it was very dramatic. It was the end of 1971, I had been living in LA for some time now and had started toying with the idea of becoming involved in the other end of the business; even though I was still committed to being a critic I started to fool around with writing scripts. In order to support myself I'd taken a job as a reader for Columbia – you were paid $15 for a script and $25 for a novel, and you wrote a synopsis and a critique. I had written things in the most snide way possible, saying, 'If you want to do an empty-headed marital comedy then this is the script for you,' which is the kind of critique no one wants to read, and I got fired and re-hired twice before we parted company for good. So I had become very conversant with scripts and wrote one called *Pipeliner*, basically in order to teach myself how to write a script, which is really the only way you can learn.

I was in New York and seeing Pauline – it was a day or two before Christmas – and she broke the big news and said, 'I've gotten you a job – there's an opening coming up in Chicago and there's one coming up in Seattle and I want you to go to Seattle. It's the best movie town in the country; it has great repertory cinema, and you have the chance to create a body of work and influence the movie-going public.'

I think the reason she wanted me in Seattle was because she had no one out there – it was like the height of the British Empire: 'You take Rhodesia.' I said, 'Yes, this is fabulous – this is exactly what I have wanted to do and have been working towards for the last five years. But there's this other thing. I've been living in LA for some time and I've been writing this script, and if I take the Seattle job I would always wonder what would have happened if I had stayed on as a screenwriter.'

Pauline said, 'They need an answer.' I said, 'Let me go back to LA and think about it and I'll tell you next week.' She said, 'No. They need an answer now.' I said, 'I can't give you answer now because going to Seattle would be a big a change in my life. It would be a five-year commitment at least.' Pauline said, 'They need an answer now, and if you don't tell me yes now, then the answer is no.'

I remember standing up and saying, 'I guess the answer is no,' and I walked out and that was the end of our close relationship. I remember flying back on the plane to LA thinking, 'Well, you just fucked up your whole career. Everything you've ever wanted to do was just handed to you and you turned it down. You can't make a living, you're in debt, and you've turned down the chance to become a major critic. Well, if you've turned this job down then it just means you're not a critic any more. You just have to give up, pack it all in and try to be a film-maker.'

Notes

1 John Cassavetes's *Faces* (1968) depicts, in the director's customary semi-documentary style, the mid-life discontents of a group of affluent characters. Among its leading players is Gena Rowlands, whom Schrader was later to cast in *Light of Day*.

2 In May 1968, the Cannes Film Festival was abandoned after protests (supported by François Truffaut, Jean-Luc Godard and others) against the commercialism and triviality of many of the films on show at a time of national crisis.

3 *Masculin/Féminin (Masculine/Feminine)* (1966); *A Bout de Souffle (Breathless)* (1959); *La Chinoise* (1967) were all made by Jean-Luc Godard (1930–   ).

4 The highly influential French cinema journal which developed out of *La Revue du Cinéma* (1951), edited by André Bazin and others. Many of the young critics who worked on *Cahiers* in the mid 1950s went on to become the leading directors of the *Nouvelle Vague*: Jean-Luc Godard, François Truffaut, Jacques Rivette, Claude Chabrol, Eric Rohmer. In the late 1960s, *Cahiers* abandoned its earlier commitment to the *politique des auteurs* in favour of structuralist and Marxist methods. An English version of *Cahiers* was produced by the American critic Andrew Sarris from 1965 to 1967; earlier, Sarris had been the leading American proponent of the auteur theory.

5 John Ford's *Young Mr Lincoln* (1939), one of the director's finest films, is based on a real-life murder trial at which Abraham Lincoln (played by Henry Fonda) was the defence lawyer. The lengthy *Cahiers* analysis of Ford's film appeared in *Screen*, Vol. 13, No. 3, Autumn 1972, as 'John Ford's *Young Mr Lincoln*; a collective text by the editors of *Cahiers du Cinéma*', translated by Hélène Lackner and Diana Matias.

6 Schrader's article on Roberto Rossellini's *La Prise de Pouvoir par Louis XIV (The Rise of Louis XIV)* appeared in his magazine *Cinema*, Vol. 6, No. 3 (1971). See p. 57.

CHAPTER 3

Critical Writings

Like the early writings of Godard, Truffaut and Rivette, Schrader's criticism has a double interest: for the light it casts on the history of cinema, and for the light it casts on the films he would go on to make. Most of the readers who have bothered to hunt down these articles in the files have done so for the latter reason, but, as was argued in the Introduction, this kind of retrospective clue-hunting can tend to draw attention away from the intrinsic merits of the pieces.

The selection from his early writings brought together here represents a variety of strands in Schrader's critical work. The *L.A. Free Press* review of *Easy Rider*, which got him fired from the paper, is a fair indication of the ways in which the young critic was willing to go against the grain of contemporary opinion. The review of *Pickpocket* and the article on Boetticher both touch on some of the arguments treated at greater length in *Transcendental Style in Film*; the Boetticher article also outlines some of his arguments against the auteurist position.

In addition to being studies of directors he personally admired, the articles on Rossellini and Peckinpah are examples of Schrader in missionary spirit, trying to create or correct the reputations of men who had been neglected or misunderstood. 'Notes on *Film Noir*', something of a pioneering study of the form, expresses Schrader's dissatisfaction with what he regards as the sociological bias of American criticism. And 'Poetry of Ideas' (which Schrader regards as the best of his pieces) explains in greater detail the experience which 'overturned my world': the discovery that 'the Eames aesthetic introduces the new way of perceiving ideas into a medium which has been surprisingly anti-intellectual'.

But if Eames was the man who ultimately enabled Schrader to become a director, there is no shortage of early hints as to the kind of director he would eventually become. Bresson's influence has been cited many times; these articles also point to some less obvious masters. Schrader was drawn, on the one hand, to the intellectual detachment of *La Prise de Pouvoir par Louis XIV* (judged by most critics at the time to be 'cold' and 'boring'); on the other, to *The Wild Bunch*, a film which 'uses violence to excite and then applies more violence to comment on the excitement'. Might not an attempted synthesis of these seemingly contrary approaches look very like a Schrader film? And at least one passage in 'Notes on *Film Noir*' sounds directly predictive of Schrader's most anguished protagonist: ' . . . 1949–53 was the period of psychotic action and suicidal impulse. The *noir* hero, seemingly under the weight of ten years of despair, started to go bananas.' Travis Bickle was not far away.

Easy Rider

In a recently published book-length interview with Jorge Luis Borges the Argentinian poet told how he had first met Federico Garcia Lorca when they both were young, and how Borges had taken an instant dislike to the Spanish poet–playwright.

Lorca wanted to astonish us. He said to me that he was very much troubled about a very important character in the contemporary world. A character in whom you could see all the tragedy of American life. And then he went on in this way until I asked him who was this character and it turned out the character was Mickey Mouse. I suppose he was trying to be clever. And I thought, that's the kind of thing you might say when you are very young and you want to astonish somebody. But after all, he was a grown man, he had no need, he could have talked in a different way. But when he started in about Mickey Mouse being a symbol of America, there was a friend of mine there and he looked at me and I looked at him and we both walked away because we were both too old for that kind of game, no? Even at the time.

In Dennis Hopper's *Easy Rider*, Hopper asks hippie commune leader Robert Walker, 'Have you ever wanted to be someone else?' After a contemplative pause, Walker solemnly replies, 'I've often thought of being Porky Pig.' And the group falls into a respectful silence. *Easy Rider* is permeated with the sententiousness Borges found in the young Lorca, the sophomoric desire to 'astonish' (not in Cocteau's sense), the self-congratulatory piety of an aphorist who has just demolished a series of straw men.

Easy Rider is a very important movie – and it is a very bad one, and I don't think its importance should be used to obscure the gross misman-agement of its subject-matter. Dennis Hopper's film about two drug-culture motorcyclists (Hopper and Peter Fonda) who, in the words of the *Easy Rider* ad, 'set out to discover America', has captured the imagination of the above- and underground press alike.

The underground identification was instant and understandable. *Easy*

Rider fuelled the paranoia which is the staple item of the youth culture (often rightly so). As a friend said, 'It's a picture that doesn't cop out,' presumably meaning that the young idealists are senselessly massacred and the audience is left without hope. The reservations of the *Life* and *Newsweek* reviewers were overridden by their eagerness to agree with the film's propositions. As Joseph Morgenstern wrote, '*Easy Rider*'s essential truth is brought home by what we ourselves know of our trigger-happy, hate-ridden nation in which increasing numbers of morons bear increasing numbers of arms.' The mass media, having exploited every other youth truth, was now usurping youth's paranoia.

My complaint is that *Easy Rider*, for all its good intentions, functions in the same superficial manner 'liberal' Hollywood films have always functioned. *Easy Rider*'s superficial characterizations and slick insights stem from the same soft-headed mentality which produced such anathema 'liberal' films as Elia Kazan's *Gentleman's Agreement* and Stanley Kramer's *Defiant Ones*. But because liberals and leftists of all varieties so desperately need the strong statement *Easy Rider* makes, they are willing to overlook the film's shallow, conventional method of argument.

The Defiant Ones (a 1958 sincere, mushy fable about race relations) had a fleeting sociological value (like *Easy Rider*), but its value as art was negligible and today nobody would take its black-and-white moral seriously. The characters of *Easy Rider* will become a joke too because Hopper has not taken the first step to protect them from the ravages of time, he has not withdrawn them from the puppet world of propaganda and made them real human beings.

Easy Rider draws its characters and situation from a bag of stock movie tricks which have historically been used to 'prove' any number of contradictory premises. Haven't you met all these characters before? – the good-hearted prostitute, the simple man of the soil, the bully cop, the redneck townsfolk, the good-natured drunk, and the stolid picaresque hero who is constantly staring into the future. The flapper movies of the twenties always included a scene of a whimsical character-actor getting drunk, spilling over himself, making faces, and finally conking out.

Today we have Jack Nicholson, the small-town, ACLU lawyer, momma's boy, getting high on grass, making faces, and finally conking out. The sentiments are the same, and so are the giggles. (And when he said with a straight face, 'You know this used to be a hell of a good country. I don't know what happened,' I, for one, couldn't stop laughing.)

When the freshly turned-on Nicholson is murdered and Peter Fonda mumbles something about his being a good man I thought I could see for one fleeting moment, in double exposure, the bulky figure of John Wayne hovering over the trusty old Walter Brennan's fresh grave. We are deep in the heart of the Old West when Fonda visits a hippie commune and tells the seed-sowing inhabitants, 'They're going to make it.'

Instead of the musical redundancies of Max Steiner, we now have Jimi Hendrix and the Steppenwolf to reinforce every thematic passage. One could take such trite set-ups in a better spirit if Hopper hadn't revealed his sensitivity to be sophomoric at most every turn. He crudely intercuts the shoeing of a horse with the changing of a motorcycle tyre, dwells on graffiti about Jesus in a jail and a statue of Christ in (of all places!) a whorehouse.

Hopper's idea of making a point is something like this: long tracking shot of rich white Southern mansions: cut: long tracking shot of poor black hovels. Even poor Stanley Kramer, who is every film student's stock example of liberal pretentiousness, is more subtle than this. Hopper finds no new metaphors for the drug culture, but simply adapts moviedom's hoary situations to the contemporary scene. The liberal clichés have changed, but they are still clichés.

Hopper's villain is every liberal's favourite scapegoat: the redneck. There is no need to motivate, characterize, or develop the killers – movie past has taught us that Southern poor whites commit such heinous crimes as a matter of course. Fonda has said that they could have just as well set the killing in the North. This is true, but it would have made Hopper define his villains more precisely (unless he wanted to transport Southerners to the North), and would have deprived him of the fun of whipping the Southern stereotype. Surrounded by majorettes (a sure sign of decadence) and speaking in a drawl, the redneck is the ideal villain for a jejune director – being for that villain would be like being against, for gosh sakes, LOVE.

The college students who complain about Sidney Poitier's two-dimensional Superspade gobble up Hopper's Superbigots with no qualms. I guess it matters which side of the paranoiac fence you are on.

A friend of mine who likes *Easy Rider* admits the film is superficial, but says, 'That's the beauty of it. It gets only about one inch into these hippie characters, but that is all there is to them anyway.' I refuse to believe that anyone is as superficial as Hopper's hippies and rednecks – even when they act that way. There are feelings (perhaps undesirable) I share with both groups and I want a film to explore and comment on that identification.

What makes *Easy Rider* look like every other gutless piece of Hollywood marshmallow liberalism is Hopper's refusal to play with anything but a stacked deck. You cannot lose when you plot stereotypes against straw men. The problem for a propagandist like Hopper is that humans are always more infectious than slogans, and to risk characterization is to risk failure. If the characterization is too honest the audience might not identify with the right group, as in the first half of Leo McCarey's 1952 anti-communist film, *My Son John*, where McCarey portrayed communist Robert Walker too conscientiously. One can imagine the format of *Easy Rider* being used to convey any type of agit-prop.

It could be a Nazi film with Hitler and Goering reviewing their choppers through the Rhineland, finally being gunned down by a rabid, motley, heavily accented group of Jewish bankers, scientists, and artists (at least it would have been funny that way). At the risk of being facetious one could say that *Easy Rider* was a Sam Yorty fund-raising film. The right-wing voters would have filled Mayor Sam's coffers after one viewing. There is no danger that conservatives would be moved or changed by seeing the film; they react as automatically as the leftists.

Easy Rider deals with the most important issues facing America – and for that reason its superficiality is the more deplorable. I find it helpful to make a distinction between documentary and fiction films about political trends. I recently saw a powerful documentary called *American Revolution 2* which dealt with an attempt to unite two ghetto militant organizations, one poor Southern white, the other the Panthers. *American Revolution 2* goes no deeper into its characters than *Easy Rider* and is just as superficial, yet I was much more affected by it than by *Easy Rider*. There is a need for an honest portrayal of events which, however superficial, can inform viewers of trends around the country. But when a film-maker weaves people and places out of his own imagination, he is responsible for much more – he is responsible for their souls and minds as well as their actions.

Easy Rider would have been a powerful film if Hopper had been able to catch these events as they happen (and I don't doubt they do happen), but as a work of art and imagination it falls completely short. I demand more of art than I do of life; I desire the sensitivity and insight that only an artist can give. And the more important the subject-matter, the more crucial that insight becomes.

If the mass media decides to exploit the Hopper–Fonda paranoia it will acquire something as worthless as last year's mod fashions and nude plays. Hopper and Fonda are too infatuated with the idea of themselves as pundits, Christs, martyrs, and Porky Pigs to examine their heroes, villains, or themselves – and this form of harmless paranoia is easily stolen and marketed throughout the media. But we are all too old for this kind of game, no?

L.A. Free Press, 25 July 1969

Pickpocket I

A custom of medieval architecture holds that the final portion of a structure should be left unfinished, perhaps a cupola or fillip of design, as a testament to man's humility and his faith in God's power to complete the building. The work of Robert Bresson strikes us as just that final touch of architecture, so pure it could have scarcely been made by man, and yet so consummate it caps and sanctifies the whole human effort.

Ascetic, proud, saintly, the films of Bresson rank among the finest expressions of the human spirit. To find another who affects us as deeply and permanently we must press the limits of media and time: Dostoevsky, Shakespeare, Beethoven, Breughel. Bresson attempts and achieves the highest function of art; he elevates the spirit, not only of his characters and viewers, but somehow of the system which has entrapped us all.

Pickpocket, Bresson's fifth film (out of eight films in a thirty-six-year career), is presently having its West Coast première ten years after it was made. It is one of those consummate works of art which in one flash pales everything you have ever seen. I would be tempted to say *Pickpocket* is the finest film I've seen if Bresson hadn't made three or four other films which affect me as deeply. Do not expect objectivity; those of us who love and admire Robert Bresson do not so much analyse him as proselytize for him.

Because *Pickpocket* is such an unmitigated masterpiece, and because Bresson is relatively unknown to the mass audience, I hope to discuss *Pickpocket* over a two-week period. This week I want to point out some of the landmarks of Bresson's rigid personal style, and next week demonstrate how Bresson brings the viewer to his knees in the moment of 'transformation'. I'll admit that this two-week plan has some personal reasons. Firstly, I'll get two pay-cheques for one article, and, secondly, just as when Jack or Bob Kennedy's body was still above the ground I could not bring myself to leave that pale TV image, similarly as long as *Pickpocket* is showing in town I don't have the desire to talk about any other picture.

Pickpocket, like all of Bresson's films, concerns the progression of a soul from confinement to freedom. Sometimes his heroes are caught in actual prisons (*A Man Escaped*), sometimes they are subject to the divine agony (*Diary of a Country Priest*), and sometimes, as in *Pickpocket*, they are the victims of a life of crime. Their progression occurs slowly, fitfully, yet as inevitably as the Stations of the Cross. And when Bresson arrives at the final station, the sepulchre of the old self, whether that be death, physical freedom or incarceration, the film abruptly ends.

Michel is a compulsive pickpocket; not for money or pleasure, but

7 Robert Bresson's *Pickpocket* (1959): Martin Lassalle.

simply because it is a project and a fulfilment. He robs his dying mother, yet weeps at her bedside. Like Dostoevsky's Raskolnikov, Michel is in a continual debate with the police inspector. Also like the hero of *Crime and Punishment*, Michel contends that some men, because of their indispensability to society, are above the law. 'But how do they know who they are?' the inspector asks. 'They ask themselves,' Michel replies. In long, ballet-like, silent sequences Michel perfects his craft, but like Raskolnikov he is compulsively drawn back to the police, the cell, and the love of Jeanne, a long-time family friend. In a shatteringly tender scene he kisses her forehead, she his hand, and he says through the prison bars, 'How long it has taken me to come to you.'

The elevation of the spirit is never accidental in Bresson's films. Although they look very human, his films are highly stylized. Bresson is one of cinema's great formalists. Briefly, this means that his intentions are always expressed by his style ('The film is not a spectacle, it is in the first place a style'). He has worked out a form which expresses exactly what he wants to say. This is different from directors whose form is what they want to say, or those who use form as form because they have nothing to say. It is Bresson's rigid, repetitive directorial influence which brings meaning to *Pickpocket*. This is the opposite from the sort of thing Gene Youngblood is usually talking about, and from the spectacle tradition of Brecht and Godard.

Bresson's style is, as Susan Sontag says, of the 'reflective mode'. Miss Sontag continues: 'In reflective art the form of the work of art is present in an emphatic way. The effect of the spectator's being aware of form is to elongate or retard the emotions.' This is why Bresson seems so perverse to the uninitiated viewer; Bresson relentlessly destroys traditional emotional constructs, which he calls 'screens'. Even essentials like plot and acting can become screens which provide cheap thrills and spectacle, giving the viewer an easy way out of the dramatic situation. And Bresson is determined not to let anything interfere with his spirit and the viewer's. The viewer can have no special interests; he must be prepared to give all or nothing. A brief rundown will reveal Bresson's unconventional attitudes toward basic movie elements.

Acting. Bresson detests acting – 'it is for theatre, a bastard art'. All his characters are amateurs who, at his insistence, mouth their lines in the most banal manner, and who, in fact, look like Bresson himself. When an actor acts, Bresson contends, he simplifies himself, being false both to the character and to the audience. 'We are complex. What the actor projects is not complex.' He is also fearful of an actor exerting competitive imaginative power. 'You cannot be inside an actor. It is he who creates. It is not you.' And in a Bresson film, it is Bresson who does all the creating.

Plot. Bresson has little interest in 'how it will come out'. Although he is an excellent photographer and cutter, Bresson will not allow the viewer to see *Pickpocket* just for the action. His elliptical style can reveal a complex plot manoeuvre in three bland shots. By denying a motion picture its motion, he spurns the most basic of cinematic 'screens'. The spectator can no longer exert emotional control over a screen action (for when the viewer sympathizes with an action he can later be smug in its completion). Bresson has described his film *A Man Escaped* as a single sequence with each shot leading only to the next.

Cinematography. Compositional beauty for itself is an indulgence Bresson cannot afford. 'Painting', he says, 'taught me to make not beautiful images but necessary ones.' He is able to create the vacuous prettiness of *Elvira Madigan* yet also knows how dangerous it can be. Bresson insists that his images, like his acting and plot, be flat and unexpressive.

Music. For the most part Bresson's films are without any music, just natural sounds: footsteps, latches opening, doors creaking. Music, of course, is the most primitive and overworked of the emotional constructs. But often in *Pickpocket* Bresson will conclude a scene with a great blast of classical music by Jean-Baptiste Lully. It is a cocky, defiant gesture by a man who knows just when to make the grand editorial gesture but the circumstances under which he employs his technique will be discussed in the next article.

Realism. Bresson's use of realism shows him at his cunning and pawky best. Bresson insists on the most realistic of settings: in *Pickpocket* it is the Gare de Lyon. Yet by using narration, journals, and pleonastic dialogue Bresson undermines his meticulous realism. One scene in *Pickpocket* shows Michel writing in his diary, and the narrator reiterates what we have read: 'I sat in the lobby of one of the great banks of Paris.' Next we see Michel going into the lobby of a great bank and sitting. When the same thing starts happening three times simultaneously we know we're beyond simple realism and into the spiritual world of Robert Bresson. As Bresson says, 'I want to and, indeed, do make myself as much of a realist as possible, using only raw material taken from real life. But I end up with a final realism that is not simply "realism".'

Examples such as these can be found in abundance in *Pickpocket*, or any of Bresson's films. Bresson deprives the viewer of every superficial pleasure, yet keeps him in tow by hinting greater and more lasting pleasures.

I'm afraid I haven't convinced you of Bresson's greatness, simply told you that he hates the things we enjoy most and that there is a good chance that *Pickpocket* will bore the hell out of you. But Bresson is not shunning your emotions, he's postponing them and fully intends to reap a bumper crop when the film is over. Because a viewer's feelings are denied doesn't mean he has no feelings. Bresson is cutting short of a superficial run-off of emotion, trying to keep it together submerged, intact, so that in one final moment he can make the viewer bring forth all of his emotions on a higher level.

That moment is the 'transformation' when all the bland characters, dull plots, and flat images can merge into the new images which the viewer, now naked of 'screens', will help to create. 'There must,' Bresson says, 'at a certain moment, be a transformation; if not, there is no art.'

Next week I'll try to reconstruct what that transformation might be – right before your very eyes.

L.A. Free Press, 25 April 1969

Pickpocket II

Last week in this column I wrote about the formalism of French director Robert Bresson. In *Pickpocket*, as in all his films, Bresson uses a rigid and austere style to ward off superficial emotional release, intent instead on creating a 'transformation'. He says, 'There must, at a certain moment, be a transformation; if not, there is no art.'

Transformation for Bresson is of the rarest and most difficult sort. He wants you to believe in something you don't want to believe in – the supernatural and the spiritual. And not just because his characters believe in the spiritual, but because there *is* a spiritual. He seeks to expose 'those extraordinary currents, the presence of something or someone, call it what you wish, which confirms that there is a hand guiding everything'.

Religious and sacrilegious artists have been trying to accomplish this for some time, but nowhere has their failure been so pronounced as in film. To appreciate the scope and innovation of Bresson's art one need only examine previous attempts. André Bazin has pointed out that since its origin, painting has been torn between two ambitions: the aesthetic and spiritual, exemplified by the mosaic icon, and the psychological and duplicatory, exemplified by the death mask.

The first ambition gradually succumbed to the latter, and painting became increasingly realistic. The Byzantine mosaics yielded to the sequential paintings of Hogarth. Cinema, an art of time and space, is the logical result of the mimetic tradition; it was first called 'life itself'. For those who wanted to make the supernatural real, that is make spiritual art, cinema seemed like the ideal solution. Since film was innately 'real', all one had to do was put the spiritual on film. Thus we have a history of cinematic magic: the blind are made to see, the lame to walk, the deaf to hear, all on camera. On the cynical level we had the biblical epics of De Mille and Satanic epic of Polanski; on the sincere level there were the many films produced by Gospel Films, World Vision, and other Billy Graham-oriented organizations.

But they didn't work. We knew that the divine fireball of *The Ten Commandments* was not conceived in Heaven, but in some film laboratory, and that the slapdash conversion of *The Restless Heart* was not caused by divine intervention, but by some hack scriptwriter. These films called attention to the supposedly realistic nature of the medium, and broke our faith in it.

Robert Bresson, in one of those original bursts of genius that leave the rest of us numb, uses the realistic properties of film against itself. He uses his new freedom – the innate reality of the cinema – to create icons. The films of Bresson are blatantly hieratic, the most unabashedly iconographic art the West has had since Cromwell smashed England's Catholic statuary.

The spiritual transformation incumbent to iconography must be extremely subtle. Bresson wants to leave the viewer so free, so unencumbered that he must perforce come to agree with Bresson himself. Bresson makes no secret of this:

You must leave the spectator free. And at the same time you must make yourself loved by him. You must make him love the way in which you render things. That is to say: show him things in the order and in the way that you love to see them; make him feel them, in presenting them to him, as you see them and feel them yourself, and this, while leaving him a great freedom, while making him free.

To make the viewer free all the while imprisoning him, Bresson creates realistic images, all the while undercutting them. Bresson always chooses the most realistic settings and situations. He makes a great use of two of film's most credible devices: the narration and the printed word. We trust the soothing voice of a narrator, just as we think there is something innately verifiable about words which are written on the screen. But then Bresson sets his termites on our comfortable structure. As I mentioned last week he starts doubling his action and narration, making the same realistic statement over and over again. The action becomes so ostensibly real that it is suspicious.

And in that magical process lies the secret of Bresson's peculiar genius. It takes no great talent to ignore the viewer, to deprive him of the things he enjoys. Yet Bresson both alienates the viewer and keeps him interested. His realistic and straightforward technique holds the audience's interest in lieu of the cheap vicarious thrills. Bresson makes us feel that there must be something more than what appears on the surface – and he doesn't disappoint us.

Bresson culminates his suspicious mood with a final, blatant anti-realistic gesture. He defiantly undercuts the weakened realistic structure. His films end with an inexplicably spiritual act: the death of a saint, the liberation of a soul, or, as in *Pickpocket*, an unpremeditated act of love. We have not been set up for it, yet we accept it. It is at that moment Bresson claims the 'transformation' occurs. At this moment all Bresson's flat images, bland dialogue, and dull characterization unite, transform into a new object. Bresson's speech constantly reiterates the need for this union:

I have noticed that the flatter an image is, the less it expresses, the more easily it is transformed in contact with other images . . . It is necessary for the images to have something in common, to participate in a sort of union . . . cinema must express itself not through images but through the relationship of images, which is not quite the same thing.

The moment of transition presupposes a volitional act by the viewer. The viewer, whose feelings have been shunned but who has feelings none the less, can, at the moment of transition, do one of two things: he can refuse to take the film seriously, or he can accommodate his thinking to his feelings. Having been given no emotional constructs by the director, the viewer constructs his own 'screen'. He creates a translucent shield through which he can cope with his feelings and the picture. This shield may be very simple. In the case of *Pickpocket* it could be: people such as Michel and Jeanne have spirits which are spiritually connected and they need no earthly rationale for their love. Bresson uses the viewer's own natural defences, his protective mechanism, to cause him to of his free will come to the identical decision that Bresson had determined for him.

The moment the viewer creates his own shield, the moment of transformation, Bresson has accomplished not only the task of the artist, but of the evangelist and the iconographist as well. The evangelist is theoretically a man who evokes a conversion not by his own sophistry but by bringing the listener into contact with the divine. In this sense Bresson's methods greatly resemble the Calvinist and Jansenist doctrines of predestination.

The doctrine of predestination holds that man, having already been chosen by God, is now free to choose God himself. God is truth; truth makes you free; and freedom is choosing God. It is a neat jungle of logic which seems quite preposterous from the outside. Yet when one is submitted to Bresson's version of the divine agony it seems the natural thing to do.

Consequently Bresson's characters, his movies, and Bresson himself all become icons. Bresson is often criticized for his pride, yet pride is one of the chief attributes of an icon. St Peter was intolerably cocksure and boastful, but when Roman Catholics worship him as an icon they admit that his pride was justified because he was a man of God. A saint justifies and sanctifies his own pride. Bresson's art presumes that there are men and works of art which can serve as icons, and that onlookers can be purified and edified by contemplating them. And Bresson fully intends to be one of those icons.

The final image of Bresson's films is often a blatant symbol. In *Diary of a Country Priest* it is actually the shadow of the Cross. In *Pickpocket* it is the tender love scene of Michel and Jeanne. Bresson pulls out the stops; he can apply all his emotional tricks. The music surges, the symbol is obvious. When Michel and Jeanne kiss it is no longer important whether we regard that act as plausible, but whether we are willing to worship that act. Bresson has transcended himself: he is blazed in mosaics in some moss-grown temple.

L.A. Free Press, 2 May 1969

Budd Boetticher: A Case Study in Criticism

Budd Boettcher is a 'discovered' director. His films, like those of so many directors, were not lost by time but by the simple volume of motion-picture production. A growing critical effort over the last decade, initiated by André Bazin in France and Andrew Sarris in America, has rescued him from the obscurity reserved for low-budget film-makers and brought him into a widening circle of critical attention.

But this rescue operation also situated Boetticher within a certain critical method, a method which became synonymous with the films themselves. There is a critical copyright which seems to govern new-found artists; for a certain period of time the discovering critics may exercise unhindered the critical rights over their discovery. Thus, Boetticher was an 'auteur' director, and his films were 'auteur' films.

But one must be careful not to confuse Boetticher's films with the critical method which brought them into the limelight. Critical methods have trends and histories of their own, and individual artists often get swept up in critical trends not ideally suited to them. Boetticher's films have substantial, universal qualities which surpass the limitations of his particular auteur, his personality. His films may, in fact, be better than even Boetticher or his best critics realize.

Boetticher was part of the original American-auteur cache of directors. In the spring 1963 *Film Culture*, Andrew Sarris thrust literally dozens of neglected film-makers on to a generally complacent critical establishment. Many of the directors Sarris classified already had their own following, and Sarris's own thinking derived from the auteur approach formulated by *Les Cahiers du Cinéma* six years previously, but, for all practical purposes, it was Sarris who catalysed American interest in these native directors. Sarris's original blurb on Boetticher was characteristically slight (as compared to Bazin's more substantial analysis of *Seven Men from Now* in 1957), but it did serve to midwife a succession of intelligent English-language criticisms about Boetticher. The criticism which resulted from Boetticher's 'discovery' was, naturally enough, auteur oriented.

I have no desire to rekindle the tired auteur debate, or even to pass judgement on the effect of auteurism (it's too premature); I simply want to use it as a comparative backdrop to another – and I think preferable – critical method with which to analyse Boetticher's films.

The auteur has meant many things in theory, but in practice it has usually meant a rather amiable combination of biographical and psychological criticism. Sarris constantly held up the test of 'personality' to a director, and the criteria he applied to a film were designed to reveal the personality behind it. He often pinpointed the unique, individual or idiosyncratic aspects of *mise-en-scène* which betrayed the director's personality. Auteurism's biographical–psychological orientation is most obvious in its excesses – the discussions of Hawks's 'masculinity', Lubitsch's 'touches', Tashlin's 'vulgarity', Preminger's 'cynicism', or of all forms of 'hitchcockery' in general. But even in the best of auteur criticism (which, at present, is the best practising 'school' of critics: the BFI–Cambridge group, Peter Wollen, Jim Kitses, Paddy Wannel, Alan Lovell, Robin Wood, Peter Harcourt) the biographical–psychological bias is present. Although these critics attempt (and, to varying degrees, succeed) to place auteurism within the formalist, 'textual' critical camp, an important, invaluable task, their criticism is usually, for better or worse, a formalist approach to the psychology of a particular individual. It is simply 'excellent' psychological–biographical criticism, as opposed to the 'poor' biog.–psych. criticism many writers associate with auteurism.

The knowledgeable auteur criticism of Boetticher's films has emphasized a central conflict: that of the moral man in an amoral universe. This conflict may be represented by the struggle between hero and villain, man and environment, individual and community, or intent and desire. In each instance a decision for the Right must be made and upheld by determination, intelligence, wit, and, sometimes, force. Jim Kitses in *Horizons West* contends that the heroes and villains are mirror images and that the moral struggle is essentially psychological: true individualism vs. narcissism. To Peter Wollen in an article in *New Left Review* (No. 32) the conflict is primarily environmental: the individual trapped in hostile, conformity-inducing surroundings. Opposed to Kitses, Peter Coonradt in a less substantial work (*Cinema*, IV–4) finds the struggle morally unambiguous: the just man within a moral vacuum.

All this is sound criticism, good criticism. My complaint with the Boetticher biog.–psych. criticism is not one of accuracy: the personality approach is often completely accurate. Once he gets a director on his psycho-critical couch, Sarris is remarkably adept at extracting the personality from the periphery. And Kitses' work on Boetticher, in particular, is astute and textual.

Instead, my complaint is one of adequacy: is auteurism with its psychological and biographical underpinnings a sufficient critical perspective with which to evaluate Boetticher's films? The most enduring qualities of a work of art are often not locked into the creator's personality, and no amount of auteur probing can reveal them. On the contrary, personality idiosyncrasies may be the most transitory aspects of a work of art. I don't doubt that Boetticher's personality is apparent in his films, but I doubt that a psychoanalysis of that personality, no matter how thorough, will provide the secret to their true worth.

Boetticher's reputation has and will continue to grow, and in time, I think, American critics may come to recognize him as one of the country's best directors, surpassing such presently acclaimed directors as Von Sternberg, Hitchcock, Lubitsch, or Hawks. His films do possess 'enduring' qualities, but to fully appreciate and assess them another set of critical principles will have to swing into motion.

The central conflict in Boetticher's films discussed by Kitses, Wollen, and Coonradt occurs not only on the individual level, but also on a more fundamental, archetypal level. The opposing force in his films is not only of this world, either psychological or environmental, but also of the other world: the autonomous force which, in Jungian terms, imposes itself on the human consciousness. All art is more or less archetypal (just as, I suppose, all art is more or less Marxistic), but in Boetticher's films the archetypes are overt and functional. Although his characters wear the familiar guise of individualism, in a moment of crisis they function not as individuals, but as archetypes.

The archetypal quality of Boetticher's work places it outside of the exclusive domain of auteur criticism, and situates it more within the realm of primitive and archetypal art. The primitive artist, as described by Wilhelm Worringer, is one who 'is confused and alarmed by life and seeks refuge from its apparent arbitrariness in the intuitive creation of absolute values'. In modern archetypal art the archetypes are less absolute, although none the less depersonalized and totemic. Jung's modern archetypes may be *Doppelgängers* (both *anima* and *animus*) and convey moral ambiguity within their archetypal image. But all archetypal art, whether primitive or modern, Wilbur Scott wrote, reflects a 'dissatisfaction with the scientific concept of man as, at his highest, rational'. Archetypal art stems from magic and religion, and even in its most secular forms still adheres to a vestige of the notion that there are men and objects which can serve as icons, and onlookers can be edified and sanctified by contemplating them.

Boetticher's archetypes are primitive in origin and function and strive, with varying degrees of success, toward the modern and ambiguous. Boetticher's primitivism is most noticeable in his bullfighting films, in which the archetypes function through physical acts rather than moral decisions. Boetticher's Westerns with Randolph Scott are more archetypal in modern terms, concentrating on the complexities and ambiguities of the moral decision. These modern qualities may not be exclusively Boetticher's but seem to result from the tension between Boetticher, the primitive director, and Burt Kennedy, the ironic, sophisticated screenwriter. Boetticher's Westerns will probably be his more lasting achievement, but to truly appreciate the Westerns one must go back to the bullfighting films, and a primitive view of life.

Boetticher has directed three films about bullfighting: *The Bullfighter and the Lady* (1951), *The Magnificent Matador* (1955), and the yet unreleased *Arruza*.

The bullfight has often been compared to the Mass; it is a comparison which separates bullfighting from the popular notions of 'sport' and sets it in the tradition of ritual. The matador can be, like the priest, a depersonalized, faceless man who does what no other man can do – mediate between this world and the next. It is possible for the priest to have a personality, it is even possible for others to be aware of that personality, but he must, in the process of ritual, function archetypally. It is not important to determine how a priest feels (or even who he is) during the Mass; similarly it may be not important to determine how a matador feels during the bullfight. At his purest each can be a totem to which spectators can respond collectively. As a priest becomes purified he becomes like an icon; as a matador becomes purified he becomes like the statues surrounding Plaza Mexico. It is not surprising that the Mass and the bullfight are often intertwined in Mexican life (and in Boetticher's films); they often are the reverse sides on the same archetypal coin.

The difference between sport and ritual in bullfighting is also the difference between individualistic and archetypal art. Sport is based on individual performance; we admire a 'sports star' for his peculiar skills. Ritual is based on form; we respect the archetype because he can embody certain ideals greater than himself. In ritualistic bullfighting, like primitive religion, the spectator appreciates the symbolic form, the conventions of confrontation between man and bull, between human nature and the forces of mystery and death. Bullfighting can be considered as sport, but its oldest, most fundamental affinities are with ritual.

In all of Boetticher's films there is a continuing tension between sport and ritual, individual and icon. This tension, which turns out to be an ironic asset in the Ranown Westerns, is an awkward liability in the bullfighting films. The contradiction between these two forms of characterization is at the surface of the bullfighting films, and the quicksilver transitions between individual and icon often strain credibility.

In *The Bullfighter and the Lady* the archetypal quality is called *stature*. The ageing matador Manolo Estrada (Gilbert Roland) and his wife Ceilo (Katy Jurado) have stature; the young American producer Chuck Regan (Robert Stack), who aspires to be a bullfighter, does not. Regan is initially presented in human terms, Manolo in archetypal terms. Regan is aggressive, exhibitionistic, inconsiderate; Manolo is mature, contented, serene. Regan is an individualist; Manolo is a formalist. Manolo studies the form of bullfighting, not just the skill, and when he performs, he performs formalistically. He is aware that his task as *el numero uno* entails more than exhibition of individual skill, but also something more universal and ritualistic.

Regan asks Manolo to teach him the skill of bullfighting, and Manolo reluctantly agrees. Regan quickly learns the craft, but gains none of the stature. Regan's bullfighting is an extension of his exhibitionism, and rather than follow the slow, methodical course of an apprentice matador, Regan wants to leap ahead to the big *corrida*. In his first major bullfight, however, he is about to be gored when Manolo saves him and is himself fatally gored in the process.

Then the predictable transformation occurs: Regan returns to the ring, wins the fight, and retires a sadder but wiser man. But this transformation occurs not only on the predictable level of melodrama; it also occurs on a more inexplicable level: Regan mysteriously gains stature. Not just maturity, skill, or wisdom, but an archetypal stature of the type Manolo possessed. He takes on Manolo's qualities: he prays to Manolo for strength and when he successfully completes the *pas de morte* he tells the crowd that it was Manolo's hand that guided the cape, not his. He becomes a surrogate for Manolo, who himself was a surrogate for the crowd.

The surprising thing about Regan's transformation is that he accomplishes it in the same manner he caused his downfall: through exhibitionism. Regan caused Manolo's death because he sought to show off, because he had mistaken the skill for the essence of bullfighting and tried to aggrandize himself as a matador. Yet it is through exhibitionism that he also gains stature. He re-enters the ring with a suicidal bent (having been warned by two authorities that this bullfight could mean his death); he seeks to hide from his disgrace in victory or death. Yet once Regan is in the ring, Boetticher justifies his exhibitionism. His exhibitionism becomes the exhibitionism of an archetype: he is permitted to show off because he presents more than himself, because he is Manolo come back to life. Exhibitionism is a fault in the individual, but a virtue in the archetype; and Boetticher makes no attempt to unravel this contradiction.

Boetticher's dilemma seems to be this: (1) he sees the matador as a person through the conventional perspective of psychology and individual achievement, (2) he sees the bullfight itself as a ritual, a mysterious primitive act, (3) but he has no convenient mechanism for putting the matador in the bullring, for transforming the individual into an archetype. It is natural that Regan's character flip-flops when he enters the bullring for the final time because it probably flip-flops in Boetticher's mind. Once Regan forgoes his safety and pride, mystically commits himself to the spirit of Manolo, and makes the pass of death, he is no longer the old Chuck Regan, but has been transformed into an enduring type, the matador performing a timeless ritual. It is fitting that *Bullfighter and the Lady* closes with a shot of the bullfighter's icon: one of the statues of Plaza Mexico.

Boetticher's next film about bullfighting, *The Magnificent Matador*, never confronted the latent contradiction in *Bullfighter*: the paradoxical combination of individual and icon in one man. *The Magnificent Matador* centres around a human, psychological struggle, the fear of a bullfighter who does not want his son to follow in his steps. It concentrates on the human side of the matador and never seems to catch that magic Boetticher feels about the bullring. Boetticher's dilemma, however, becomes very obvious again in his latest film and magnum opus, *Arruza*.

Arruza is unique in film history; it is a documentary about Boetticher's matador friend, Carlos Arruza, made over a ten-year period from 1956 to Arruza's death in 1966. Not only does the film offer dazzling footage of one of the world's top bullfighters at work, but it also offers the perspective of one artist upon another.

Arruza intermittently follows Arruza's family and friends, but for the most part traces his career from voluntary retirement to comeback success as a *rejoneador* (bullfighter on horseback). As a director, Boetticher does not have any *cinéma-vérité* scruples; he brazenly intercuts between staged and 'live' scenes. In fact, *Arruza* is more the product of its director than most documentaries. On several occasions Arruza complained that Boetticher was forcing him to undertake risks for the sake of the film that he would have ordinarily refused. Before the final triumphant fight at Plaza Mexico, Arruza reportedly told Boetticher that 'You're going to get me killed for the sake of your damn film.' Throughout the film the viewer is never sure if he is being treated to the 'true' Arruza or not.

Arruza was made, says Boetticher, 'because my best friend happened to be the best bullfighter in the world'. This contradiction permeates *Arruza*: best friend or best bullfighter? The tension between the bullfighter–friend and the bullfighter–archetype is as obvious in *Arruza* as in *The Bullfighter and the Lady*.

On one hand Boetticher sees Arruza as a pal and a longtime companion. He is interested in Carlos's emotions, his personality quirks, his relationship to his family and friends. There are many scenes designed to show the human side of Arruza, scenes with his wife, his children, and his bulls at Pasteje. For the most part these are the 'staged' scenes, contrived to demonstrate Arruza's humanity as if it were evidence to be presented in a courtroom. For example, Arruza in close-up looks wistfully over his farmland as the narrator (Anthony Quinn) states, 'Arruza was bored.' Such a scene fails first of all on the level of audience psychology: Boetticher cannot force audiences to read emotions into inexpressive faces, and the audience in turn reacts hostilely at being asked to. But, more importantly, the scene fails because it misdirects Boetticher's own interest in Arruza. Arruza's most interesting and worthwhile characteristic is not his emotions, and Boetticher seems to know it. These commonplace emotions are too petty and mundane for a character of the size Boetticher has made Arruza. Boetticher's heart does not seem to be in this textbook psychology.

On the other hand, Boetticher sees Arruza as an icon, an archetype in the longstanding ritual of the bullfight. It is in this that Arruza is truly unique, and it is for this, one expects, that Boetticher admires him. The 'live' bullfighting scenes are structured formalistically; they are based on the principles of return and repetition. Once in the ring, Arruza is an Everyman in an unchanging morality play. Arruza, whenever he performs, does essentially the same things, makes the same moves and passes, and the viewer assumes the same attitude, that of distant and attentive spectator. The viewer now sees Arruza two-dimensionally; any pretence of a psychological study vanishes. *Arruza* ends the same way it began, and the same way *Bullfighter and the Lady* ends, with a shot of one of the statues surrounding the Plaza Mexico – but this time the statue is of Arruza himself. The film concludes with a freeze-frame of Arruza in action, and the narrator, after briefly telling of his senseless death (he was killed in a car crash), states that no man is dead as long as he is remembered. The film then cuts to a concluding, long-angle shot of Arruza's statue. The mood and intent are consciously idolatrous; Arruza has been transformed into an icon, and now stands permanently, hieratically, at the gate of the bullfighter's temple. The shot is in direct contradiction to another of the final scenes, that of Señora Arruza and her children watching Carlos on TV. Arruza, now cast in iron before the Plaza Mexico, has no distinctive personality, no wife or children, and it seems unimportant whether or not he ever did. Nothing becomes Arruza's personality like the losing of it.

Again Boetticher's dilemma is painfully apparent. Boetticher-the-friend sees Carlos as a skilful, talented man with problems and neuroses much like anyone else's. Boetticher-the-spectator sees Arruza as many Mexicans have always intuitively seen the matador, as a primitive symbol of their collective unconscious. As in *Bullfighter*, Boetticher can shift his attitude quickly and without warning. Before the final bullfight there is a striking shot taken from within Arruza's car as it enters the Plaza. The point of view is Arruza's, and the viewer senses his fear and trepidation. But once inside the bullring the point of view becomes that of the spectator, and Arruza himself is part of a larger drama.

Budd Boetticher is probably the most primitive film-maker in American history. Movies were born of the twentieth century, a by-product of capitalism and technology, and although they were often naive, simple-minded and sentimental, they were seldom primitive. Many films presently considered primitive are only terse or simplistic. Films have often studied the individual plight, seldom the collective one.

Boetticher is intuitively obsessed with the primitive dilemma: at what point does the individual become archetypal? It is a theme of considerable intellectual depth (although Boetticher himself may not be a man of intellectual depth) and goes to the origins of art. It is primitive in the best sense of the word, neither vulgar nor jejune, but hieratic and archetypal.

The remarkable achievement of Boetticher's Westerns is that they can make the transition from individual to icon, becoming more modern and ambiguous in the process. Burt Kennedy's screenplays seemed to have provided Boetticher with the bridge he needed. Kennedy's scripts 'sophisticate' Boetticher's archetype: they force him into a world filled with irony, dark humour, pessimism and moral ambiguity. The intense pressure of adapting Kennedy's scripts (some of the Westerns were made on twelve-day shooting schedules) temporarily forced Boetticher out of his dilemma: Scott became a modern archetype, a man who sensed the difference between individual and icon and could vacillate between them.

The difference between Arruza and Scott is the difference between a morality based on action (good works) and decision (grace). In an article on morality plays (to which Boetticher's films have many affinities) Marvin Halverson makes a contrast between medieval and modern moralities, and it is a contrast very applicable to Boetticher's bullfighting films and Westerns.

The medieval morality play is based on the belief that man justifies himself before God by his good deeds. Man proves himself worthy of God's acceptance by the multitude of his good works. Thus *Everyman* sets forth the medieval notion that man, assisted by the various instrumentalities of the church, saves himself. However, the experience of twentieth-century man does not substantiate such a view, for he has found the sign NO EXIT posted at the dead-end road of autonomy.

Thus the differences between morality plays symbolize not only the changes in drama during the intervening centuries but they also embody a contemporary way of understanding life and a different comprehension of Christianity. *Therefore one might properly assert that there are two types of moralities: a morality of works and a morality of grace.*

The concept of grace is crucial in modern morality films (such as Robert Bresson's *A Man Escaped*) and it thrusts Boetticher's primitive archetype into a modern context. In the Ranown Westerns Randolph Scott does not save himself by his skill as the primitive, Arruza, had to. Instead, his weapons are intelligence, wit, and, most of all, a thoroughgoing sense of morality. With the exception of *Seven Men from Now*, Scott is not a particularly skilful gunfighter; he often finds himself at the mercy of others. In each Western his life is saved by his enemy at least once, and in *Buchanan Rides Alone* he is spared five times. He survives simply because he is Right, just as his foes fail because they are Wrong. There is no earthly reason why Scott should be victorious; in any 'normal' course of events he would be dead by the second reel. Time after time he recklessly lays his life on the line for his moral sense of right, and time after time he is exonerated. He seems sustained and guided by an external source he knows will justify him. Boetticher's Scott is, in a strange way, like Bresson's Joan of Arc, a person who lives by a special call and is not rationally responsive to the dangers of earthly existence.

It is through this mysterious grace that Scott exists, and it is his decision for grace that allows him to function archetypally, like a horseback Everyman. Grace, even in its secular form, is not something a man does like good works, but it is something that is both given to him and something he must choose. The dilemma of the Ranown Westerns, like modern morality plays, is not one of works but of grace, not of action but of decision. But the decisions are not easy; they are complex and ambiguous: a man must be aware that grace exists, know that it is possible for him to make a decision for it, make that decision, and stand by it to the point of death.

In the Ranown cycle the Boetticher–Kennedy characters save or damn themselves through moral decisions. Scott continuously confronts his enemy with the moral question. In *Comanche Station* Richard Rust says of a dead companion, 'It ain't his fault. All he knew was the wild side.' Scott replies, 'A man can cross over any time.' And Rust returns, 'It ain't that easy, it ain't that easy at all.'

'Crossing over' is not a matter of physical action, but of moral decision. Scott knows that crossing over 'ain't easy', but he also knows that it can be done, and therefore he never vacillates from his moral stance. Grace, this extraordinary power Scott possesses, is available to every character if he will only choose it. Sometimes the villains (who are very much like Scott himself) seem predestined to rejection of this grace. 'I come too far to turn back now,' Claude Akin says in *Comanche Station* before he shoots it out with Scott. But Scott rejects moral defeatism; when Richard Boone in *Tall T* states that 'Sometimes you don't have a choice,' Scott replies, 'Don't you?' And rarely – very rarely – it is possible for a villain to cross over and make the decision for the right, as Pernell Roberts does in *Ride Lonesome*.

Humour, or more accurately wit, is a measure of the 'modernity' of the Scott archetype. Manola and Arruza are relatively humourless men; they perceive and execute their task in a straightforward manner. In contrast, Randolph Scott has an endearing, laconic sense of humour. He dislikes confronting an opponent physically, preferring to use word-play and parable. He employs a crackerbarrel Socratic method: questioning, teasing, suggesting. Scott's task is only straightforward in principle; in reality it is ambiguous and circular. Scott not only finds irony in existence, but delights in it. Scott's wit is a defence mechanism: he knows that if he is patient time will justify his virtue, and irony provides the necessary distance so that he can be patient and wait for events to take their inevitable course. Virtue personified in an expedient world is an *ironic* situation, and Scott's irony allows him to exist in the world.

Scott's deep irony is unique in Boetticher's films and is probably a by-product of the working relationship with screenwriter Burt Kennedy. One might hypothesize the Boetticher–Kennedy interaction like this: Kennedy sought to 'play with' the Scott character, leading him into confusing, embarrassing, and demeaning situations. The scripts have often led Scott into degrading circumstances designed if not to demean an archetype at least to 'humanize' him: in *Tall T* he awkwardly bumps his head, in *Comanche Station* he hobbles about, howling in pain after an ointment is poured on his knee, and in *Decision at Sundown* he learns that his supposedly virtuous wife was not so pure after all. Perhaps Burt Kennedy is not directly responsible for these specific incidents, but this much is true: they are the type of indignities which Kennedy likes to inflict upon the heroes of his later Westerns (*The Rounders*, *The War Wagon*, *Support Your Local Sheriff*), and they do not occur in Boetticher's bullfighting films which were not scripted by Kennedy. Into each of these potentially demeaning situations comes Boetticher's matador archetype, determined to accomplish his task formalistically, precisely, and succinctly. But he can't: instead, he must avoid the snares Kennedy has laid for him. Out of this Boetticher–Kennedy tension evolves a modern, ironic archetype. Scott gains self-consciousness and insight, seeing the irony and seeming futility of life, yet none the less chooses Virtue, becoming a modern archetype – that is, a primitive figure who can exist in a contemporary situation.

Scott's decision for grace is exemplified by ironic wit because it often takes a sense of irony to accept grace in a modern world. The emphasis on *decision* in the Ranown Westerns situates them in the modern archetypal tradition: in the bullfighting films, as in *Everyman*, the archetype must only perform the ritual, the good work, whereas in the westerns, as in contemporary morality plays like Charles Williams's *Grab and Grace*, the archetype must make the decision in receiving grace to function archetypally. Randolph Scott can function as a primitive archetype like Arruza, but he can also function in a much more demanding and rewarding manner, like a modern archetype. Scott can bridge the gap between individual and icon because he knows that the gap is moral, not physical, and that the bridge is made of decision and grace.

The outer shell of this article has been the metaphor of critical method. The ambivalence that Boetticher can have about his characters is like the ambivalence a critic can have about Boetticher. Carlos Arruza may be considered a great exhibitionistic sports star, or he may be considered a faceless archetype; Budd Boetticher may be considered an idiosyncratic director, or he may be considered an archetypal director.

The choices open to Boetticher and his critics may be compared to what Jung called individualization and individuation. Both methods were open to a psychiatrist; both were accurate. Individualization concentrated on the uniqueness of a single personality. Individuation, which Jung favoured, searched out the non-idiosyncratic, universal qualities of the human psyche. Individualization sought to discover how men were different; individuation sought to discover how they were alike.

Some artists see the world as an extension of their own personality, and individualization serves them all. Other artists, like Boetticher, integrate their personality with universal, pre-existing archetypes, and individuation best reveals their contribution.

The auteur approach, to the extent that it emphasizes the *uniqueness* of Boetticher's personality, resembles individualization in psychiatry; it seeks out his superficial characteristics. When auteur criticism concentrates on Boetticher's personality it misses the crucial, archetypal qualities of his art. Kitses faults *Arruza* because 'its power is diminished by the nature of its fundamentally static hero'. An archetypal analysis, however, reveals the stasis is basic to Arruza's character as Boetticher understands it, and that stasis is, in fact, responsible for the power of the film. In describing Boetticher's art as individualistic, Wollen writes, 'For individualism, death is an absolute limit which cannot be transcended'; yet the ending of *Arruza* seems to contend just the opposite, that death is precisely the limit which the individual-become-archetype can transcend.

The psychological–biographical critical method bypasses the most enduring qualities of Boetticher's art. Carlos Arruza's most endurable quality was neither his personality nor his emotional depth, but his ability to function archetypally. Budd Boetticher's most endurable quality is neither his 'personality' nor his neuroses, but his intuitive need to integrate his personality into archetypal structures.

Boetticher's films have not found wide acceptance in the American critical community. Partially this is because many mass-media reviewers condescendingly reject 'discovered' auteur directors out of hand (Stanley Kauffmann's jab at Boetticher criticism in a review of Don Siegel's *Two Mules for Sister Sara* is a recent example); partially it is because of the limitations of the biographical–psychological method itself – Boetticher's 'personality' is certainly less rich than those of many other American directors: Welles, Chaplin, Hitchcock, Hawks, Peckinpah. But primarily it is because audiences and critics have often been slow to appreciate the great intuitive, primitive art that is all around them. The dilemmas of archetype and grace are situated in such commonplace conventions in Boetticher's films that many intellectuals cannot recognize them. They search for transcendence in the year 2001, in 'Jupiter and beyond', when perhaps the closest thing to an archetypal 'transcendence' has occurred in these neglected Randolph Scott Westerns.

W. H. Auden, in 'For the Time Being', contrasts the two groups of visitors to the manger, the Wise Men who spent an 'endless journey' through ideas and ideas to reach the Christ child, and the Shepherds who came immediately, instinctively to the same place. Other artists have found different metaphors for saying the same thing. In Bresson's *Pickpocket* Michel, after his spiritual 'liberation' in prison, says to Jeanne, 'How long it has taken me to come to you.' In Boetticher's *Ride Lonesome* Pernell Roberts, after he has finally 'crossed over' (the only one to ever do so successfully in a Boetticher Western), says to Scott, 'Funny, how a thing looks one way and turns out to be the other.'

Cinema, Volume 6, No. 2, 1971

Roberto Rossellini: *The Rise of Louis XIV*

Roberto Rossellini's *The Rise of Louis XIV* was made in 1966 and first shown in the United States at the 1967 New York Film Festival. It was an unpropitious première. The theme of the festival was 'The Social Film in Cinema' and there was a special seminar on the subject 'Reality Cinema: Whose Truth?' These were the halcyon (some would say corrupt) days of *cinéma vérité*: four of the many documentary films shown at the festival went on to obtain general release and a hitherto unknown degree of box-office success: *Titicut Follies, Don't Look Back, Warrendale, Portrait of Jason*, as did a documentary reconstruction film making free use of *cinéma vérité* techniques, *Battle of Algiers*. Lost in this rush for cinema truth was one of the pioneers of the techniques of hand-held camera and documentary reconstruction himself, Roberto Rossellini, and few took time to notice that the master had gone his own way, bypassing many of his disciples. Because of the cold critical reception of *The Rise of Louis XIV* at the festival, Rossellini was unable to get either the television or theatrical release for which he had been negotiating.

The New York Festival was only a microcosm for Rossellini's difficulties in the sixties. On several occasions he had publicly quarrelled with the leaders of the *cinéma vérité* movement. At the 1963 UNESCO film conference he accused Jean Rouch of substituting superficial and immediate truth for moral truth. ('Rouch,' Rossellini told the director of *La Punition* and *Chronicle of a Summer*, 'you have a talent to create and you use it to tear down' (*Artsept*, April–June 1963). In turn *cinéma vérité* theorist Louis Marcorelles accused Rossellini of 'forget(ting) his own early films' and of 'pointless aestheticism' (*Sight and Sound*, Summer 1963). The *cinéma vérité* spokesmen carried the day; their films were released, exhibited and praised. Rossellini was unable to work in the commercial cinema and like Jean Renoir turned to French television for support. His 1957 film *India* was never released in France and his subsequent documentary reconstructions, *Age of Iron* (1965) and *The Rise of Louis XIV* (1966), were only exhibited commercially in France and Italy.

But last year (1970) when *The Rise of Louis XIV* was finally released in New York the critical apathy had turned to enthusiasm. The *New York Times*, which in 1967 had described *Louis* as 'a mounting bore', now wrote that 'it is surely a masterpiece'. The *New Yorker*, *Newsweek*, and *New Republic* all followed suit with laudatory reviews, and *Louis* had an unexpected six-week New York run, outgrossing Truffaut's *Wild Child* in the same art-house circuit. After a decade of *cinéma vérité* films, audiences and critics seemed more willing to accept a documentary approach, which sought truth not in the immediate moment but in study and reflection. The successful 1970 release of *The Rise of Louis XIV* may signal a return to what Rossellini calls 'moral responsibility' in documentary films, and it will hopefully return Rossellini to a pre-eminent place in the field of documentary and documentary reconstruction. Rossellini is pioneering a method of film reconstruction of the distant past which may have as far-reaching implications as did his post-war reconstructions of the immediate past.

The Rise of Louis XIV reconstructs the kingship of Louis (Jean-Marie Patte) from the death of his godfather Mazarin (Silvagni) in 1661, when Louis was twenty-two, to his construction of Versailles in the 1680s. At the outset of the film the king is a fop and a pawn of his guardians. After Mazarin's protracted death he unexpectedly announces 'I will govern' and begins to consolidate his power. The Queen Mother, Anne of Austria (Katharina Renn), is gracefully removed from her position of power and the vain Foquet (Pierre Barrat) is gracelessly arrested in his own capital. Louis' rise is climaxed when he constructs the immense Versailles, populates it with sycophants, and establishes extravagant rules of court manners and dress to woo the noble class away from their local power bases and place them under his financial mien. His 'dandyism' is transformed into a power structure, and his elders are the pawns. These Machiavellian manoeuvres completed, the king, in the final scene of the film, slowly strips himself of his many outer garments and contemplates a maxim by La Rochefoucauld: 'Neither death nor the sun can be faced steadily.' The ultimate fantasy of the aristocrat has been fully achieved and the world's last great monarch is firmly established.

The Rise of Louis XIV is the second in a series of nonfiction historical films Rossellini has made since 1964. The others include: *The Age of Iron* (1964) in five one-hour episodes, *Acts of the Apostles* (1968) in four one-hour and one hour-and-a-half episodes, and *Socrates* (1970). In addition he has completed a script about Caligula and is presently writing a script on the American Revolution (for the US bicentennial celebration).

Louis is evidence of a theory and method of film-making Rossellini has developed throughout the sixties. The theory, at its simplest, is one of didacticism: film must set its roots in information and ideas. But unlike cinema's other great contemporary didacticist, Godard, Rossellini has turned to history for his subject-matter. It is only in the past that ideas can be isolated and defined. Rossellini seems more interested in understanding what has happened than effecting what will happen.

As early as 1958 Rossellini stated these 'humble' intentions: 'What I am trying to do is a piece of research, a documentation, on the state of man all over the world . . . as I find dramatic subjects I may move towards fiction film. But the first stage has to be research, the observation, and this has to be systematic' (*Sight and Sound*, Winter 1958–9). The first stage of Rossellini's method is, similarly, study and research. A film-maker must learn everything he can about his subject-matter, both from history and art, documents of the period and subsequent studies. These historically verifiable facts must then be presented on screen in the most coldly objective manner possible: they cannot be tampered with. The film-maker cannot let his ego or emotions (or those of his actors, cameraman or editor) editorialize upon or empathize with those facts. (Rossellini faults Fellini's *Satyricon* and Visconti's *The Damned* for doing this.) The past cannot be predicated upon present-day knowledge and attitudes. No one involved in a Rossellini film can project, act, or interpret what he does; there can be no attempt to directly evoke audience empathy.

This false 'objectivity' (pretending the past is beyond interpretive alteration), of course, is an interpretation of its own, but its effect on the viewer is crucially different from conventional film interpretations of history. Because Rossellini makes no attempt to plunge the viewer into the drama of the past, making the past relevant to his immediate feelings (much of *Louis* seems rightly irrelevant), the viewer has a sense of detachment rather than involvement, of awareness rather than empathy. He can fix his attention on the subtler, more revealing aspects of the past – the way meetings are conducted, gestures are made, curtains are hung. It is at this level, within rather than beyond history, that one finds Rossellini's 'interpretation' of Louis XIV.

The second stage of Rossellini's method, therefore, is aesthetic: organization and refinement. If it is also entertaining, ironic and interpretive, as it is, then these qualities are extensions of the aestheticism. The facts of the past must be framed and organized in such a manner as to reveal *their* – not Rossellini's, not our – intrinsic truth. This truth must not only correspond to history, but to art, not only to the political legacy of Louis XIV, but to the moral and artistic legacy as well.

Here, then, is the paradox of Rossellini's method: on one hand the film-maker must be factually faithful to the past, not interjecting his emotions or interpretations; on the other hand he must have a sufficient aesthetic vision to structure scenes and events so that they reveal their intrinsic 'truth' and are not simply anecdotal yarns or *cinéma vérité* snatches of life. How does a film-maker frame and organize the past so that it reveals its essential truth, both factual and moral, without himself becoming the creator of that past?

Rossellini is exploring some near-virgin territory in the fields of documentary reconstruction and historical presentation, and it is difficult to know what yardstick of success or failure can be applied to a film like *Louis*. One must be careful not to apply inappropriate criteria, such as those used by Marcorelles; it makes little sense to fault Rossellini for not being Don Pennebaker. Rossellini's method is certainly opposed to that of the *cinéma vérité* film-makers, but it is also in opposition to almost every previously successful method of historical film presentation. It is unlike that of John Ford, which seeks the mythological truth of the past; it is unlike that of Penn and Peckinpah, which seeks the moral truths of the present in the past; it is unlike that of the *Encyclopedia Britannica* documentarians, which seeks the factual truth of the past. Those who search out past models for every current success (*O tempora, O mores,* Herman Weinberg!) will have a difficult time finding suitable precedents for Rossellini's recent series of historical documentaries.

The Rise of Louis XIV should be analysed, I think, first and foremost as

Rossellini intended it, as history. It should not be initially thought of as a Roberto Rossellini film, or as a parable for modern times. *Louis'* filmic past should have a validity as past. The test of the past should be as thorough as possible and should include, one, the test of factuality: is *Louis* true to the letter of history book law? Two, the test of past credibility: do the actions and ideas of the film naturally spring from its mood and style, or does it falsely use a contemporary sensibility to portray past events? Three, the test of present credibility: without violating the necessary isolation of past credibility, does the film contain the seeds for subsequent cultural and political events? Four, the test of art and artefacts: is the film true to the *spirit* of the relics of Louis' reign, in art, literature, songs, religious texts?

If *Louis XIV* passes the test of the past, then it is only natural (and necessary) to ask why. How can a film seem to be true to the past when it is necessarily the collaboration between present-day artists and modern film communication? Asked in this way, the question can give a clue to Rossellini's true aesthetic 'interpretation' of the past.

To document the reign of Louis XIV Rossellini sought the aid of scholar Philippe Erlanger, whose monumental study of Louis has recently been published in English. Erlanger supplied the original story and data, ensuring the film's adherence to the historical evidence. They did not stack Louis' career, but instead attempted to present all sides of it equally: his success as well as failure, his cleverness as well as his blinding vanity. Louis is both politically brilliant: he ensures his power by cutting the ties between the nobility and the peasantry; and short-sighted: he implicitly rejects his Economic Minister's advice to tie himself to the peasantry by cutting taxes. Neither of these events is given weight over the other; they contain equally important information about a politically complex figure.

Louis XIV not only gives facts, however, it also conveys the sense of time and place in which those facts have meaning. This sense is not only revealed in the obvious characteristics of the period, like rampant sycophantism, the political vacuum of the upper echelons of power, and the total lack of moral direction from the Church, but also in the subtler social aspects such as dress, gait and gesture.

The film opens, for example, with the death of Cardinal Mazarin, the King's godfather. At Mazarin's bedside the court doctors one by one sniff a basin of his urine and after some contemplation or debate they decide that although his death is imminent Mazarin should be bled anyway. The bleeding begins: the livid, sweating Mazarin winces in pain as the blood is drained from his emaciated body. From this point the excretory smell only grows stronger. Several hours later, shortly before the young king's last visit to his bedside, Mazarin paints himself with rouge and make-up to give himself the illusion of health. The falseness and sham are apparent to everyone, yet they are none the less essential and effective for being false. Such is Louis' world.

The compositions and editing reinforce the cumulative smell of stench. Each frame has an ornate, sickly love of detail. There are few clear-cut lines: reds and yellows bleed into each other. There are few wide open spaces: most scenes take place in claustrophobic, baroque rooms with the sycophants crowding the frame for a place near Louis. Until the concluding, thematic scene Louis is never seen alone. All of his activities, love-making, eating, dressing, strolling, are public spectacles. Louis does not alleviate this claustrophobic decadence: he heightens and manipulates it. At the outset of the film the members of the court wear relatively sombre, black and white costumes, but when Louis introduces his new sybaritic mode of dress, the frame becomes increasingly cluttered with trains and ruffles and unfriendly, clashing colour schemes.

Yet Rossellini's stoical camera never reacts against this accumulation of discordant detail. It does not, like Visconti's camera in *The Damned*, zoom, track and jump about these lurid settings. The stolid camera simply sits, soaking everything into its dispassionate gaze. Rossellini's camera is like one of Louis' courtiers: it watches, it knows, it obeys. For the modern viewer it is as if Mazarin's basin of urine is sitting on a pedestal at the front of the theatre; everyone knows it is there, the smell growing increasingly rank, yet no one gets up to remove it.

The Rise of Louis XIV has an almost terrifying sense of past credibility: those ludicrous costumes and risible court manners are no longer the senseless affectations one always thought they were, but are the precise machinations of power. No action seems too silly, no pretence too great: these are the marks of a truly totalitarian government which can transform vanity into a source of power. Without violating this immediate sense of the past, *Louis* also offers a present-day credibility: the seeds of anarchy and revolution lie everywhere dormant. As the spectator's desire to clean out the cluttered frame, to overturn that basin of dead man's piss, grows, so does his comprehension of the unrestrained frenzy of the French Revolution. In Rossellini's film there is both the image of complete order and restraint and the suppressed rage for chaos.

Louis XIV is also true, at the fourth level, to the art of the period it portrays. There remains nothing today which has survived Louis XIV quite as well as Versailles itself. Long after his power has vanished, his legend faded, his political effect diminished, Louis' masterwork still tells

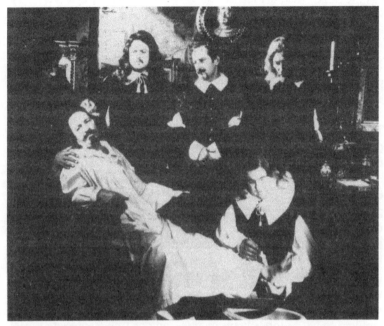

8 'Claustrophobic, baroque rooms with sycophants crowding the frame':
Rossellini's *The Rise of Louis XIV* (1966).

his story. It has an order, a symmetry, a totally unfunctional ornateness which represents Louis better than all the historical records. In these halls, balustrades and gardens the Sun King still shines. *The Rise of Louis XIV* has the same order, decadence and vanity as Versailles. Like Versailles, Rossellini's film has both a sense of symmetry and circuitousness. There are no clean lines, no functionality: everything seems pomp and circumstance, and the underlying structure is everpresent. Like Versailles, *Louis XIV* gives the modern spectator the immediate sense of an anachronistic past: like the old relic, it has survived to give us information about and ideas of the past.

There is a natural tendency to say that the past of the film is Rossellini's past and its Louis is Rossellini's Louis (as José Luis Guarner does in his recent book on Rossellini), but this is unfair to the intent of Rossellini's method and misses the true value of his work. Rossellini does not care to make the past 'relevant' or 'personal'; he only desires to give it validity as past. If the past is valid as past, Rossellini would say, then it is necessarily relevant to all humans. When asked how *Louis XIV* relates to us today, Rossellini replied, 'I don't know and I don't care. What is relevant is to know the facts of history and because we are the same it is good to know' (*Medium*, Winter 67–8). The filmic Louis is first of all history's Louis, and it is Rossellini's method which has enabled history to take such a meaningful form. Not until one first realizes the audacity and genius required to put history's Louis on film, can one truly appreciate Rossellini's accomplishment.

Rossellini's contribution is simple but crucial; he allows the past to stand in its own right; he assembles the many threads of history and art so that they reveal their intrinsic truth. Like other masters of visual composition and structure, Rossellini's power lies in his ability to *let* an image reveal itself rather than *make* it reveal itself. No emotional or editorial contrivances are forced upon the image: it is not made to twist or turn, to run or jump, to hide or camouflage. Rossellini has great respect for the power of the photographed image, for its composition and lines of force, for its 'inner dynamic'.

The Rise of Louis XIV evidences a thoroughgoing economy of artistic means. There are many long two or more minute takes and a minimum of lateral camera movement. The action and décor are precisely organized within the frame and the camera examines them from a fixed position. The settings are fixed: the characters enter into them, discuss matters trivial and weighty, and exit. The emphasis throughout the film remains on the ornate décor, the elaborate, meticulously constructed late-baroque world of Versailles and seventeenth-century France. There is little 'acting' per se. The actors are non-professionals who recite their lines by rote and without inflection. The editing is also extremely functional: it is the necessary glue which affixes one tableau to the next.

Yet all these seemingly anonymous techniques are guided by Rossellini's directorial hand. It is he who frames each image and sets each shot next to its neighbour, and if the accumulation of these frames seems to reveal Louis' true history, its vanity, power and moral vapidity, then it is Rossellini who has allowed it to happen.

Rossellini's formal techniques do not mean that Louis was any more quiescent than ourselves or that his regime is somehow best represented by the long take. These are instead the techniques which best enable the viewer to understand the past. Like history itself, Rossellini's film asks to be analysed rather than participated in. This may not seem unusual for the historian, but it is relatively unique for the film-goer. Rarely is a viewer able to intellectually analyse a subject *as he is watching it*: detached comprehension is inevitably sacrificed to the relentless march of melodrama. *What's the use of history if the kids don't dig it?* The bookish historian may want film to help him *experience* the past, but the intellectually starved movie-goer needs film to help him *understand* it. And Rossellini, like a few great didacticists, can walk this tightrope between empathy and awareness.

The value of analysing a subject *as you see it* is simply that you see more. The viewer can study the seemingly insignificant events and objects which would normally pass him by. It is like seeing a film for the second time the first time. There are no compelling plots or strong characterizations to monopolize the viewer's interest, the viewer has the time and inclination to examine all that Rossellini presents: not only the themes but the details, not only the dialogue but the compositions. In this detached perspective *Louis'* colour scheme plays as important a role as its politics. The truth of the past lies as much in the forgotten gesture as in the consequential execution, and if the viewer can be aware of them both simultaneously then he understands it more. When a viewer makes the connections between the seemingly trival and the supposedly weighty, he goes beyond history-book facts to a comprehension of the unity of a time and place: its facts, customs, morality, ideas.

Rossellini's 'interpretation' of history, therefore, is elusive because it is aesthetic. On the one hand Rossellini, like a philosopher and historian, has a firmly rooted understanding of and respect for man's past, on the other hand, like an artist, he has the ability to recreate it. Neither of his occupations, historian and artist, seems subservient to the other, and his recent films have the unexpected impact of both history and art.

Some reviewers, such as Penelope Gilliatt of the *New Yorker*, were a bit taken aback to find Rossellini 'of all people' espousing a cold, factual cinema. This certainly seems at odds with his textbook reputation, which presently has him cast as the neo-realist director of *Open City* and *Paisan*, films whose 'realism' was more personal than cold, more political than unbiased, more naturalistic than objective. To many film-goers Rossellini is still the neo-realist hero of Siegfried Kracauer and John Howard Lawson, and they find it difficult to realize that he has grown while their viewpoint has remained fixed. (Like a star, a director can become critically typecast.) The evolution of Rossellini's documentary aesthetic, however, could catch even the most astute movie-goer by surprise: in the same month (March, 1963) Rossellini was attacking Rouch for cinematic immorality, Truffaut was explaining the debt of Rivette, Godard, Rouch and himself to the director of *Open City* and *Paisan* (*Roberto Rossellini*, Éditions Seghers).

André Bazin, in 1957, was one of the first to defend Rossellini from the charges which would be levelled against him in the sixties. Bazin contended that Rossellini's *Voyage in Italy* (1953) was not a break from the neo-realist principles, but a continuation and extension of them. 'With him,' Bazin wrote, 'neo-realism naturally rediscovers the style and the means of abstraction. For to respect reality does not mean to accumulate details; on the contrary, it means to strip reality of everything that is not essential, to achieve totality in simplicity' (*Qu'est-ce que le Cinéma? IV*). If Bazin were alive today I'm sure he could adapt the term *neo-realism* to describe *The Rise of Louis XIV*, but the essential point is not one of semantics. Rossellini's recent films are a refinement of his neo-realist techniques, not a break from them. What many viewers thought was the heart of his neo-realist style turned out to be the vignettish, personal periphery, and he has gradually stripped it away. The heart of his 'neo-realist' documentary approach is aesthetic perception: the setting of realist tableaux side by side in such a manner as to reveal their lasting value, their autonomous validity as events and ideas.

It is this rare, elusive aesthetic perception which so many historical films and documentaries lack. Of all the documentaries which received greater favour than *Louis XIV* at the 1967 New York Festival, none could offer its moral and intellectual complexity. The *cinéma vérité* documentarians played an indispensable role in the film-making of the sixties, they revitalized film technique and brought the man on the street in front of the camera. But it is time, I think, for the *cinéma vérité* film-makers to be revitalized themselves, and for this they can do no better than to return to the footsteps of their old mentor Roberto Rossellini.

The recent Maysles brothers *cinéma vérité* film *Gimme Shelter*, for example, is a shameless mixture of pandering and profiteering. Their subject-matter ranges from the death of a man to the death of a movement, yet they pretend to be the everpresent innocents. The Maysles could point their camera in the right direction, but they simply were not equipped to give their subject-matter the moral and historical perspective it demanded. The ageing youth movement desperately needs a Rossellini: one who respects the integrity of his material, understands it, and can organize it.

For the third time in his career Rossellini has returned to the creative forefront of his trade. In his first *Open City* period, in his early fifties films with Ingrid Bergman, and now in his historical documentaries, Rossellini has shown film-makers a new, distinctly moral direction. When the treatment of reality on screen is again at a crucial stage, when Godard is drifting away into rhetoric, when many *cinéma vérité* film-makers have opted for the facile truth and the quick dollar, when the Newsreel documentarians proceed as if there were no past, Rossellini has again shown us the way.

Cinema, Volume 6, No. 3, 1971

Sam Peckinpah Going to Mexico

'*The Wild Bunch* is simply,' says director Sam Peckinpah, 'what happens when killers go to Mexico.' And in the beleaguered career of Sam Peckinpah Mexico has become increasingly the place to go. It is a land perhaps more savage, simple, or desolate, but definitely more expressive. Sam Peckinpah's Mexico is a spiritual country similar to Ernest Hemingway's Spain, John London's Alaska, and Robert Louis Stevenson's South Seas. It is a place where you go 'to get yourself straightened out'.

The Wild Bunch is Peckinpah's first unhampered directorial effort since *Ride the High Country* in 1962. The intervening seven years had brought personal bickerings, thwarted projects, blacklisting – and belated critical acclaim. Critics called *Ride the High Country* an 'American classic', and Peckinpah wrangled for TV writing assignments. When Peckinpah finally regained his voice he found it had changed. The violence had lost its code, becoming instead something deeper and more deadly. The new violence responded to the years fresh in Peckinpah's memory, the new mood of the country, but, more importantly, to a feature of his personality which had previously worn more polite guises.

After working for director Don Siegel and on 'The Westerner' TV series, Peckinpah's first film was a small-budget Western, *Deadly Companions* (later called *Trigger Happy*), which he now describes as 'unmanageable' and a 'failure'. But it did catch the attention of Richard Lyon who brought Peckinpah to MGM and produced *High Country* that same year. A year later in the Winter 1963 issue of *Film Quarterly*, editor Ernest Callenbach wrote about *High Country*: 'When it appeared no one took it terribly seriously. But as time wore on, its unobtrusive virtues began to seem more appealing, and by now it is hard to see what American picture of 1962 could be rated above it.' But in 1962 MGM, like the daily reviewers, was unprepared for this leisurely moral fable; *High Country* filled out the second half of double bills in neighbourhood theatres and drive-ins.

Ride the High Country was painfully an old man's picture, all the more painful because its director was only thirty seven years old. Two old gunfighters, Joel McCrea and Randolph Scott, are reduced to guarding a $20,000 gold shipment from a small mining town. In an extention of their earlier roles McCrea extols the virtues of the classic Western code of honour and Scott tempts him to run off with the gold they both admit they well deserve for their selfless past of gunfights and wound-mending. After a scuffle Scott becomes reconciled to McCrea's code, not because the code is particularly appropriate, but simply because they are old Westerners. Together they stand off three coarse, half-crazed brothers. In the fusillade McCrea is killed and dies a hero's death saying, 'I want to go it alone,' as his bullet-ridden corpse sinks to the bottom of the frame. *Ride the High Country* had it both ways: it presented old Westerners caught up in their own outdated myth, and also justified their existence in terms of that myth. British critic Richard Whitehall wrote that *High Country* 'is not only a celebration of the myth, it is also a requiem'. Sam Peckinpah's film more acutely captured the Westerner's old age pangs than did two films of the same period by old Westerners about old Westerners, John Ford's *The Man Who Shot Liberty Valance* and Howard Hawks' *Rio Bravo*. Like McCrea and Scott, Ford and Hawks could close their careers with honour and dignity: Peckinpah had to look beyond the myth and situate it in time. In retrospect the Sam Peckinpah of *High Country* seems to be playing the game of Western directors like Ford, Hawks, George Sherman, Delmer Daves and Budd Boetticher. In many ways he was playing the game better, but it still wasn't Peckinpah's game. *Ride the High Country* was a prologue, not an epilogue.

Ride the High Country and Peckinpah's TV programmes demonstrate certain values which, prior to *The Wild Bunch*, have invariably been associated with the director. In 1963 he told *Film Quarterly*, 'My work has been concerned with outsiders, losers, loners, misfits, rounders – individuals looking for something besides security.' These heroes, often old in body as well as mind, fall back on certain virtues: biblical stoicism, practicality, primitivism, and honour. When a Peckinpah character makes the effort to verbalize his desires, which is rare, they are often banal. In Peckinpah's Dick Powell Theater episode 'The Losers' (1963) Lee Marvin tells Keenan Wynn, 'Peace of mind and an understanding heart. That's all we need.' This is not obvious satire, but pure Peckinpah hokum; the insidious parody comes in when his characters, in rare moments, can actually come near to obtaining such a goal.

The crucial line in *Ride the High Country*, a line by which Peckinpah has often been characterized, was a simple profession by Joel McCrea: 'I want to enter my own house justified.' The line originally came from Peckinpah's father, a Superior Court Judge of Fresno County, California, and before that it came from the Gospel of St Luke, the parable of the Pharisee and the Publican. Some of Peckinpah's most vivid memories of his Madera County, California, childhood were his family's dinner table discussions about justice, law and order. 'I always felt like an outsider,' he says. It was in the strong biblical sense of the Publican that Peckinpah sought to justify his characters – and himself – and it has been his desire to justify himself in his own way that has informed his early work. In *High Country* McCrea, Scott, and a fanatically religious farmer swap biblical texts, each trying to make his point. McCrea loses the battle of the text, but wins justification in the battle of honour. The farmer deprives his daughter of a full life; McCrea returns it to her by sacrificing himself meaningfully. Both the farmer and the gunslinger died, but only one went to his home justified. Peckinpah has no qualms about adding the second half of the biblical injunction regarding justification, 'Whom he justified, them he also glorified.' McCrea's glorification was explicit, unsubtle, and shattering.

Honesty and purity of intent (and thereby justification) no longer come naturally to the Westerner (as they did to the Virginian); they must be fought for and defended. Peckinpah's characters are ruthlessly cynical about ways to protect the Westerner's code against the corrosive influence of 'civilization'. The code is not a game, but must be defended in every way possible, even unsporting ways. In 'Jeff', Peckinpah's favourite episode of 'The Westerner' series, a bare-knuckled boxer-pimp complains that the Peckinpah hero, David Blasingame (Brian Keith), isn't being a good sportsman. 'You're a bad loser, Mr Blasingame,' the heavy says. 'I sure am,' replies Blasingame. 'This isn't a game.'

As in all Westerns, the gun is immediately behind the code. Sooner or later it comes down to killing. Like the code, the gun is not a plaything. In another 'Westerner' episode, 'Hand on the Gun', Blasingame tells a cocky Easterner, 'A gun ain't to play with. It's to kill people. And you don't touch it unless you plan to shoot, and you don't shoot unless you plan to kill.' Implied in that logical progression were the tenets that you don't kill unless you have to, or you don't kill without a purpose. In his early work Peckinpah clung tenaciously to the Western code. *Ride the High Country* was great as a 'Western' – at heart it functioned the way Westerns were supposed to function. But there was also a strong sense of expectation. Sam Peckinpah was young and strong; the code was old and weak. Something had to give.

But nothing had a chance to give. After *High Country* came Sam Peckinpah's seven lean years. Peckinpah underwent a series of reputation-damaging producer clashes. And as Orson Welles learned so well, once a film-maker's reputation is damaged in Hollywood nothing short of a miracle can retrieve it. No longer is the bum script, the meddling producer, the restrictive budget to blame, but the fault always falls on 'that' director, the kiss of death.

Major Dundee was Charlton Heston's idea. He had seen *High Country*, loved it, and proposed Harry Julian Fink's script to Peckinpah. *Major Dundee* was Peckinpah's first big budget film (costing $2½ million compared with $813,000 for *High Country*). Producer Jerry Bresler (*The Vikings, Diamond Head, Love Has Many Faces*) was described by a member of the cast as 'wall-to-wall worry'. In a power play with the studio, Columbia, Heston and Peckinpah won the right to shoot the entire film on location in Mexico, and also, supposedly, final cut privileges. But after the film was shot Heston and Peckinpah's influence began to wane. Peckinpah's final cut ran three hours. Columbia wanted it shortened, and Peckinpah cut it to two hours and forty minutes, suggesting that ten minutes should go back in. But Bresler got nervous, Peckinpah assumes, and cut the film to under two hours. Peckinpah asked that his name be left off the credits, contending that the film was neither the long powerful film he intended, nor the short action film it could have been. Peckinpah still regards his two hour forty minute version as an excellent film, but there are few to verify his opinion. Against contractual obligations neither of Peckinpah's cuts was ever previewed. Heston was one of the few who saw it, and he liked it so much that he offered to turn back his salary if the picture were left untouched. Peckinpah also offered to defer most of his salary, but Columbia won the day and *Major Dundee* premiered as a double-bill feature in multiple situations. The anonymous *Newsweek* reviewer knew where to set the blame for the *Dundee* fiasco. His review began, 'Think of Yosemite Falls, or suicides from the top of the Empire State Building, or the streaking of meteorites downward toward the earth, and you get some idea of the decline in the career of Sam Peckinpah.' Like Welles after the *Journey into Fear* débâcle, Peckinpah saw his reputation plummet without being able to do a thing about it.

Another Hollywood producer played the next part in the decline of Peckinpah's career. He accused Peckinpah of being a 'perfectionist', adding that Peckinpah wanted to make a dirty movie (sex is a remarkably minor factor in Peckinpah's films, and whatever there is is far from titillating). Peckinpah found himself on the street. A projected film for MGM and another for Heston failed to materialize. 'I got angry and named names,' Peckinpah says. 'Then I spent three and a half years without shooting a camera. That's what you call black-listing,' Peckinpah says. 'I made a living, but for a director there can be nothing but making a film. It was a slow death.' During those three and a half years he wrote a Western called *The Glory Guys*, which was filmed by Arnold Laven in 1965, and *Villa Rides*, which was rewritten by Robert Towne and directed by Buzz Kulik. Peckinpah's only minor triumph during this period came when he filmed Katherine Ann Porter's *Noon Wine* for ABC's 'Stage 67' programme. Peckinpah's adaptation starred Jason Robards, Olivia DeHavilland, Per Oscarsson, and Theodore Bikel, and won the praise of critics as well as Miss Porter. That year the Screen Directors' Guild ironically selected Peckinpah one of the ten best television directors.

In late 1967 producer Phil Feldman selected Sam Peckinpah to direct *The Wild Bunch*, Feldman's second producing effort (the first was Francis Ford Coppola's *You're a Big Boy Now*). 'It was nice to get picked off the street and given a $5 million picture,' Peckinpah reflects. 'This picture came about only because of two wonderful reasons: Phil Feldman and Ken Hyman.' Although Peckinpah didn't have final cut rights, *The Wild Bunch* was shot and edited the way he desired. 'A good picture is usually 70 per cent of your intentions. *Ride the High Country* was 80 per cent for me. I'd say *The Wild Bunch* was about 96 per cent. I'm very satisfied.'

Peckinpah's original cut of *The Wild Bunch* ran over three hours.

Warner Bros. was understandably queasy about many of the graphic scenes of killing. Two disastrous previews (one in Kansas City and the other in Hollywood) had indicated some degree of audience revulsion. 'I hope you drown in a pool of Max Factor Technicolor blood,' one UCLA graduate film student told Peckinpah. Warner Bros. stuck with Peckinpah, however, letting him cut the film down to its present two hours and twenty-three minutes. 'There was never danger of an "X" rating for violence,' Peckinpah says. 'We had an "R" right from the beginning. I actually cut out more than Warners requested. There were certain things Warners wanted cut, but I went farther. I had to make it play better.' To make the film play better Peckinpah excised much of the explicit violence in the initial fight scene, particularly the disembowellings, letting the violence come at the audience more gradually. Included in the 4 per cent Peckinpah regretted losing was a flashback of William Holden (in addition to the present two flashbacks of Robert Ryan and Holden). The flashback, which is curiously included in the international print, revealed how Holden had received a leg wound.*

At one point in the pre-release intrigue of *The Wild Bunch* Peckinpah feared that it would receive the inadequate distribution of his earlier films. 'It was a funny thing,' he says. 'The European distributor saw it and said, "Roadshow". The domestic distributor saw it and said, "Double-bill".' This time Peckinpah won the battle and *The Wild Bunch* came to be regarded as Warner Bros.' 'picture of the summer' and received a massive publicity campaign.

The Wild Bunch is again about old Westerners and killing. Like McCrea and Scott, the Wild Bunch are battle-weary veterans of many movie Westerns: William Holden (8 Westerns), Robert Ryan (14), Ernest Borgnine (10), Edmund O'Brien (10), Ben Johnson (16) and Warren Oates (8). Warner Bros. wanted to cast a 'young leading man' in the role of Holden's sidekick, but Peckinpah balked. 'Someone said what about old Ernie

---

*On 18 July Warner Bros. cut five minutes from the domestic print of *The Wild Bunch*. The original idea was, Peckinpah says, to cut out the flashbacks in two theatres. Instead three scenes were excised in 400 theatres. The flashback of Ryan's capture and Holden's escape in a brothel was cut out, as was the flashback to the death of Syke's nephew Crazy Lee (Bo Hopkins, who says 'I'll hold 'em here till Hell freezes over or you say different, Mr Pike'). Particularly damaging was the deletion of the entire Las Trancas battle scene, mentioned later in this article. The battle sequence revealed the other side of Mapache's character, the *machismo* in battle and defeat. Without the sequence, Mapache is only comic relief, a drunken sot. The reason for the 18 July cut, the *New York Times* News Service reported, was to shorten the picture, thereby allowing the distributors more screening times per day. One theatre, however, the Pacific Pix in Hollywood, used the extra time to insert a 'Tom and Jerry' cartoon. Peckinpah is no longer 'very satisfied'. – P.S.

Borgnine and I said, "Go to it." ' The year is 1914, the pickings are slim, and the killers are tired. 'This is about what Bill Holden is today,' Peckinpah says, 'fifty, middle-aged, wrinkled, no longer the glamour boy.' Holden talks wistfully about giving up the Bunch's outlaw existence. 'We're getting old. We've got to think beyond our guns . . . I'd like to make one good score and back off,' he tells Borgnine. 'Back off to what?' Borgnine replies.

On the action level, *The Wild Bunch* is the most entertaining American picture in several years. The scenes flow evenly and quickly, and the highpoints seem to pile on top of each other. The editing (by Lou Lombardo, assisted by Peckinpah) is superb, if only for its unostentatiousness. Although *The Wild Bunch* has more cuts than any other picture in Technicolor – 3643 – it flows naturally and smoothly. Lombardo skilfully intercuts slow motion shots (taken at 25, 28, 32, 48, and 64 frames per second) with normal action, demonstrating Eisenstein's theory of collision montage even better than the master himself, whose assemblages always seemed more didactic than natural. Someone suggested to Peckinpah that the editing of *The Wild Bunch* was as good as any in the Kurosawa samurai epics. 'I think it's better,' he replied.

'*The Wild Bunch* is a very commercial picture, thank God,' Peckinpah says. 'I just happened to put some of myself into it.' It is important to Peckinpah that *The Wild Bunch* be a 'commercial' picture and play to large audiences, and not only to retrieve its large budget (approaching, by common estimate, $8 million), Peckinpah's film speaks in common, proletarian themes and is effective for even the most unsophisticated audiences. Its first appeal is to the vulgar sensibility: callous killings, bawdy jokes, boyish horse-play. *The Wild Bunch* flaunts the vulgar exhilaration of killing. Like the best of American films of violence, *The Wild Bunch* has it both ways: it uses violence to excite and then applies more violence to comment on the excitement. And like such indigenous, murderous American masterpieces as *Underworld*, *Scarface*, *The Killing*, *Bonnie and Clyde*, *The Wild Bunch* puts the stinger in the butterfly; the violence moves beyond itself, becoming something much more virulent: artifice.

Peckinpah carefully manages his violence, bargaining between the violence the audience wants and the violence he is prepared to give. Peckinpah uses violence the way every dramatist has, to make the plot turn. Then he applies vicarious violence to the plot mechanism. We don't really care whether it's logical if so-and-so is killed; we need more blood to satiate our appetite. Most 'serious' war films do not progress beyond vicariousness; we simply want to be better war heroes. At the final level, the most difficult, Peckinpah goes beyond vicariousness to superfluity. We no longer want the violence, but it's still coming. Violence then can either become gratuitous or transcend itself. Peckinpah enjoys walking the thin line between destructive and constructive violence. For much of the film he allows the violence to verge on gratuity, until, at one moment, it shifts gears and moves beyond itself. For Peckinpah, this moment occurs during the literal Mexican stand-off at Mepache's Aqua Verde encampment. Holden shoots the general as two hundred soldiers watch on. A silence falls; no one moves. A few soldiers tentatively raise their hands; the Wild Bunchers look at each other and begin to laugh. This is what their lives have led to, one brief moment between life and death. And into death they plunge, the gore and bodies mounting higher and higher.

Robert Warshow wrote that the Western was popular because it created a milieu in which violence was acceptable. After years of simplistic Westerns, Peckinpah wants to define that milieu more precisely. Violence, Peckinpah seems to say, is acceptable and edifiable primarily for the spectator. It may also be edifiable for the participant, but only to the extent that it is suicidal. Like the Western code, it succeeds most when it is self-destructive. To be of any value, violence must move from vicariousness to artifice. The spectator must be left 'disinterested' in the Arnoldian sense, evaluating what he had previously revelled in.

In the post-slaughter epilogue of *The Wild Bunch* Peckinpah rubs the spectator's nose in the killing he has so recently enjoyed. New killers arrive to replace the old. A way of life has died, but the dying continues. In a departing gesture of shocking perversity Peckinpah brings back the fade-in fade-out laughing faces of each of the Wild Bunch killers to the stirring chorus of 'La Golondrina'. This is Sam Peckinpah's Mount Rushmore: four worn-out frontiersmen who ran out of land to conquer and went to Mexico to kill and be killed. It is a blatant parody of Ford's *Long Grey Line* and the petulant perversity of it, like the final gunning down of Bonnie and Clyde, throws the viewer out of the movie and into the realm of art. It is one of the strongest emotional kickbacks of any film. The viewer leaves the theatre alone, shattered, trying to sort out the muddle Peckinpah has made of his emotions. A friend after seeing *The Wild Bunch* for the first time remarked, 'I feel dirty all the way through.' Peckinpah wouldn't have it any other way.

The Westerners of *The Wild Bunch* have only the remnants of the code. They mouth many of the familiar platitudes but the honour and the purpose are absent. The cynicism has hardened; it no longer protects another set of values, but is a way of life in itself. When Angel, the only Mexican Wild Buncher, grieves over his recently murdered father, Holden perfunctorily admonishes him, 'Either you learn to live with it or we leave you here.' As Holden explains later, '$10,000 cuts an awful lot of family ties.' The Wild Bunch do have their particular code, which they like to think separates them from the others. Concerning Mapache, Borgnine remarks, 'We ain't nothing like him. We don't kill nobody.' When Ben Johnson threatens to leave the Bunch, Holden warns him, 'I either lead this Bunch or end it right now.' And later, 'When you side with a man you stay with him. If you can't do that you're no better than animal. You're finished. We're finished.' But the irony of the Wild Bunch is that they are finished, and that they are little more than animals. The Bunch has taken on the characteristics which McCrea repudiated in *High Country*. Warren Oates, playing one of the vulgarized, psychopathic Hammond brothers in *High Country*, explodes in frustrated anger during the final shoot-out, wildly shooting at some nearby chickens. In *The Wild Bunch* there is a similar scene when Ben Johnson, after he and Oates have refused to pay a young whore an honest wage, plays with a baby sparrow, killing it. Unlike Blasingame in *The Westerner*, the Wild Bunch draw their guns often, with little purpose and obvious delight. McCrea and Scott have died, the Hammond brothers have firmed up and headed for Mexico. It could be said that the Bunch represents 'better' Westerners, in contrast to the broad comedy bounty hunters, but this was not Peckinpah's primary intent. 'I wanted to show that each group was no better than the next,' he says. The only thing that distinguishes the Wild Bunch is their ability to die appropriately.

The Wild Bunch is not a 'Western' in the sense of *Ride the High Country*. (Peckinpah claims that neither is a Western. Although he doesn't mind being labelled a 'Western director', he states, 'I have never made a "Western". I have made a lot of films about men on horseback.') The film is not about an antiquated Western code, but about Westerners bereft of the code. The Bunch are not Westerners who kill, but are killers in the West. *Ride the High Country* gave a perspective on why the code was valuable; *The Wild Bunch* gives a perspective on the age that could believe the Western code was valuable.

The metaphor for the old men of *The Wild Bunch* becomes, ironically, children. Peckinpah does not emphasize their honour, but their infantilism. The film begins with the frame of the naïvely cruel village children. After Mapache's disastrous defeat at the hands of Villa, a young messenger boy proudly struts with the general away from the bloody Las Trancas battle scene. It is a child who, in the final battle, terminates the massacre by killing Holden. At Angel's village (a scene which Peckinpah considers the most important in the film), an old villager and peasant revolutionary, Chano Ureuta, characterizes the Bunch in a conversation with Holden and O'Brien. 'We all dream of being children,' he says, 'even the worst of us. Perhaps the worst more than others.' 'You know what we are then?' Holden asks. 'Yes, both of you.' Ureuta replies. 'All three of us!' Holden laughs. Peckinpah conceived of his characters as children and made object lessons of them the way we do of children. 'They are all children,' Peckinpah says. 'We are all children.'

In *The Wild Bunch* Peckinpah comes to terms with the most violent aspects of his personality. A long-time acquaintance of Peckinpah recently said of him, 'I think he is the best director in America, but I also think he is a fascist.' He was using the term 'fascist' personally rather than politically. Peckinpah has a violent, domineering streak. There is in Peckinpah the belief that the ultimate test of manhood is the suppression of others. He maintains an impressive collection of guns, and his California home is kept up by 'Spanish domestics', householders who do not speak English. Peckinpah is, in a sense, a colonial in his own home. A good friend of Peckinpah recalled that once he came into the director's office and found him intently watching a cage on his desk. In the cage was a resting rattlesnake and a petrified white mouse. The rattler had already eaten one mouse; probably the survivor's mate, and was now contentedly digesting the large bulge in its stomach. 'Who do you think will win?' Peckinpah asked his friend. 'You will, Sam,' the friend replied.

The fascist edge of Peckinpah's personality does not make him particularly unique. It is a trait he shares with directors like Don Siegel, Howard Hawks, Samuel Fuller, Anthony Mann and all the rest of us who have always wanted to believe that those horse-riding killers were really making the West safe for the womenfolk. What makes Peckinpah unique is his ability to come face to face with the fascist quality of his personality, American films, and America, and turn it into art. (I realize that 'fascist' is a particularly vicious epithet. But its viciousness implies pain – and pain is the cathartic emotion Peckinpah experiences as he moves away from the old West of youth.)

In *The Wild Bunch* Sam Peckinpah stares into the heart of his own fascism. What had been formerly protected by the code is laid bare. The Western genre is ideally suited to such an examination; Jean-Luc Godard has noted that the Western is the only surviving popular fascist art form. In the past the Western had been able to perpetuate the myth of its own altruism, but, for Peckinpah, that myth had died its honourable death in *High Country*. The Westerners of *The Wild Bunch* have lost their code – only the fascism remains. The power of *The Wild Bunch* lies in the fact that this fascism is not peculiar to Peckinpah, but is American at heart. The America which created the Western (and the Communist Conspiracy) is the America Peckinpah determined to evaluate in his own life.

Like America's former macho-in-residence, Ernest Hemingway, Sam Peckinpah fights his private battles in public, both in life and art, but unlike Hemingway Peckinpah comes increasingly to terms with his own persona as he ages. As Hemingway approached death he relied increasingly on his code; as Peckinpah grows older he progressively discards his, preferring to confront death head-on. *The Wild Bunch* is *The Old Man and the Sea* without a boat, a great fish, or a native boy. The great anguish of *The Wild Bunch* is the anguish of a fascist personality coming to terms with itself: recognizing its love of domination and killing, and attempting to evaluate it.

The new psychopaths in the best of recent American films – *Bonnie and Clyde, Point Blank, Pretty Poison* – have had a strong environmental context in which to make their killings plausible, whether it be the rural Texas of the Depression era, garish new Los Angeles, or the polluted Massachusetts countryside. Codeless, Sam Peckinpah goes to the land he loves best to recreate and understand his violence: Mexico. Peckinpah has lived in Mexico off and on during the past few years (a refuge from the Hollywood ordeal) and is a student of Mexican customs and history. 'Mexico is the greatest place,' Peckinpah says. 'You have to go there, just to sit back and rest. You have to go there to get yourself straightened out.'

Peckinpah thinks of *The Wild Bunch* as a Mexican film. 'It is what really happens when killers go to Mexico. It is my comment on Richard Brooks and *The Professionals*.' Brooks's 1966 south-of-the-border adventure story treated Mexico as facilely as it did the Americans who went there; John Huston's 1948 *Treasure of Sierra Madre* is much more to Peckinpah's liking. '*Treasure of Sierra Madre* is one of my favourite films. In fact, *The Wild Bunch* is sort of early Huston. Ever since I saw that film I've been chasing Huston.' It was not so much Huston's moralistic story which impressed Peckinpah, but his expressive use of the Mexican milieu (of *Treasure* the late James Agee wrote, 'I doubt we shall ever see a finer portrait of Mexico and Mexicans'). Mexico had lent a depth to *Treasure*, a depth Peckinpah wanted to pursue in *The Wild Bunch*.

Agee to the contrary, Huston's characterization of Mexicans was not so much incisive as it was stereotyped – a fault which Peckinpah unfortunately shares. Mexicans fit into pre-existing categories: federalistas, rurales, caudillos. Like Huston's Mexican bandits, Peckinpah's bandoleros speak broken English, have bad breath, and possess a charming sense of humour. Alfonso Bedoya's Gold-Hat in *Treasure* ('Badges? We don't need no stinking badges') is the prototype of Jorge Russek's Lt Zamorra in *The Wild Bunch* ('I want to congratulate you on great bravery you have done'). Peckinpah wanted to show that the Mexicans (all varieties) were no less psychopathic than the Americans, but compared to the Bunch the Mexicans (with a few notable exceptions like Angel's girl Teresa and the old Urueta) seem colonial subjects.

But *The Wild Bunch* is only secondarily about the individual psychology of the Mexicans; it is primarily concerned with the mood of their country. Peckinpah's film is not about Mexicans, but murderous Americans who go to Mexico. Peckinpah's Mexico is much more powerfully drawn than Huston's and more accurately resembles the Mexico of Luis Buñuel's films. Although Peckinpah does not achieve the individual Mexican psychology of films like *Los Olvidados*, *Subdida al Cielo*, *Ensayo de un Crimen*, *Nazarin*, he is able to capture the irrationally savage mood of Buñuel's Mexico. The comparison would please Peckinpah. 'I loved *Los Olvidados*,' he says. 'I know that territory well. I've lived there. I would like to make *Children of Sanchez* one day. *The Wild Bunch* is only a beginning.' The opening shot of the taunted scorpion in *The Wild Bunch* is almost identical to the opening shot of Buñuel's 1930 *L'Age d'Or*, although Peckinpah says he has never seen the Buñuel film (the idea for the ant-scorpion battle in *The Wild Bunch* originated with actor-director Emilio Fernandez, who plays Mapache). Peckinpah's Mexico, like Buñuel's, is a place where violence is not only plausible, but inescapable.

Peckinpah was recently asked which films stood out best in his memory. He started to reply, '*Breaking Point, Rashomon, My Darling Clementine, Ace in the Hole*,' and then he abruptly added, 'If you really want to know about *The Wild Bunch* you should read a book by Camilo José Cela called *La Familia de Pascual Duarte*.' It is from the sensibility of *Pascual Duarte*, a seminal book in modern Spanish literature, that Peckinpah draws the frame in which to make the violence of *The Wild Bunch* meaningful. On the most immediate level there is an instant meeting of the minds between Cela and Peckinpah. Cela's dedication to *Pascual Duarte* could serve as the frontpiece for *The Wild Bunch*: 'I dedicate this thirteenth and definitive edition of my *Pascual Duarte* to my enemies who have been of such help to me in my career.' *The Wild Bunch* shares themes and sentiments with *Pascual Duarte* which do not figure in Peckinpah's earlier films. 'I'm not made to philosophize,' Pascual writes in his diary, 'I don't have the heart for it. My heart is more like a machine for making blood to be spilt in a knife fight . . .' McCrea and Scott were philosophers first, killers second: Holden and Borgnine are laconic psychopaths like Duarte. Pascual's wife says to him, 'Blood seems a kind of fertilizer in your life.' Pascual dedicates his diary to 'The memory of the distinguished patrician Don Jesus González de la Riva, Count of Torremejía, who, at the moment when the author of this chronicle came to kill him, called him Pascualillo, and smiled.' Peckinpah tells a similar story: 'I once lived with a wonderful man in Mexico. He was the most trustworthy man I have ever met. I would have done anything for him; I would have put my family in his care. He took me for every cent. A true friend is one who is really able to screw you.'

Like Pascual, the Wild Bunch disguise their barbarity in boyish innocence. Whenever Pascual mentions hogs or his behind he adds 'begging your pardon' and then goes on to describe the most savage acts. Just before the initial massacre in *The Wild Bunch* the Bunch stroll insouciantly down the main street, helping an old woman across the street. Like the scorpion-torturing children of *The Wild Bunch*, the children of *Pascual Duarte* tease injured dogs, sheep, and drown kittens in the watering-trough, lifting them out of the water from time to time 'to prevent their getting out of their misery too quickly'. Like Pascual, the Wild Bunch are picaros, men who roam the country in a never-ending war, spawning a rich heritage of death and suffering. It is into this tradition of Spanish suffering, the tradition of Cela, that Peckinpah thrusts his battle-weary Westerners.

Mexico represents an older, more primitive culture, a place where violence can still have meaning on the functional level. As the works of Oscar Lewis indicate, the Mexican peasant still regards the *macho* – the Mexican Westerner – as a practical prototype, and not just a mythological figure. Mexico is the ideal place for an old Westerner to go to give his violence meaning. The American frontier has been superseded by the more sophisticated mayhem of the city, but in Mexico there is an on-going tradition of significant violence. There you can fill a hero's grave, even if it is a shallow one. In Mexico you can extend the external frontier, and postpone the conquest of the internal frontier. The Mexico of 1914 was the Wild Bunch's Vietnam, a place where the wolf of fascism goes to wear the sheepskin of purpose.

Mexico cannot justify the Westerner's fascism, but it can bring the Westerner to an honourable end. If Holden, Borgnine, Oates and Johnson do enter their homes justified it is not because of any intrinsic virtue, but because of their enthusiastic demise. Deprived of both the mythical and functional qualities of his character, Holden dies the only way he knows how – with his boots on. But Peckinpah has the sensitivity, self-awareness, and feeling for America and Mexico to give his death poignancy and art.

The Wild Bunch is a powerful film because it comes from the gut of America, and from a man who is trying to get America out of his gut. The trauma of ex-patriotism is a common theme in American art, but nowhere is the pain quite so evident as in the life of Sam Peckinpah. *The Wild Bunch* is the agony of a Westerner who stayed too long, and it is the agony of America.

Cinema, Volume 5, No. 3, 1970

Notes on *Film Noir*

In 1946 French critics, seeing the American films they had missed during the war, noticed the new mood of cynicism, pessimism and darkness which had crept into the American cinema. The darkening stain was most evident in routine crime thrillers, but was also apparent in prestigious melodramas.

The French cinéastes soon realized they had seen only the tip of the iceberg: as the years went by, Hollywood lighting grew darker, characters more corrupt, themes more fatalistic and the tone more hopeless. By 1949 American movies were in the throes of their deepest and most creative funk. Never before had films dared to take such a harsh uncomplimentary look at American life, and they would not dare to do so again for twenty years.

Hollywood's *film noir* has recently become the subject of renewed interest among movie-goers and critics. The fascination *film noir* holds for today's young film-goers and film students reflects recent trends in American cinema: American movies are again taking a look at the underside of the American character, but compared to such relentlessly cynical *film noir* as *Kiss Me Deadly* or *Kiss Tomorrow Goodbye*, the new self-hate cinema of *Easy Rider* and *Medium Cool* seems naïve and romantic. As the current political mood hardens, film-goers and film-makers will find the *film noir* of the late forties increasingly attractive. The forties may be to the seventies what the thirties were to the sixties.

Film noir is equally interesting to critics. It offers writers a cache of excellent, little-known films (*film noir* is oddly both one of Hollywood's best periods and least known), and gives auteur-weary critics an opportunity to apply themselves to the newer questions of classification and transdirectorial style. After all, what is a *film noir*?

Film noir is not a genre (as Raymond Durgnat has helpfully pointed out over the objections of Higham and Greenberg's *Hollywood in the Forties*). It is not defined, as are the Western and gangster genres, by conventions of setting and conflict, but rather by the more subtle qualities of tone and mood. It is a *film 'noir'*, as opposed to the possible variants of film grey or film off-white.

Film noir is also a specific period of film history, like German Expressionism or the French New Wave. In general, *film noir* refers to those Hollywood films of the forties and early fifties which portrayed the world of dark, slick city streets, crime and corruption.

Film noir is an extremely unwieldy period. It harks back to many previous periods: Warners' thirties gangster films, the French 'poetic realism' of Carné and Duvivier, Von Sternbergian melodrama, and, farthest back, German Expressionist crime films (Lang's Mabuse cycle). *Film noir* can stretch at its outer limits from *The Maltese Falcon* (1941) to *Touch of Evil* (1958), and almost every dramatic Hollywood film from 1941 to 1953 contains some *noir* elements. There are also foreign offshoots of *film noir*, such as *The Third Man*, *Breathless* and *Le Doulos*.

Almost every critic has his own definition of *film noir*, and a personal list of film titles and dates to back it up. Personal and descriptive definitions, however, can get a bit sticky. A film of urban nightlife is not necessarily a *film noir*, and a *film noir* need not necessarily concern crime and corruption. Since *film noir* is defined by tone rather than genre, it is almost impossible to argue one critic's descriptive definition against another's. How many *noir* elements does it take to make a *film noir noir*?

Rather than haggle definitions, I would attempt to reduce *film noir* to its primary colours (all shades of black), those cultural and stylistic elements to which any definition must return.

At the risk of sounding like Arthur Knight, I would suggest that there were four conditions in Hollywood in the forties which brought about the *film noir*. (The danger of Knight's *Liveliest Art* method is that it makes film history less a matter of structural analysis, and more a case of artistic and social forces magically interacting and coalescing.) Each of the following four catalytic elements, however, can define the *film noir*; the distinctly *noir* tonality draws from each of these elements.

War and post-war disillusionment. The acute downer which hit the US after the Second World War was, in fact, a delayed reaction to the thirties. All through the Depression, movies were needed to keep people's spirits up, and, for the most part, they did. The crime films of this period were Horatio Algerish and socially conscious. Towards the end of the thirties a darker crime film began to appear (*You Only Live Once*, *The Roaring Twenties*) and were it not for the war *film noir* would have been at full steam by the early forties.

The need to produce Allied propaganda abroad and promote patriotism at home blunted the fledgling moves towards a dark cinema, and the *film noir* thrashed about in the studio system, not quite able to come into full prominence. During the war the first uniquely *films noirs* appeared: *The Maltese Falcon*, *The Glass Key*, *This Gun for Hire*, *Laura*, but these films lacked the distinctly *noir* bite the end of the war would bring.

As soon as the war was over, however, American films became markedly more sardonic – and there was a boom in the crime film. For fifteen years the pressures against America's amelioristic cinema had been building up, and, given the freedom, audiences and artists were now eager to take a less optimistic view of things. The disillusionment many soldiers, small businessmen and housewife/factory employees felt in returning to a peacetime economy was directly mirrored in the sordidness of the urban crime film.

This immediate post-war disillusionment was directly demonstrated in films like *Cornered*, *The Blue Dahlia*, *Dead Reckoning* and *Ride a Pink Horse*, in which a serviceman returns from the war to find his sweetheart unfaithful or dead, or his business partner cheating him, or the whole society something less than worth fighting for. The war continues, but now the antagonism turns with a new viciousness towards the American society itself.

Post-war realism. Shortly after the war every film-producing country had a resurgence of realism. In America it first took the form of films by such producers as Louis de Rochemont (*House on 92nd Street*, *Call Northside 777*) and Mark Hellinger (*The Killers*, *Brute Force*), and directors like Henry Hathaway and Jules Dassin. 'Every scene was filmed on the actual location depicted,' the 1947 de Rochemont–Hathaway *Kiss of Death* proudly proclaimed. Even after de Rochemont's particular 'March of Time' authenticity fell from vogue, realistic exteriors remained a permanent fixture of *film noir*.

The realistic movement also suited America's post-war mood; the public's desire for a more honest and harsh view of America would not be satisfied by the same studio streets they had been watching for a dozen years. The post-war realistic trend succeeded in breaking *film noir* away from the domain of the high-class melodrama, placing it where it more properly belonged, in the streets with everyday people. In retrospect, the pre-de Rochemont *films noirs* look definitely tamer than the post-war realistic films. The studio look of films like *The Big Sleep* and *The Mask of*

Dimitrios blunts their sting, making them seem polite and conventional in contrast to their later, more realistic counterparts.

The German influence. Hollywood played host to an influx of German expatriates in the twenties and thirties, and these film-makers and technicians had, for the most part, integrated themselves into the American film establishment. Hollywood never experienced the 'Germanization' some civic-minded natives feared, and there is a danger of over-emphasizing the German influence in *film noir*.

But when, in the late forties, Hollywood decided to paint it black, there were no greater masters of chiaroscuro than the Germans. The influence of Expressionist lighting has always been just beneath the surface of Hollywood films, and it is not surprising, in *film noir*, to find it bursting out full bloom. Neither is it surprising to find a large number of Germans and East Europeans working in *film noir*: Fritz Lang, Robert Siodmak, Billy Wilder, Franz Waxman, Otto Preminger, John Brahm, Anatole Litvak, Karl Freund, Max Ophüls, John Alton, Douglas Sirk, Fred Zinnemann, William Dieterle, Max Steiner, Edgar G. Ulmer, Curtis Bernhardt, Rudolph Maté.

On the surface the German Expressionist influence, with its reliance on artificial studio lighting, seems incompatible with post-war realism, with its harsh unadorned exteriors; but it is the unique quality of *film noir* that it was able to weld seemingly contradictory elements into a uniform style. The best *noir* technicians simply made all the world a sound stage, directing unnatural and Expressionistic lighting on to realistic settings. In films like *Union Station, They Live by Night, The Killers* there is an uneasy, exhilarating combination of realism and Expressionism.

Perhaps the greatest master of *noir* was Hungarian-born John Alton, an Expressionist cinematographer who could relight Times Square at noon if necessary. No cinematographer better adapted the old Expressionist techniques to the new desire for realism, and his black-and-white photography in such gritty *films noirs* as *T-Men, Raw Deal, I the Jury, The Big Combo* equals that of such German Expressionist masters as Fritz Wagner and Karl Freund.

The hard-boiled tradition. Another stylistic influence waiting in the wings was the 'hard-boiled' school of writers. In the thirties authors such as Ernest Hemingway, Dashiell Hammett, Raymond Chandler, James M. Cain, Horace McCoy and John O'Hara created the 'tough', a cynical way of acting and thinking which separated one from the world of everyday emotions – romanticism with a protective shell. The hard-boiled writers had their roots in pulp fiction or journalism, and their protagonists lived out a narcissistic, defeatist code. The hard-boiled hero was, in reality, a soft egg compared to his existential counterpart (Camus is said to have based *The Stranger* on McCoy), but they were a good deal tougher than anything American fiction had seen.

When the movies of the forties turned to the American 'tough' moral understrata, the hard-boiled school was waiting with pre-set conventions of heroes, minor characters, plots, dialogue and themes. Like the German expatriates, the hard-boiled writers had a style made to order for *film noir*; and, in turn, they influenced *noir* screenwriting as much as the Germans influenced *noir* cinematography.

The most hard-boiled of Hollywood's writers was Raymond Chandler himself, whose script of *Double Indemnity* (from a James M. Cain story) was the best written and most characteristically *noir* of the period. *Double Indemnity* was the first film which played *film noir* for what it essentially was: small-time, unredeemed, unheroic; it made a break from the romantic *noir* cinema of *Mildred Pierce* and *The Big Sleep*.

(In its final stages, however, *film noir* adapted then bypassed the hard-boiled school. Manic, neurotic, post-1949 films such as *Kiss Tomorrow Goodbye*, *D.O.A.*, *Where the Sidewalk Ends*, *White Heat*, *The Big Heat* are all post-hard-boiled: the air in these regions was even too thin for old-time cynics like Chandler.)

Stylistics. There is not yet a study of the stylistics of *film noir*, and the task is certainly too large to be attempted here. Like all film movements *film noir* drew upon a reservoir of film techniques, and given the time one could correlate its techniques, themes and causal elements into a stylistic schemata. For the present, however, I'd like to point out some of *film noir*'s recurring techniques.

– The majority of scenes are lit for night. Gangsters sit in the offices at midday with the shades pulled and the lights off. Ceiling lights are hung low and floor lamps are seldom more than five feet high. One always has the suspicion that if the lights were all suddenly flipped on, the characters would shrink from the scene like Count Dracula at noontime.

– As in German Expressionism, oblique and vertical lines are preferred to horizontal. Obliquity adheres to the choreography of the city, and is in direct opposition to the horizontal American tradition of Griffith and Ford. Oblique lines tend to splinter a screen, making it restless and unstable. Light enters the dingy rooms of *film noir* in such odd shapes – jagged trapezoids, obtuse triangles, vertical slits – that one suspects the windows were cut out with a penknife. No character can speak authoritatively from a space which is being continually cut into ribbons of light. The

Anthony Mann/John Alton *T-Men* is the most dramatic but far from the only example of oblique *noir* choreography.

– The actors and setting are often given equal lighting emphasis. An actor is often hidden in the realistic tableau of the city at night, and, more obviously, his face is often blacked out by shadow as he speaks. These shadow effects are unlike the famous Warner Brothers lighting of the thirties in which the central character was accentuated by a heavy shadow; in *film noir*, the central character is likely to be standing *in* the shadow. When the environment is given an equal or greater weight than the actor, it, of course, creates a fatalistic, hopeless mood. There is nothing the protagonist can do; the city will outlast and negate even his best efforts.

– Compositional tension is preferred to physical action. A typical *film noir* would rather move the scene cinematographically around the actor than have the actor control the scene by physical action. The beating of Robert Ryan in *The Set-Up*, the gunning down of Farley Granger in *They Live by Night*, the execution of the taxi driver in *The Enforcer* and of Brian Donlevy in *The Big Combo* are all marked by measured pacing, restrained anger and oppressive compositions, and seem much closer to the *film noir* spirit than the rat-tat-tat and screeching tyres of *Scarface* twenty years before or the violent expression actions of *Underworld U.S.A.* ten years later.

– There seems to be an almost Freudian attachment to water. The empty *noir* streets are almost always glistening with fresh evening rain (even in Los Angeles), and the rainfall tends to increase in direct proportion to the drama. Docks and piers are second only to alleyways as the most popular rendezvous points.

– There is a love of romantic narration. In such films as *The Postman Always Rings Twice, Laura, Double Indemnity, The Lady from Shanghai, Out of the Past* and *Sunset Boulevard* the narration creates a mood of *temps perdu*: an irretrievable past, a predetermined fate and an all-enveloping hopelessness. In *Out of the Past* Robert Mitchum relates his history with such pathetic relish that it is obvious there is no hope for any future: one can only take pleasure in reliving a doomed past.

– A complex chronological order is frequently used to reinforce the feelings of hopelessness and lost time. Such films as *The Enforcer, The Killers, Mildred Pierce, The Dark Past, Chicago Deadline, Out of the Past* and *The Killing* use a convoluted time sequence to immerse the viewer in a time-disoriented but highly stylized world. The manipulation of time, whether slight or complex, is often used to reinforce a *noir* principle: the how is always more important than the what.

Themes. Raymond Durgnat has delineated the themes of *film noir* in an excellent article in British *Cinema* magazine ('The Family Tree of *Film Noir*', August 1970), and it would be foolish for me to attempt to redo his thorough work in this short space. Durgnat divides *film noir* into eleven thematic categories, and although one might criticize some of his specific groupings, he does cover the whole gamut of *noir* production (thematically categorizing over 300 films).

In each of Durgnat's *noir* themes (whether Black Widow, Killers-on-the-run, *Doppelgängers*) one finds that the upwardly mobile forces of the thirties have halted; frontierism has turned to paranoia and claustrophobia. The small-time gangster has now made it big and sits in the mayor's chair, the private eye has quit the police force in disgust, and the young heroine, sick of going along for the ride, is taking others for a ride.

Durgnat, however, does not touch upon what is perhaps the most overriding *noir* theme: there is a passion for the past and present, but a fear of the future. The *noir* hero dreads to look ahead, but instead tries to survive by the day, and if unsuccessful at that, he retreats to the past. Thus *film noir*'s techniques emphasize loss, nostalgia, lack of clear priorities, insecurity; then submerge these self-doubts in mannerism and style. In such a world style becomes paramount; it is all that separates one from meaninglessness. Chandler described this fundamental *noir* theme when he described his own fictional world: 'It is not a very fragrant world, but it is the world you live in, and certain writers with tough minds and a cool spirit of detachment can make very interesting patterns out of it.'

Film noir can be subdivided into three broad phases. The first, the wartime period, 1941–6 approximately, was the phase of the private eye and the lone wolf, of Chandler, Hammett and Greene, of Bogart and Bacall, Ladd and Lake, classy directors like Curtiz and Garnett, studio sets and, in general, more talk than action. The studio look of this period was reflected in such pictures as *The Maltese Falcon, Casablanca, Gaslight, This Gun for Hire, The Lodger, Woman in the Window, Mildred Pierce, Spellbound, The Big Sleep, Laura, The Lost Weekend, The Strange Love of Martha Ivers, To Have and To Have Not, Fallen Angel, Gilda, Murder My Sweet, The Postman Always Rings Twice, Dark Waters, Scarlet Street, So Dark the Night, The Glass Key, The Mask of Dimitrios, The Dark Mirror.*

The Wilder–Chandler *Double Indemnity* provided a bridge to the postwar phase of *film noir*. The unflinching *noir* vision of *Double Indemnity* came as a shock in 1944, and the film was almost blocked by the combined efforts of Paramount, the Hays Office and star Fred MacMurray. Three years later, however, *Double Indemnity*s were dropping off the studio assembly lines.

The second phase was the post-war realistic period from 1945–9 (the dates overlap and so do the films; these are all approximate phases for which there are many exceptions). These films tended more toward the problems of crime in the streets, political corruption and police routine. Less romantic heroes like Richard Conte, Burt Lancaster and Charles McGraw were more suited to this period, as were proletarian directors like Hathaway, Dassin and Kazan. The realistic urban look of this phase is seen in such films as *The House on 92nd Street, The Killers, Raw Deal, Act of Violence, Union Station, Kiss of Death, Johnny O'Clock, Force of Evil, Dead Reckoning, Ride the Pink Horse, Dark Passage, Cry of the City, The Set-Up, T-Men, Call Northside 777, Brute Force, The Big Clock, Thieves Highway, Ruthless, Pitfall, Boomerang!, The Naked City.*

The third and final phase of *film noir*, from 1949–53, was the period of psychotic action and suicidal impulse. The *noir* hero, seemingly under the weight of ten years of despair, started to go bananas. The psychotic killer, who had in the first period been a subject worthy of study (Olivia de Havilland in *The Dark Mirror*), in the second a fringe threat (Richard Widmark in *Kiss of Death*), now became the active protagonist (James Cagney in *Kiss Tomorrow Goodbye*). James Cagney made a neurotic comeback and his instability was matched by that of younger actors like Robert Ryan and Lee Marvin. This was the phase of the 'B' *noir* film, and of psychoanalytically inclined directors like Ray and Walsh. The forces of personal disintegration are reflected in such films as *White Heat, Gun Crazy, D.O.A., Caught, They Live by Night, Where the Sidewalk Ends, Kiss Tomorrow Goodbye, Detective Story, In a Lonely Place, I the Jury, Ace in the Hole, Panic in the Streets, The Big Heat, On Dangerous Ground, Sunset Boulevard.*

The third phase is the cream of the *film noir* period. Some critics may prefer the early 'grey' melodramas, others the post-war 'street' films, but *film noir*'s final phase was the most aesthetically and sociologically piercing. After ten years of steadily shedding romantic conventions, the later *noir* films finally got down to the root causes of the period: the loss of public honour, heroic conventions, personal integrity, and, finally, psychic stability. The third-phase films were painfully self-aware; they seemed to know they stood at the end of a long tradition based on despair and disintegration and did not shy away from that fact. The best and most characteristically *noir* films – *Gun Crazy, White Heat, Out of the Past, Kiss Tomorrow Goodbye, D.O.A., They Live by Night, The Big Heat* – stand at the end of the period and are the results of self-knowledge. The

9 *Film Noir*: Rudolph Mate's *D.O.A.* (1950), the source for Schrader's
unfilmed script *Covert People*: Neville Brand, Edmond O'Brien,
Michael Ross.

third phase is rife with end-of-the-line *noir* heroes: *The Big Heat* and *Where the Sidewalk Ends* are the last stops for the urban cop, *Ace in the Hole* for the newspaper man, the Victor Saville-produced Spillane series (*I the Jury, The Long Wait, Kiss Me Deadly*) for the private eye, *Sunset Boulevard* for the Black Widow, *White Heat* and *Kiss Tomorrow Good-bye* for the gangster, *D.O.A.* for the John Doe American.

By the mid-fifties *film noir* had ground to a halt. There were a few notable stragglers, *Kiss Me Deadly*, the Lewis–Alton *The Big Combo*, and *film noir*'s epitaph, *Touch of Evil*, but for the most part a new style of crime film had become popular.

As the rise of McCarthy and Eisenhower demonstrated, Americans were eager to see a more bourgeois view of themselves. Crime had to move to the suburbs. The criminal put on a grey flannel suit and the footsore cop was replaced by the 'mobile unit' careering down the expressway. Any attempt at social criticism had to be cloaked in ludicrous affirmations of the American way of life. Technically, television, with its demand for full lighting and close-ups, gradually undercut the German influence, and colour cinematography was, of course, the final blow to the *noir* look. New directors like Siegel, Fleischer, Karlson and Fuller, and TV shows like *Dragnet, M-Squad, Lineup* and *Highway Patrol*, stepped in to create the new crime drama.

Film noir was an immensely creative period – probably the most creative in Hollywood's history; at least, if this creativity is measured not by its peaks but by its median level of artistry. Picked at random, a *film noir* is likely to be a better-made film than a randomly selected silent comedy, musical, Western and so on. (A Joseph H. Lewis 'B' *film noir* is better than a Lewis 'B' Western, for example.) Taken as a whole period, *film noir* achieved an unusually high level of artistry.

Film noir seemed to bring out the best in everyone: directors, cameramen, screenwriters, actors. Again and again, a *film noir* will mark the high point on an artist's career graph. Some directors, for example, did their best work in *film noir* (Stuart Heisler, Robert Siodmak, Gordon Douglas, Edward Dmytryk, John Brahm, John Cromwell, Raoul Walsh, Henry Hathaway); other directors began in *film noir* and, it seems to me, never regained their original heights (Otto Preminger, Rudolph Maté, Nicholas Ray, Robert Wise, Jules Dassin, Richard Fleischer, John Huston, André de Toth, Robert Aldrich); and other directors who made great films in other moulds also made great *films noirs* (Orson Welles, Max Ophüls, Fritz Lang, Elia Kazan, Howard Hawks, Robert Rossen, Anthony Mann, Joseph Losey, Alfred Hitchcock, Stanley Kubrick). Whether or not one agrees with this particular schema, its message is irrefutable: *film noir* was good for practically every director's career. (Two interesting exceptions to prove the case are King Vidor and Jean Renoir.)

Film noir seems to have been a creative release for everyone involved. It gave artists a chance to work with previously forbidden themes, yet had conventions strong enough to protect the mediocre. Cinematographers were allowed to become highly mannered, and actors were sheltered by the cinematographers. It was not until years later that critics were able to distinguish between great directors and great *noir* directors.

Film noir's remarkable creativity makes its long-time neglect the more baffling. The French, of course, have been students of the period for some time (Borde and Chaumenton's *Panorama du Film Noir* was published in 1955), but American critics until recently have preferred the Western, the musical or the gangster film to the *film noir*.

Some of the reasons for this neglect are superficial: others strike to the heart of the *noir* style. For a long time *film noir*, with its emphasis on corruption and despair, was considered an aberration of the American character. The Western, with its moral primitivism, and the gangster film, with its Horatio Alger values, were considered more American than the *film noir*.

This prejudice was reinforced by the fact that *film noir* was ideally suited to the low-budget 'B' film, and many of the best *noir* films were 'B' films. This odd sort of economic snobbery still lingers on in some critical circles: high-budget trash is considered more worthy of attention than low-budget trash, and to praise a 'B' film is somehow to slight (often intentionally) an 'A' film.

There has been a critical revival in the US over the last ten years, but *film noir* lost out on that too. The revival was auteur (director) oriented, and *film noir* wasn't. Auteur criticism is interested in how directors are different; *film noir* criticism is concerned with what they have in common.

The fundamental reason for *film noir*'s neglect, however, is the fact that it depends more on choreography than sociology, and American critics have always been slow on the uptake when it comes to visual style. Like its protagonists, *film noir* is more interested in style than theme; whereas American critics have been traditionally more interested in theme than style.

American film critics have always been sociologists first and scientists second: film is important as it relates to large masses, and if a film goes awry it is often because the theme has been somehow 'violated' by the style. *Film noir* operates on opposite principles: the theme is hidden in the style, and bogus themes are often flaunted ('middle-class values are best') which contradict the style. Although, I believe, style determines the theme in *every* film, it was easier for sociological critics to discuss the themes of the Western and gangster film apart from stylistic analysis than it was to do for *film noir*.

Not surprisingly it was the gangster film, not the *film noir*, which was canonized in *The Partisan Review* in 1948 by Robert Warshow's famous essay, 'The Gangster as Tragic Hero'. Although Warshow could be an aesthetic as well as a sociological critic, he was interested in the Western and gangster film as 'popular' art rather than as style. This sociological orientation blinded Warshow, as it has many subsequent critics, to an aesthetically more important development in the gangster film – *film noir*.

The irony of this neglect is that in retrospect the gangster films Warshow wrote about are inferior to *film noir*. The thirties gangster was primarily a reflection of what was happening in the country, and Warshow analysed this. The *film noir*, although it was also a sociological reflection, went further than the gangster film. Towards the end *film noir* was engaged in a life-and-death struggle with the materials it reflected; it tried to make America accept a moral vision of life based on style. That very contradiction – promoting style in a culture which valued themes – forced *film noir* into artistically invigorating twists and turns. *Film noir* attacked and interpreted its sociological conditions, and, by the close of the *noir* period, created a new artistic world which went beyond a simple sociological reflection, a nightmarish world of American mannerism which was by far more a creation than a reflection.

Because *film noir* was first of all a style, because it worked out its conflicts visually rather than thematically, because it was aware of its own identity, it was able to create artistic solutions to sociological problems. And for these reasons films like *Kiss Me Deadly*, *Kiss Tomorrow Goodbye* and *Gun Crazy* can be works of art in a way that gangster films like *Scarface*, *Public Enemy* and *Little Caesar* can never be.

The selection of the following seven films by the Los Angeles International Film Exposition reflects a desire to select not only the best *noir* films, but also some of the less well known.

Kiss Me Deadly. Made in 1955, *Kiss Me Deadly* comes at the end of the period and is the masterpiece of *film noir*. Its time delay gives it a sense of detachment and thoroughgoing seediness – it stands at the end of a long sleazy tradition.

The private-eye hero, Mike Hammer, undergoes the final stages of degradation. He is a small-time 'bedroom dick', and has no qualms about it because the world around him isn't much better. Ralph Meeker, in his best performance, plays Hammer, a midget among dwarfs.

Robert Aldrich's teasing direction carries *noir* to its sleaziest, and most perversely erotic. In search of an 'eternal whatsit' Hammer overturns the underworld, causing the death of his friend in the process, and when he finally finds it, it turns out to be – joke of jokes – an exploding atomic bomb. The cruelty of the individual is only a trivial matter in a world in which the Bomb has the final say. Hammer can be seen struggling to safety as the bomb ejaculates, but for all practical purposes the forties private-eye tradition is defunct. Written by A. I. Bezzerides. Photographed by Ernest Laszlo. Produced by Victor Saville. With Ralph Meeker, Maxine Cooper, Nick Dennis, Gaby Rodgers, Juano Hernandez, Paul Stewart, Albert Dekker, Cloris Leachman, Jack Elam.

Gun Crazy. An early Bonnie and Clyde variant, Joseph H. Lewis's *Gun Crazy* incorporates both the Black Widow and on-the-run themes. John Dall and Peggy Cummins play a winsome couple spinning at a dizzying rate into the exhilarating world of action, sex, love and murder. Dall is confused, innocent and passive, Cummins is confused, vindictive and active; together they make an irresistibly psychopathic pair. And their deadliness is sanctified by the fact that they know they are special people and will be given the right by the American ethic to act out their symbolic fantasies.

Gun Crazy's lighting is not as *noir* as other films of the period, but its portrayal of criminal and sexual psychopathy very much is. There are no excuses for the gun craziness – it is just crazy.

Gun Crazy has three *tour de force* scenes: the brilliantly executed Armour robbery, the famous one-take Hampton heist, and the meeting at the carnival which is a ballet of sex and innuendo more subtle and teasing than the more famous sparring matches of Bogart and Bacall or Ladd and Lake. 1949. Written by Mackinlay Kantor and Millard Kaufman. Produced by the King Brothers. Photographed by Russell Harlan. With John Dall, Peggy Cummins, Barry Kroeger, Annabel Shaw, Harry Lewis, Frederick Young.

They Live by Night. Made in the same year as *Gun Crazy*, Nicholas Ray's *They Live by Night* is another Bonnie and Clyde/on-the-run film. Ray's heroes, Farley Granger and Cathy O'Donnell, as the title implies, really do live by night, and the choreography is strictly *noir*.

Unlike *Gun Crazy*, Granger and O'Donnell are not psychopathic; rather, the society is, as it makes them into bigger and bigger criminals and finally connives to gun down the unsuspecting Granger. There's an excellent bit by Ian Wolfe as a crooked Justice of the Peace, and Marie

Bryant sings 'Your Red Wagon' in the best *noir* tradition. Written by Charles Schnee. Photographed by George E. Diskant. Produced by John Houseman. With Farley Granger, Cathy O'Donnell, Howard Da Silva, Jay C. Flippen, Helen Craig, Will Wright, Ian Wolfe, Harry Harvey.

White Heat. There was no director better suited to portray instability than Raoul Walsh, and no actor more potentially unstable than James Cagney. And when they joined forces in 1949 for *White Heat*, they produced one of the most exciting psycho-sexual crime films ever. Cagney plays an ageing Oedipal gangster who sits on his mother's lap between bouts of pistol-whipping his cohorts, planning robberies and gunning down police.

In an exuberantly psychotic ending Cagney stands atop an exploding oil tanker yelling, 'I made it, Ma! Top of the World!' We've come a long way from *Scarface* where Paul Muni lies in the gutter as a neon sign ironically flashes, 'Cook's Tours. See the World'. Cagney, now the *noir* hero, is not so much interested in financial gain and power as he is in suicidal showmanship. Cagney tapped the same vein the following year when he produced and starred in Gordon Douglas's *Kiss Tomorrow Goodbye*, one of the best of the late *noir* films. What Douglas lacked as a director, Cagney made up in just plain craziness. 1949. Written by Ivan Goff and Ben Roberts. Photographed by Sid Hickox. Produced by Louis Edelman. With James Cagney, Virginia Mayo, Edmund O'Brien, Margaret Wycherly, Steve Cochran, John Archer.

Out of the Past. Jacques Tourneur's *Out of the Past* brilliantly utilizes the *noir* element of narration as well as the themes of Black Widow and on-the-run. A gangster (the young Kirk Douglas in one of his best roles) sends his best friend Robert Mitchum to retrieve his girlfriend, Jane Greer, who has run off with his money. Mitchum, of course, teams up with Greer and they hide from Douglas.

Mitchum narrates his story with such pathetic relish that he obviously draws comfort from being love's perennial fool. Tourneur combines Mitchum's narration, Jane Greer's elusive beauty and a complex chronology in such a way that there is no hope for any future; one can only take pleasure from reliving a doomed past. 1947. Written by Geoffrey Homes. Produced by Warren Duff. With Kirk Douglas, Robert Mitchum, Jane Greer, Rhonda Fleming, Steve Brodie.

Pickup on South Street. Sam Fuller's 1953 film sacks in with an odd *noir* bedfellow – the Red scare. The gangsters undergo a slight accent shift and become communist agents; no ideological conversion necessary.

Richard Widmark, a characteristic *noir* actor who has never done as well outside the period as within it, plays a two-time loser who picks the purse of a 'commie' messenger and ends up with a piece of microfilm. When the State Department finally hunts him down and begins the lecture, Widmark replies, 'Don't wave your flag at me.'

The scenes on the waterfront are in the best *noir* tradition, but a dynamic fight in the subway marks Fuller as a director who would be better suited to the action-crime school of the middle fifties. Written by Samuel Fuller. Photographed by Joe MacDonald. Produced by Jules Schermer. With Richard Widmark, Jean Peters, Thelma Ritter, Murvyn Vye, Richard Kiley.

T-Men. Anthony Mann's 1947 film was photographed by John Alton, the most characteristically *noir* artist of the period. Alton also photographed Joseph H. Lewis's *The Big Combo* eight years later and the cinematography is so nearly identical that one has momentary doubts about the directorial difference between Mann and Lewis. In each film light only enters the scene in odd slants, jagged slices and vertical or horizonal strips.

T-Men is a bastard child of the post-war realistic school and purports to be the documented story of two Treasury agents who break a ring of counterfeiters. Complications set in when the good guys don't act any differently from the bad ones. In the end it doesn't matter anyway, since they all die in the late-night shoot-outs. 1948. Written by John Higgins. Photographed by John Alton. Produced by Edward Small and Aubrey Schenck. With Dennis O'Keefe, Alfred Ryder, Mary Meade, Wallace Ford, June Lockhart, Charles McGraw, Art Smith.

Originally published 1971 (pamphlet to accompany short season programmed by Schrader for Los Angeles Film Festival); *Film Comment*, Volume 8, No. 1, Spring 1972

Poetry of Ideas: The Films of Charles Eames

They're not experimental films, they're not really films. They're just attempts to get across an idea.

– Charles Eames

Charles Eames was baffled by the fact that anyone would want to write an article about his films. 'When asked a question like that, about "my approach to film",' Eames said, 'I would almost reply, "Who me, film?" I don't think of it that way. I view film a little bit as a cheat; I'm sort of using a tool someone else has developed.'

Because of his casual attitude toward 'Film' – his debunking of the romantic myth of the 'artist personality' and his concept of film as a primarily informational medium – Charles Eames has been able, in his recent films, to give 'Film' what it needs most: a new way of perceiving ideas. As films move away from a period in which they were content to show only what they felt, and attempt little by little to also tell what they think, many of the most talented film-makers, young and old, are trying to graft on to movies the cerebral sensibility they have so long resisted. Eames personifies this sensibility, a sensibility so synonymous with his life and work that he cannot conceive of himself as only a 'film-maker'.

There are many ways one can think about Charles Eames. He defies categorization; he is architect, inventor, designer, craftsman, scientist, film-maker, professor. Yet in all his diversity Eames is one creator, and his creation is not a series of separate achievements, but a unified aesthetic with many branch-like manifestations. Eames's films do not function independently, but like branches; they do not derive from film history or tradition, but from a culminant culture with roots in many fields. A capsulized biography can give, in the most vulgar way, the scope of his career; but, as always, Eames remains greater than the sum of his avocations.

Born in St Louis in 1907, Eames studied architecture at Washington University, in 1930 started his own practice, and in 1940 married Ray Kaiser, a painter with whom he subsequently shared credit for all his work. In 1940 Eames and Eero Saarinen collaborated on designs for the Museum of Modern Art's Organic Furniture Competition. From these designs came a generation of Eames chairs: from the luxurious black-leather Eames lounge chair to the omnipresent moulded fibreglass stacking chairs, which, within twenty years, had received such mass acceptance that Eames's way of sitting was, in a fundamental sense, everybody's way of sitting. In 1941, to encourage the wartime production of their first chair prototypes, Charles and Ray perfected an inexpensive lamination process for wood veneers, and in the same year Charles went to work, temporarily, for the art department of MGM. In between chairs, the Charles Eames Workshop produced toys, furniture, gliders, leg splints, and magazine covers. In 1949 Eames designed the Santa Monica House (where he still lives), which, like the chairs, was a model of simplicity and variety, and soon became a standard textbook illustration.

The Eames films commenced in 1950 and over the next fifteen years they won awards at the Edinburgh, Melbourne, San Francisco, American,

Mannheim, Montreal and London film festivals. 'A Rough Sketch for a Sample Lesson for a Hypothetical Course', presented by Charles and Ray (with George Nelson and Alexander Girard) in 1953 at the University of Georgia and UCLA, was the first public presentation of multi-media techniques. In 1960 Eames's rapid cutting experiments in the CBS 'Fabulous Fifties' special won him an Emmy for graphic design. During this period Eames designed a series of World's Fair presentations: in 1959 the multi-screen presentation for the US exhibit at Moscow, in 1962 a multi-screen introduction to the US Science Exhibit at Seattle (where it is still shown), in 1964 the IBM Ovoid Pavilion, and the film presentations in it, at the New York Fair. Over the years Eames has prepared courses and lectured across the world, and will this fall hold the Charles Eliot Norton Chair of Poety at Harvard.

Charles Eames can weave in and out of these diverse occupations because he is not committed to any of them. He is, in the final account, committed to a way of life which encompasses them all. The toys, chairs, films are the available tools through which Eames can actualize his lifestyle. The common denominator of Eames's occupations is that he is, elementally, one thing: a problem-solver, with aesthetic and social considerations. He approaches life as a set of problems, each of which must be defined, delineated, abstracted, and solved. His architect's mind visualizes complex social patterns, twisting and folding like a three-dimensional blueprint. He respects the 'problem' not only as a means to an end but as an aesthetic pleasure in itself. Although Eames rarely rhapsodizes about anything, his most 'emotional' prose is saved for a description of the problem-solving process:

The ability to make decisions is a proper function of problem solving. Computer problems, philosophical problems, homely ones: the steps in solving each are essentially the same, some methods being elaborate variations of others. But homely or complex, the specific answers we get are not the only rewards or even the greatest. It is in preparing the problem for solution, in the necessary steps of simplification, that we often gain the richest rewards. It is in this process that we are apt to get a true insight into the nature of the problem. Such insight is of great and lasting value to us as individuals and to us as a society. – from Think, the IBM New York Fair presentation

For Eames, problem solving is one of the answers to the problem of contemporary civilization. Not only does his problem-solving process provide beauty and order, but it constitutes the only *optimistic* approach to the future. He is currently working for the Head Start programme, a task he feels is vital because:

you have to teach children to have a genuine respect for a large number of events and objects which are not of immediate gain to them. It is the only thing which puts a human being in a situation where he can promptly assess the next step. Whether it is in the ghetto or Appalachia, kids get their beginning having respect only for things which have an immediate payoff, and this is no way to run a railroad, particularly when you don't know what the next problem will be.

Eames will not indulge in the despair of a complete overview, not because it is illegitimate, but because it can't solve the problems. 'You can't take too broad a perspective,' he says, quoting Nobel Prize-winning physicist Richard Feynman; 'you have to find a corner and pick away at it.'

Charles Eames is, in the broadest sense of the word, a scientist. In his film introduction to the US Science Exhibit at the Seattle Fair, Eames prescribed what that rare creature, the true scientist, should be, and it is a description of Charles Eames:

Science is essentially an artistic or philosophical enterprise carried on for its own sake. In this it is more akin to play than to work. But it is quite a sophisticated play in which the scientist views nature as a system of interlocking puzzles. He assumes that the puzzles have a solution, that they will be fair. He holds to a faith in the underlying order of the universe. His motivation is his fascination with the puzzle itself – his method a curious interplay between idea and experiment. His pleasures are those of any artist. High on the list of prerequisites for being a scientist is a quality that defines the rich human being as much as it does the man of science, that is, his ability and his desire to reach out with his mind and his imagination to something outside himself. – *from* House of Science

To counter that the puzzles don't have a solution and are not fair is to beg the question, because the scientist does not admit these possibilities into his working definition. Because his pleasures 'are those of any artist' the scientist sustains his world not necessarily by empirical proof, but by his 'faith in the underlying order of the universe'. In this way Eames's scientist may seem similar to the scientists of the Enlightenment who constructed elaborate fictions of order, only to have them collapse with the next wave of data. But unlike the Newtonian cosmologist, Eames does not state that the solvable problem is necessarily a microcosm for the universe, which may have no solution. Eames is describing a *Weltanschauung*, not the universe. A corollary argument levelled (often by artists) against Eames's scientist accuses him of being shallowly optimistic, unaware of man's condition. C. P. Snow defended scientists against this charge in his 'Two Cultures' lecture: 'Nearly all of them [the scientists] – and this is where the colour of hope genuinely comes in – would see no reason why, just because the individual condition is tragic, so must the social condition be.' It is a fallacy of men of letters to equate contemporaneity with pessimism – as if Beckett's 'it' crawling in the mud was unavoidably the

man of the future. One of the exciting things about Eames's film-maker,
like his scientist, is that he challenges the hegemony of pessimism in the
contemporary arts.

Although Eames's structuring of the problem may seem antiquated (and
this is debatable), his solutions are undeniably modern. His statement
about the designing of a chair is not only a remarkable account of the
creative process, but also a pioneering approach to art in a society in which
the individual has become progressively functionalized and collectivized:

How do you design a chair for acceptance by another person? By not thinking of
what the other guy wants, but by coming to terms with the fact that while we may
think we are different from other people in some ways at some moments, the fact of
the matter is that we're a hell of a lot more like each other than we're different, and
that we're certainly more like each other than we're like a tree or a stone. So then
you relax back into the position of trying to satisfy yourself – except for a real trap,
that is, what part of yourself do you try to satisfy? The trap is that if you try to
satisfy your idiosyncrasies, those little things on the surface, you're dead, because it
is in those idiosyncrasies that you're different from other people. And in a sense
what gives a work of craft its personal style is usually where it failed to solve the
problem rather than where it solved it. That's what gives it the Noguchi touch, or
whatever. What you try to do is satisfy your real gut instincts and work your way
through your idiosyncrasies, as we have tried in the stuff we've done, the furniture
or the ideas. You know it's tough enough just to make the first step of understanding without trying to introduce our personality or trying to outguess what the other
guy's thinking.

The Eameses have constructed structures – a house, chair, film – in
which people can define themselves not by their idiosyncrasies but by their
similarities. These structures permit problem solving – and therefore give
the scientist hope. To some these structures will seem artificial and
solipsistic, but in an age which has so ruthlessly degraded man's individu-
ality any attempt to restructure the concept of humanism will necessarily
seem artificial.

From Eames's sensibility have come two contributions: one pertaining
primarily to architecture and design, which has already been incorporated
into the international cultural mainstream, and another most applicable to
film, which is being developed and exists only as potential for mass
audiences.

Eames's first contribution concerns what British critic Peter Smithson
calls 'object-integrity'. The Eames aesthetic respects an object for what it
is, whether machine-made or hand-crafted, and is based on 'careful
selection with extra-cultural surprise, rather than harmony of profile, as its
criteria – a kind of wide-eyed wonder of seeing the culturally disparate
together and so happy with each other.' Smithson goes on, 'This sounds

like whimsy, but the vehicles are ordinary to culture.' Eames's vehicles, his 'structures', make it possible for an object to have integrity.

The Eames aesthetic brought art into the marketplace through the assembly line. There was neither fear of nor blind obedience towards the machine. The machine, like its heir the computer, are tools which must be used by the artist as well as the entrepreneur. It is proletarian art: 'We want to get the most of the best to the most of the least,' Eames has said; 'in the final analysis I want to try to reach the greatest number of people'. The Eames chair stands as a tribute to the universality of his aesthetic; at the same time beautiful and functional, it is being manufactured in every continent except Africa. 'By the late fifties,' writes Smithson, 'the Eames way of seeing things had in a sense become everybody's style.'

Eames's aesthetic is in opposition to one of the older canons of art criticism, Ruskin's theory of 'invention'. In 'The Nature of the Gothic' Ruskin instructed customers to purchase only goods which showed the hand of the inventor, rejecting anything copied or undistinctive, even to the point of preferring the rough to the smooth. The Eames aesthetic contends that the customer, who organizes the life context in which objects exist, is as much a creative agent as the artist, and that it is his creative imperative to organize and respect the 'inventive' as well as the commonplace objects. 'If people would only realize', Eames said, 'that they have the real stuff in their hand, in their back yards, their lives could be richer. They are afraid to get involved.'

The second Eames contribution results when the Eames aesthetic of object-integrity is carried into the electronic age. There are two reasons: first of all, a computer cannot have object-integrity the way a chair or a toy train does. A chair is essentially shape, colour, and movement, but a computer is much more. To respect a computer one must understand how it thinks, must appreciate Boolean Logic. As Eames's objects became more complex, his approach necessarily became more cerebral.

Secondly, the object-integrity aesthetic is now confronted by an object-less society. 'The conscious covetors are growing tremendously,' Eames has said,

and the covetables in our society are shrinking tremendously. There's not much worth coveting. I feel that a lot of this vacuum is going to be beautifully filled by certain mastery of concepts, mastery of, say, the French or Russian language. And the beauty of this is that the coin of the realm is real. It means involvement on the part of the guy that's getting it. He's got it, all he has to do is give of himself. A lot of this is going to have to come through film.

Eames's second contribution, then, concerns the presentation of ideas through film. His method is information-overload. Eames's films give the viewer more data than he can possibly process. The host at the IBM Pavilion succinctly forewarned his audience:

Ladies and gentlemen, welcome to the IBM information machine. And the information machine is just that – a machine designed to help me give you a lot of information in a very short time. – *from* Think

Eames's information machine dispenses a lot of data, but only one idea. All the data must pertain directly to the fundamental idea; the data are not superfluous, simply superabundant. Eames's innovation, it seems to me, is a hypothesis about audience perception which, so far, is only proved by the effectiveness of his films. His films pursue an Idea (Time, Space, Symmetry, Topology) which in the final accounting must stand alone, apart from any psychological, social, or moral implications. The viewer must rapidly sort out and prune the superabundant data if he is to follow the swift progression of thought. This process of elimination continues until the viewer has pruned away everything but the disembodied Idea. By giving the viewer more information than he can assimilate, information-overload short-circuits the normal conduits of inductive reasoning. The classic movie staple is the chase, and Eames's films present a new kind of chase, a chase through a set of information in search of an Idea.

To be most effective the information cannot be random, as in a multi-media light show, or simply 'astounding', as in the multi-media displays at Expo '67 which Ray described as 'rather frivolous'. The Idea conveyed by the information must have integrity, as evidenced by its problem-solving potential, intellectual stimulation, and beauty of form. The multi-media 'experience' is a corruption of information-overload in the same way that the Barbara Jones and Peter Blake 'found-art' collages are corruptions of object-integrity – they present the innovation without the aesthetic. Through information-overload, the Idea becomes the new covetable, the object which has integrity in an objectless society. To paraphrase Eames, it is in the quest of the Idea that we often gain the richest rewards.

The films of Charles and Ray Eames fall into two categories. The first, the 'Toy Films', primarily use the first Eames contribution, object-integrity; the second the 'Idea Films', use the second Eames contribution, information-overload.

Through precise, visual, non-narrative examination the toy films reveal the definitive characteristics of commonplace objects. The toy films were the natural place for the Eameses to begin in film, for they found in simple, photographed objects – soap-water running over blacktop, toy towns and soldiers, bread – the characteristics they were trying to bring out in the furniture design:

In a good old toy there is apt to be nothing self-conscious about the use of materials – what is wood is wood; what is tin is tin; and what is cast is beautifully cast. – *from* Toccata for Toy Trains

Eames's film career is often equated with his toy films. Because of this mistaken assumption, the Eames films have already seen a critical rise and fall. Eames's films received their initial recognition during the heyday of the Norman McLaren pixillation, the early fifties, when the Museum of Modern Art and the Edinburgh Film Festival acclaimed the early toy films, *Bread, Blacktop, Parade*. Eames's reputation rose with McLaren's, and fell with it. The Eameses became typed as the toy film-makers, and critical interest died off.

The Eameses continued to make films, toy films as well as idea films. The toy films have progressed throughout the intervening years, using 'toys' of varied complexity, the Santa Monica House, baroque churches, toy trains, the Schuetz calculating machine, the Lick Observatory. Each toy film presents a structure in which objects can 'be themselves', can act like 'toys' in the same way that humans, given a certain structure, can act like children. The object need not be only functional; it can assume a number of positions. The Lick telescope is at one time practical, cumbersome, odd, and beautiful. One feels the same respect for the telescope that the Lick astronomer must feel after years of collaboration with the instrument. It cohabits the same structure, has meaning, both functional and aesthetic, and, in brief, has integrity.

The latest toy film, and the best, is *Tops*, a seven-minute study of just what the title says, tops. *Tops* is a refinement of the toy film technique. The structures are simplified: there is no narration, scantier backdrops, less plot; and the object assumes a greater importance within the structure. Tops of every variety are presented. The viewer studies the ethnic impulses, the form variations, the coloration, and the spinning methods of tops. The first half of *Tops* presents tops in all their diversity, gradually narrowing the scope of its investigation to simpler and simpler forms: a jack, a carrom, and, finally, a spinning tack. This is a moment of object-integrity: all the complexity and variation of tops have resolved into the basic form of two planes, one of them suspended by the balanced forces of gravity and gyroscopic momentum. The unaware viewer realizes that he has never really understood even an insignificant creation like a top, never accepted it on its own terms, never *enjoyed* it. The second half of *Tops*, which depicts the 'fall' of the tops, moves back to more complex tops, against blank backgrounds, giving the viewer a chance to see the same tops again, but with the new eyes of insight and sensitivity.

Eames feels that the toy films are as essential as the idea films. 'I don't think it's an overstatement', he remarked, 'to say that without a film like *Tops* there would be no idea films. It's all part of the same process, and I think I could convince IBM of that, if necessary.'

From the outset of their film-making, the Eameses were also making another sort of film, a film which dealt with objects with cerebral integrity. Eames's first idea film, *A Communications Primer*, resulted from a problem Eames realized he had to state before he could solve. He says,

I had the feeling that in the world of architecture they were going to get nowhere unless the process of information was going to come and enter city planning in general. You could not really anticipate a strategy that would solve the increase in population or the social changes which were going on unless you had some way of handling this information. And so help me, this was the reason for making the first film, because we looked for some material on communications. We went to Bell Labs and they showed us pictures of a man with a beard and somebody says, 'You will invent the telephone', or something. And this is about all you get. So we made a film called *Communications Primer*, essentially for architects.

Innovation is often a by-product of Eames's problem solving, as when Charles and Ray developed a lamination process for wood veneers to permit mass manufacture of their chairs. Similarly, Eames, in his desire to solve the complex, non-immediate problems of the city, and in his desire to bring integrity to the computer, developed a revolutionary method of information presentation. In 1953 Charles and Ray presented 'A Rough Sketch for a Sample Lesson for a Hypothetical Course', the first multi-media demonstration. 'A Rough Sketch' not only featured three concurrent images, but also a live narrator, a long board of printed visual information, and complementary smells piped through the ventilation system.

Eames's technique of information-overload has progressed just as his toy-film technique has, and some of the first 'revolutionary' films look rather primitive compared to his recent work. Eames has developed several methods of information-overload. The most basic, of course, is fast cutting (*Two Baroque Churches* has 296 still shots, roughly one every two seconds). He often has several screens (the most being twenty-two at the NY Fair, although not all the images were projected simultaneously), but has realized that a multiplicity of action on one screen can often have more impact than a single action on several separate screens. He has often used animation to simplify data, so that it can be delivered faster with clarity. One of Eames's most successful techniques is to split the screen between live action and animation, each of which affects the mental process differently. Eames also counterpoints narration, sound effects, music, and images to present several related bits of data simultaneously.

These techniques will certainly fade, just as did the McLaren aspects of his earlier films. Multi-media projections are a bit passé just now, and Eames isn't designing any at the moment. But, none the less, Eames's films hold up phenomenally well, because they are based on an aesthetic, not just an innovation. (Eames's specific techniques have several competent practitioners: Wheaton Galentine's 1954 *Treadle and Bobbin* corresponds to Eames's toy films, Don Levy's 1964 *Time Is* corresponds to Eames's idea films.) Even though the specific techniques and in some cases the very ideas of his earlier films may become antiquated, Eames's way of living seems as immediate today as ever. The solutions may no longer seem pressing, but his problem-solving process still offers beauty and intellectual stimulation.

Two of Eames's recent films, *Powers of Ten* and *National Aquarium Presentation*, are refinements of the idea-film technique just as *Tops* is a refinement of the toy films. These two films represent the two sorts of ideas Eames designs, the single or the environmental concept, and are more universal than Eames's earlier computer ideas. Because of the richness of the aesthetic Eames brings to these films, the ideas they portray inevitably strike deeper than originally intended.

Powers of Ten was a 'sketch film' to be presented at an assembly of one thousand of America's top physicists. The sketch should, Eames decided, appeal to a ten-year-old as well as a physicist; it should contain a 'gut feeling' about dimensions in time and space as well as a sound theoretical approach to those dimensions. The solution was a continuous zoom from the farthest known point in space to the nucleus of a carbon atom resting in a man's wrist lying on Miami Beach. The camera zooms from the man's wrist to a hypothetical point in space and zooms back again, going through the man's wrist to the frontier of the inner atom.

Going out, the speed of the trip was $10^{t/10}$ metres per second* – that is, in each 10 seconds of travel the imaginary voyager covered 10 times the distance he had travelled in the previous 10 seconds. In this schema a trip from the nucleus of the carbon atom to the farthest-known reaches of the universe takes 350 seconds. This information is presented in several ways: the right central section of the screen pictures the actual zoom, at the left of the screen a dashboard with several clocks shows the total distance travelled, the power of ten achieved, the traveller's time, the earth time, and the percentage of the speed of light. A dispassionate female voice – a robot stewardess – describes every second of the journey in full, rapid

*Time divided by 10 is the 'power' – in other words, after 40 seconds, you are 10-to-the-fourth metres away, or one followed by four zeros (10,000).

detail. The narrator also supplies extraneous, unexpected information. 'We have now reached the point where we can see the distance light travels in one minute,' she says, and a short burst of light, one minute long, passes before our eyes. In addition, there is an eerie score supplied by Elmer Bernstein on a miniature Japanese organ.

Handling information in such a way, *Powers of Ten* is able to give more data more densely than a multi-screen presentation. The pictorial area of the screen in itself has more visual information than the mind can assimilate. Every spot on the image is a continuous transformation: skin becomes a wrist, wrist a man, man a beach, beach a peninsula, and so on, each change the square of the previous change, and each faster than the viewer can adjust his equilibrium. The zooming image, in itself, is only an 'experience' and could easily be used in a light show (as it has been at the Whiskey A Go Go in Los Angeles). But the irony of *Powers of Ten* is that the narration and the dashboard demand exactly what the viewer is unable to do: make cerebral sense of the fantastic voyage. The monotone narration and animated dashboard affect the other side of perception; they use the conventional methods of appealing to reason. From the first frame of this eight-minute film the spectator is at a perceptual fail-safe point; both his mental and emotional facilities are over-taxed. As the viewer backs off from such a fail-safe point, as he has to, he takes with him certain souvenirs – individual data which in each case will be different, but mostly an Idea which in this case is about the dimensions of time and space.

The interstellar roller-coaster ride of *Powers of Ten* does what the analogous sequence in *2001: A Space Odyssey* should have: it gives the full impact – instinctual as well as cerebral – of contemporary scientific theories. (In comparison *2001*, like Expo '67, seems 'astounding'.) It popularizes (in the best sense of the word) post-Einsteinian thought the way the telescope popularized Copernicus; and the effect is almost as upsetting. The spectator is in perspectiveless space; there is no one place where he can objectively judge another place. Just as the vacationing hayseed begins to think of himself as a citizen of the country rather than of just Sioux Center, and the jet-setter begins to think of himself as a citizen of the world rather than of just the United States, so the time–space traveller of *Powers of Ten* thinks of himself as a citizen of the universe, an unbounded territory.

Eames approached the problem in universal terms (to please the ten-year-old as well as the nuclear physicist) and, as in designing a chair, sought to find what was most common to their experience. Sophisticated scientific data was not the denominator (although the film had to handle such matters with complete accuracy to maintain credibility), but it was that inchoate 'gut feeling' of new physics which even the most jaded scientist, as Eames says, 'had never quite seen in this way before'. Just as it took a more complex and intellectual structure to give a computer integrity than a toy train, so it took a more complex and intellectual structure to give the powers-of-ten-extended-through-space-and-time idea integrity than Boolean Logic. *Powers of Ten* goes beyond a simple explanation of the powers of ten (which Eames had done in his *IBM Mathematics Peep Show* by using the parable of the chessboard and sacks of grain), and concretizes a concept of the universe true to contemporary experience. And the Idea is covetable.

National Aquarium Presentation resulted from a more earthly problem. *Aquarium* is, simply enough, a report of the Department of Interior on a proposed National Aquarium. After two years of research and design, the Eames office presented the Department of the Interior not with a voluminous sheath of blueprints, but with a ten-minute colour film and an illustrative booklet. The problem was not only to develop the design and rationale for the Aquarium, but also to persuade an economy-minded Congress to lay out the cash for such a project. When dealing with the government, film is the petitioner's ideal medium: 'I've discovered', says Eames, 'that not even a senator dares to stand up and interrupt a film.'

Again Eames had to state the problem before he could solve it:

Aquarium wasn't a selling job, it was a report. Mike Kerwin, a venerable member of Congress, was interested in this and this was to be Mike Kerwin's monument. But Mike Kerwin didn't have any idea really of what an aquarium should be. As he or someone else said, 'Anything to keep those little children from peeing in the Capitol.' This is about the level these projects get started. The only thing you can do is try to create a level someone else would be embarrassed to fall below.

National Aquarium Presentation constructs the Aquarium in ten minutes, from overall conception to minute detail. Step by rapid step the film discusses the rationale, decides on a location, landscapes the environment, constructs the building, details the departments, and takes the viewer on a guided tour of the finished institution. Diverse methods of information presentation are used: graphs, animation, models, live-action, narration, music.

The guiding principles of the Aquarium are not simply aquatic curiosity or research. Like all of Eames's creations, the Aquarium is founded on organization, practicality, intelligence, and enjoyment. *Aquarium* makes sure that the viewer doesn't mistake those fish for something inessential to man. One who wishes to attack the Aquarium must attack the principles it is based on. The true function of the Aquarium is stated in the concluding lines of narration:

Still the greatest souvenirs of the Aquarium may be the beauty and intellectual stimulation it holds. The principal goal is much the same as science, to give the visitor some understanding of the natural world. If the National Aquarium is as good as it can be, it will do just that. – *from* National Aquarium Presentation

Even though Congress has yet to give final approval, the National Aquarium exists. It exists not only to the architects, to whom it always exists, but also to those who have seen Eames's film. After seeing the film, viewers speak of the Aquarium in the present; the fact that they cannot go to Washington and experience the Aquarium tactilely is only a chronological misfortune. The viewer has already experienced the full delights of the Aquarium, its beauty and intellectual stimulation. When the Aquarium is finally built, it seems to me, it will not be because the government really felt that it was needed, but because the Aquarium has already existed in so many minds – Congressmen, scientists, bureaucrats – that a physical structure was necessary to concretize the cinematic experience. And, if the Aquarium is built, it will be a rare demonstration of the *Realpolitik* power of an idea.

The irony and power of *National Aquarium* is that it is greater than the Aquarium ever can be. In its finest form the Aquarium exists in the mind, and the physical structure can only be a pale imitation of the dream. Eames calls *National Aquarium* a 'fiction of reality', and like the best fictions it is more meaningful than its reality. Eames has constructed the Aquarium like Borges constructed the Library of Babel in his short story of that title. Like the Aquarium the Library is real because it is definitive, it can encompass all reality. Just as the writer of 'Library of Babel' was able to define himself as a member of the Library, it is possible to define oneself as a member of the Aquarium. The Aquarium has all the virtues of a meaningful existence; it offers a way of perceiving the outside world, one's neighbour, and one's self. And even if one is only a visitor to the Aquarium, as we all must be, the Aquarium presents the virtues of beauty and intellectual stimulation that one would be embarrassed to fall below.

The radical, wonderful thing about Eames's Aquarium is that you *can* live there. One of the pleasures and limitations of Traditional cinema is that it is idiosyncratic: only Fellini can fully live in Fellini's world, Godard in Godard's, Hawks in Hawks's (great films transcend these limitations to varying degrees). Like an architect, Charles Eames builds film-structures in which many people can live, solve their problems, and respect their environment.

The three films discussed, *Tops*, *Powers of Ten*, and *National Aquarium Presentation*, total less than twenty-five minutes of screen time. To extrapolate an environmental aesthetic from a ten-minute sponsored film like *National Aquarium* many seem like the height of critical mannerism to some, and it is certainly possible that Eames's first films are not as important as I think they are. But in examining his films in detail, one finds the essential qualities of contemporary art. The Eames aesthetic personalizes assembly-line art, gives creator power to the consumer, permits individual integrity within a dehumanized collective, and allows the field to have as much value as the items within it.

In film, the Eames aesthetic introduces a new way of perceiving ideas into a medium which has been surprisingly anti-intellectual. Cinema threw every other art into the twentieth century, Wylie Sypher contends in *Rococo to Cubism*, and remained woefully in the nineteenth itself. Much of the upheaval in contemporary films has been the protest of the romantic–idiosyncratic tradition against itself. Even the best of recent films, like *Persona, Belle de Jour, The Wild Bunch*, are too inherently a part of the tradition they protest to posit an alternative cinema. The few film-makers handling ideas today, Robbe-Grillet, Rohmer, Godard, Resnais, seem to fail because they cannot escape the romantic perspective. The French intellectual cinema (the *only* intellectual cinema) verges on bankruptcy; its failures are as disastrous as Godard's *One Plus One*, its successes as minimal as Robbe-Grillet's *Trans-Europe Express*. Because Eames comes from another discipline with a pre-existing aesthetic he is able to bring innovation to an art which in the area of ideas is only spinning its wheels. It is Eames's aesthetic which is ultimately the innovation.

Eames returns to film in a limited and exploratory manner what Cubism took from it in the early 1900s. What Sypher wrote of the cubist art of Cézanne, Eliot, Pirandello, and Gide is now true of Eames's films:

Have we not been misled by the nineteenth-century romantic belief that the imagination means either emotional power or the concrete image, the metaphor alone. We have not supposed there is a poetry of ideas.

Film Quarterly, Spring 1970

CHAPTER 4

The Screenwriter: *The Yakuza* to *The Last Temptation of Christ*

JACKSON: *What approach do you have to the mechanics of writing a screenplay?*
SCHRADER: Well, first of all, screenwriting isn't really writing: it's really part of the oral tradition and it has a lot more to do with the day your uncle went hunting and the dog went crazy and the bird got away than it does with literature. One of the indispensable ways of judging whether an idea will work as a film story is oral presentation – you have to tell your story to someone.

When you first get an idea, maybe it's five minutes long, then the more you tell it, the more you elaborate on it and the longer it grows. When the story gets up to about forty-five minutes in length and is still holding your listener's attention, so that you know that if you walk out of the room they'll follow you to ask what happens next, then you know you have something that will probably work on screen. It's a very good way to weed out the ideas that aren't going to work. It's extremely debilitating to spend six months on a script getting angered and anguished and then to find out that there's really not a movie there, so working in this way saves you a tremendous amount of time on useless and counter-productive work.

Once you get to that stage you can write out an outline, a list of scenes. I favour using an outline that is paced out in terms of page counts. If you do that, you always know where you are in terms of the film's rhythm. If you're writing a scene that you projected to fall on page 49 and it's fallen on page 53, you can look back over your outline and see where those four pages have crept in and whether you want to keep them and cut four pages from elsewhere or not. I compare it to running a long-distance race where you have familiar landmarks and you can look at your watch and see whether you're faster or slower than usual.

KJ: *What sort of length is your average screenplay?*
PS: I started out thinking that a script should be about 115 pages and then I went down to 100 and then to 105. One version of *The Last Temptation of*

American Gigolo

0	1.	PRE-CREDITS	89	92	36.	SEARCHES ROOM + CAR
2	2.	CREDITS	92	93	37.	JAS ARRIVAL
3	3.	ANNE + JULIAN	93	94	38.	FOLLOWS R-MAN / ALIBI'S
6	4.	JULIAN AT AIRPORT	94	95	39.	MICHELLE + JILL
17	5.	W/MRS. DOBRUN	95	96	40.	PLANTS JEWELS
19	6.	MEETS MICHELLE #96	96	97	41.	LA SCALA
515	7.	JULIAN IN APT/LEROY CALLS 102		102	42.	JULIAN + LEROY
17	8.	JULIAN AT RIDELL S108	108	108	43.	JULIAN W/ REPORTERS
20	9.	GEORGIO'S	109	109	44.	JULIAN + DECT. + EVIDENCE
21	10.	DAISY: JULIAN + LEROY 109		110	45.	JULIAN + MICHELLE IN JAL
323	11.	MICHELLE VISITS JULIAN #2		112	46.	JULIAN W/ MICH'S LAWYER
29	12.	JULIAN + CLIENT AT VIEWING 111		113	47.	MICHELLE, SUNDAY
32	13.	JULIAN AT POOL: MICHELLE 113		114	48.	JULIAN AND MICHELLE #8
335	14.	DECT. + RIDELL				
36	15.	DECT. + JULIAN				
39	16.					
40	17.	POLITICAL RECEPTION				
42	18.	JULIAN IN WESTWOOD				
43	19.	JUL. + MICHELLE IN W.W. #4				
48	20.	JULIAN AND LILIAN				
52	21.	DECT + JULIAN AT HOTEL				
56	22.	ROOM SEARCHED				
57	23.	JULIAN AND ANNE				
60	24.	HOUCONT				
61	25.	JULIAN + HOTEL MANAGER				
62	26.	SPANISH BOY				
64	27.	VISITS ALIBI CLIENT				
66	28.	JULIAN + MICHELLE #5				
71	29.	JULIAN FOLLOWED				
73	30.	L.A. COUNTRY CLUB + HUSBAND				
78	31.	AFTER HOURS CLUB				
82	32.	MICHELLE + HUSBAND				
84	33.	LINE-UP				
89	34.	MICH, JULIAN, AT CLIENT #6				
91	35.	BOY IN PORCHE				

10 Outline of *American Gigolo*.

Christ was down to 99, and that was for a two-and-three-quarter-hour movie, but I generally think that for a two-hour movie about 105 is right.

KJ: *Do you concentrate first of all on alternating action scenes with exposition scenes, or on the disposition of the characters, or what?*

PS: Obviously there are techniques of pacing that you have to follow. Whenever two characters meet repeatedly there has to be some intervening action that will define their relationship, so that when you outline it on a single page you can see the various things that happen in between the meetings. The same thing applies to comic relief, or to action scenes: you can see at once that thirty minutes have gone by and the characters have done nothing but talk, so you say, 'Maybe I should move the scene where the car explodes back here.'

In the *American Gigolo* outline, for example, you can see at once that Julian and Michelle have to meet eight times, so you can arrange the scenes around those meetings accordingly. Writing dialogue comes fairly late, and if you've been telling your story to people as you've gone along – 'He says to her, so she says to him' – then you should already have a pretty good sense of what the dialogue should be.

KJ: *What was the first screenplay you wrote? Did it draw on ideas from the directors you had written about as a critic?*

PS: My first screenplay was called *Pipeliner*, and yes, it was sort of a Bressonian piece which all hinged on an irony. It was about a young man in LA who is told by his doctors that he has only a short time to live, so he goes back to the northern part of Michigan where he was raised and works on an oil pipeline for the winter, which is sort of a suicidal occupation. He feels that he has been released from the bonds of conventional morality by his impending death; he starts breaking and entering, and has an affair with the wife of an old friend of his who's now become the town sheriff. The upshot of it is that he causes an enormous mess, the marriage breaks up, somebody commits suicide and so on, but at the end of the film he's still alive and has gone into remission and is obviously going to be all right.

KJ: *Was anything in the film autobiographical apart from the locale?*

PS: The character really came right out of Bresson, with the sense of a higher personal morality that he takes from *Crime and Punishment* in *Pickpocket*; it was sort of a cross between *Pickpocket* and *Diary of a Country Priest*, meant to evoke that sort of barren sterility of the landscape.

KJ: *It sounds very austere. Was it ever close to being financed?*

PS: I think it was just as well that it never got made, but the business of trying to get it financed was a very good school; I had a good look at the denizens of the deep that inhabit film financing and the next time around I was much more savvy about why people put up money for films, which is an important part of being a film-maker. I've always felt that I could have made a lot of money if I had gone into business; I have a nose for it, and that's why I've never been too obsessed about making a fortune in movies. If I'd really been interested in becoming a millionaire I'd have gone into some other trade.

Anyway, around this time my marriage broke up and I had to quit the AFI, because I'd challenged George Stevens over the way he was running it. After the first year the AFI started to run out of money and they had to make cutbacks, but instead of making cuts in the side of the Institute that fed into the studios they cut back on archival, library and critical functions. So I started a petition to remove George Stevens, and eventually there was a big board meeting full of the studio heads and captains of industry who were George's friends.

It was a suicide mission, of course, but somebody had to tell the board in the most blunt, unflattering terms that the AFI was going in the wrong direction. Well, I lost, and even though George was nice about it and sent someone to say that there were no hard feelings, I knew that after publicly attacking him in the most brutal terms there was no way I could stay.

KJ: *You suddenly found yourself out of work?*

PS: I was out of work; I was out of the AFI; I was in debt. I fell into a period of real isolation, living more or less in my car. A grim time. And out of that isolation came *Taxi Driver*, which was written in just ten days; the first draft was about seven and the rewrite was three. It just jumped out of my head like an animal. As soon as I had written it I gave it to a literary agent who had been helping to support me, and then I just drifted about the country for six months.

KJ: *When was this?*

PS: The summer of 1972. I went to Michigan for a while, then up to Montreal, then Maine, and ended up in Winston-Salem, North Carolina. I was basically just living on friends' couches and trying to get myself back to psychological health. The only plan I had at the time was to negotiate with someone about opening a repertory theatre in Grand Rapids, but that never happened.

Then, when I was in Winston-Salem, I got a letter from my brother that

11 *The Yakuza* (Sydney Pollack, 1974): Robert Mitchum as
Harry Kilmer.

had been banging around the country after me. He was living in Kyoto, where he'd gone to escape the draft, as a missionary. I had a deferment on medical grounds, so I wasn't worried about Vietnam.

My brother had fallen on hard times himself and his marriage had also broken up. He had taken to watching lots of Japanese gangster movies. So I called up my agent friend in LA and said, 'I've had this fascinating letter from my brother. I think that it might be a very commercial idea to do a Yakuza film, a kind of Japanese version of the Kung-fu films.' He agreed that it was very commercial and so he paid for me and my brother to come back to LA to write it. We started writing round about Thanksgiving in a one-bedroom apartment we were sharing; we had finished by New Year and by February the script, which had been written purely on spec, got into an auction and was sold for $325,000, which was an extraordinary amount, especially at that time.

KJ: *Did this help resolve your personal crisis too?*
PS: Yes, because it gave me a clear direction. I had a place.

KJ: *You were reported not to be too happy with the way the film of* The Yakuza *turned out. What were your main objections?*
PS: My objections at the time were different from my feelings today. At the time I was being very snotty about it and I don't really think I understood how collaboratively films are made. What essentially happened was that the director, Sydney Pollack, was not terribly comfortable with making a pure gangster film so he brought in Bob Towne to heighten the international romantic element, and I think that the final film sort of fell between two stools. But once he was committed to making the film, it was my job to try to help him make the film he was best at, rather than snipe at him from the corner and assume that kind of arrogant high ground that writers like to assume.

KJ: *And you started working on other screenplays at around this same time?*
PS: Yes. When I came back to LA to work on *The Yakuza* I also started doing a little freelance criticism, and I did a review of Brian De Palma's *Sisters*, which I liked. I went to interview De Palma for an article and we struck up a friendship; I let him read *Taxi Driver* and he liked it a lot and wanted to do it.

He was living out on the beach at that time, and he walked down to a neighbouring house where Michael and Julia Phillips lived. They had just produced *The Sting* and they were interested in doing *Taxi Driver*, but

12 *Vertigo* (Alfred Hitchcock, 1958): James Stewart, Kim Novak.
13 *Obsession* (Brian De Palma, 1976): Cliff Robertson,
Genevieve Bujold.

they felt it would be ideal for De Niro and Scorsese, who was just cutting *Mean Streets*. So that was when I first met Marty. That whole summer of 1973 was very heady because every weekend a lot of people would assemble at Michael and Julia's house – myself, Gloria and Willard Huyck, John Milius, Steve Spielberg, David Ward, Scorsese; and John Dunne and Joan Didion lived right behind. John recently told me that he used to look at that house as a sort of generator for the new Hollywood – all these egos banging around.

KJ: *Did you share that feeling at all?*
PS: Yes. Even though we were relatively unknown there was a real feeling that the world was our oyster. Steven had done *Duel*; Marty was getting ready to do *Alice Doesn't Live Here Anymore*; Bobby De Niro had just got the role in *Godfather Part Two*; I had sold *The Yakuza* for this huge sum.

KJ: *If Michael and Julia Phillips were so interested in* Taxi Driver, *why did you not start in on it right away?*
PS: Well, at the time we couldn't put the film together because we still didn't have the clout. There was a chance to do it with another actor – Jeff Bridges – but we just held out and a year went by. *Alice* came on and did well; Bobby won an Oscar for *Godfather Two*; and Brian was off making the next script I wrote, 'Déjà-Vu', or *Obsession* as it was eventually called. That came out of a discussion I had with Brian about *Vertigo*, and it was essentially a sort of remake of the Hitchcock film, set in Florence and New Orleans. The film that got made had to be done quite cheaply, and my script was heavily cut so I dropped out of it.

The script of *Taxi Driver* kept banging around, and everyone would say, 'Gee, this is fabulous, but it's not for us.' But after a while we were all hot enough, the film was low budget enough at $2 million, and Michael, Julia, Bob, Marty and I just said, 'OK, we'll make it.'

Taxi Driver

KJ: *What do you think it was about the script that excited people so much?*
PS: It's a very exciting script to read. It had the same compelling urgency that the finished movie has. You read the first page of it, which is a character description of Travis Bickle, and you know you're on a ride.

KJ: *Were many changes made between the draft you gave to your agent friend and the screen version?*
PS: Very few. Marty wanted two things added: a scene for Albert Brooks and a scene for Harvey Keitel. I was opposed to this because everything in the movie should take place from the taxi driver's point of view, and if he doesn't see it, it doesn't exist. I said, 'You can't let the audience know that there's another world out there, otherwise, they won't buy into his, because his is a rather unsavoury one.' And I turned out to be right, because in the end Marty did cut the scene that he shot for Albert; and for the scene he shot for Harvey, which is the one of him and Jodie dancing, he had to put in a shot of Bobby from another scene, looking up at a window, so that it looked as if he was watching them. I think the reason that the film works is that you're given no alternative world to Travis's.

KJ: *Do you think that the film caught so many people's imaginations because of its strong sense of pent-up anger?*
PS: Yes. Godard once said that all great movies are successful for the wrong reasons, and there were a lot of wrong reasons why *Taxi Driver* was successful. The sheer violence of it really brought out the Times Square crowd.

But I have no real quarrel with that. I think that films can be extremely violent provided they understand the root causes of the violence. I think *The Wild Bunch* is a great film because it understands how deeply sick it is, and lets you know how sick it is; so it not only exploits your vicarious need for violence, but undermines it at the same time. I think films that analyse violence in that way are entirely justified.

KJ: *But the violence in Travis is not held up for analysis in a sociological or psychological way, is it? The film seems to have distinct spiritual ambitions.*
PS: Yes. Travis's is not a societally imposed loneliness or rage, it's an existential kind of rage. The book I reread just before sitting down to write the script was Sartre's *Nausea*, and if anything is the model for *Taxi Driver*, that would be it.

KJ: *And there are references to Bresson as well – the line about thinking he has stomach cancer . . .*
PS: And the scene where he makes the gun slide, which is sort of an allusion to *Pickpocket*. Originally Marty shot that scene so that it lasted ten minutes or more, dwelling on the sensuous mechanics of the process.

I think that what makes the film so vivid is what has made all my collaborations with Scorsese interesting, which is that we both have essentially the same moral background – a kind of closed-society Christian morality, though mine is rural and Protestant and his is urban and Catholic; mine is North European and his is South European. We can basically agree on everything in life, but we don't express it in the same way. I once described the film as the story of a Protestant kid from the snow country who wandered into a cathedral in the middle of New York City. That conflict of sensibilities is what makes it vibrate.

KJ: *Presumably there was something about Travis's character that reflected an aspect of your own – the loneliness, the rage, the wish for a kind of purgation?*
PS: At the time I wrote it I was very enamoured of guns, I was very suicidal, I was drinking heavily, I was obsessed with pornography in the way a lonely person is, and all those elements are upfront in the script. Obviously some aspects are heightened – the racism of the character, the sexism. Like every kind of underdog, Travis takes out his anger on the guy below him rather than the guy above. When they edited the film for TV I didn't so much mind having to lose the violence, but they had to remove huge sections of narration because of the virulent anti-black and anti-women characterizations. He appeared a very silly kind of guy because there was no edge to his anger; you just wanted to slap him in the face and say, 'Come on, come on.'

In fact, in the draft of the script that I sold, at the end all the people he kills are black. Marty and the Phillipses and everyone said, no, we just can't do this, it's an incitement to riot; but it was true to the character.

KJ: *It's curious that he should be so racist, given that your first impulse towards fiction came about because of witnessing racial bullying.*
PS: Well, that's really what art is about, you know. I think one is stung into progressive, positive behaviour by an awareness of the great lure of negative thought; it's the awareness of prejudice inside you that spurs you on to rid yourself and others of it. One of the things you should do in art is lift up the rock and look at those things inside you.

KJ: *The words in* Taxi Driver, *both the dialogue and Travis's voice-over, are terrific. Are they as you wrote them, or did they come about from improvisation?*
PS: The narration is as I wrote it. The dialogue is somewhat improvised – not to the extent of *Raging Bull*, say, but the most memorable piece of dialogue in the film is an improvisation: the 'Are you looking at me?' part.

14 Shooting *Taxi Driver*: Schrader and Martin Scorsese on location in New York.

In the script it just says, 'Travis speaks to himself in the mirror.' Bobby asked me what he would say and I said, well, he's a little kid playing with guns and acting tough. So De Niro used this rap that an underground New York comedian had been using at the time as the basis for his lines.

KJ: *Was the black comedy clear from the outset, or did that also develop from De Niro's performance?*

PS: Both Marty and I were very attracted to the perverse singularity of vision – someone who says, 'I've gotta get healthy' while he's swallowing pills – and to the self-contradictory nature of the character, which is where a lot of that humour comes from. Travis can't see that he is the one making himself lonely. He is the one making the world sordid, and you come to realize that the gimmick of the movie is to make you identify with him for simpler reasons, such as feeling oppressed by the city, and then gradually you're made aware that you have identified with someone you don't want to identify with, but now it's too late.

KJ: *One of the most disturbing qualities of Travis is his feeling of sexual disgust and rage. Does his attempted relationship with the Cybill Shepherd character amount to an attempt at health which just happens to fail, or has he somehow willed that failure?*

PS: He wills it, though not consciously. *Taxi Driver*'s plot structure is fairly simple. You have this pathologically lonely man confronted with two examples of femininity, one of which he desires but cannot have, the other of which he can have but does not desire. Now, obviously he's chosen objects which will exacerbate his own pathology – he doesn't really want a girl who will accept him, and when it seems as if the Cybill Shepherd character may, then in that unconsciously destructive way he takes her into an environment that will show her his real ugliness so that she will have to reject him.

KJ: *Taking her to the porno cinema isn't just naïvety?*

PS: It plays like naïvety – the character would say, 'Oh, stupid me, why did I go there?' – but there was something in him that really wanted to shove her face in the filth that he felt, to dirty her, to say, 'Look at this: this is what I'm really like. How could you love someone like me?'

And then, from that step where you have these two feminine figures who must be unresolved, you just move on to the two father figures. He decides to kill the father figure of the girl who rejected him, which of course is a reflection of his own father figure, and when he is thwarted by that he moves on to the pimp, the other father figure. That isn't meant to indicate that a pimp and a politician are one and the same, but in his mind they are identical as father figures. Of course the irony of the film is that society puts value on one and not the other and says he's a hero. But it didn't really make any difference to him which one he was going to get.

KJ: *Does the end of the film indicate that he's purged himself and is now safe and sane?*
PS: No, I think the syndrome is just going to start all over again.

KJ: *Did your feelings about the film change after the Hinckley affair at all?*
PS: No. I'm not opposed to censorship in principle – we can all agree on censorable things like child pornography – but I think that if you censor a film like *Taxi Driver* all you do is censor a film, not confront a problem. These characters are running around and can be triggered by anything, most often by advertisements or innocuous images.

A few years ago they did a study about incitement to rape, and one of the things that cropped up most often was the old Coppertone suntan oil ad – it had a little puppy tugging at a girl's swimsuit. It had just the right mixture for these rapists of adolescent sexuality, female nudity, rear entry, animals, violence . . . So I think that if you do get involved in this kind of censorship you still end up having Raskolnikov, you just don't have *Crime and Punishment*.

KJ: *But* Taxi Driver *now seems a different kind of film than it did before – more prophetic, more diagnostic.*
PS: When I talk to younger film-makers they tell me that it was really the film that informed them, that it was their seminal film, and listening to them talk I really can see it as a kind of social watermark. But it was meant as a personal film, not a political commentary.

There was a very good feeling around the making of the film; everything felt right about it, and I remember the night before it opened we all got together and had dinner and said, 'No matter what happens tomorrow we have made a terrific movie, and we're damn proud of it even if it goes down the toilet.' And the next day I got up and went over to the theatre for the noon show. There was a long line that went all the way around the block, but I absolutely had to be let in. And then I realized that this huge line was already for the two o'clock show, not the noon show! So I ran inside and watched the film and everyone was standing at the back and there was a sense of exhilaration about what we had done. We knew we'd never repeat it.

Rolling Thunder and Other Scripts

PS: Around 1974 to 1975 I was so full of ideas I was writing faster than I could make deals; the ideas were coming out of the toaster like pop tarts. I wrote 'Déjà-Vu', *Rolling Thunder*, *Quebecois* and others all in the same year. I look back on those days with great fondness, the ideas were so hot and heavy.

KJ: *Do you find it harder to have ideas today?*
PS: Yes, first of all because I don't have that angry passion, that *cri de cœur*, that need just to lean out of the window and yell. I have a much more resolved life and I don't need to fantasize that much. So mix that with the kind of calculation that comes after years of working – where you know you shouldn't be writing something because it won't get made . . . At that time I just didn't care: I had to write them and write them.

KJ: *Were you trying to break into directing too?*
PS: *Rolling Thunder* was going to be my first film as a director. That film has an ironic history. I originally sold it to Larry Gordon at AIP, and then Larry moved from AIP to Columbia and took it with him, and then he left Columbia and took it to Twentieth Century Fox, made it there, and then Twentieth sold it back to AIP again and they released it.

The story of *Rolling Thunder* was really botched in the rewriting. The main character in the film was meant to be the same sort of character as Travis, with that same anti-social edge. The character, as I originally wrote him, was a Texas trash racist who had become a war hero without ever having fired a gun, and came home to confront the Texas Mexican community. All his racism from his childhood and Vietnam comes out, and at the ending of the film there's an indiscriminate slaughter of Mexicans, meant as some kind of metaphor for American racism in Vietnam.

In order to get it made at Twentieth, they insisted that that racist element be taken out, which is the equivalent of giving Travis Bickle a dog. Once you take out the perverse pathology of these characters, rather than become films about fascism they become fascist films, and that's what happened to *Rolling Thunder*.

KJ: *There's an idea in common between* Rolling Thunder *and* The Yakuza *to do with the mutilation of the hand – in* The Yakuza *a ritual cutting off, in* Rolling Thunder *damage by a garbage-disposal unit.*

PS: That's a common fantasy of all writers, because you write with your hands and the self-destructive impulse in a writer takes that form. It's like a painter fantasizing about blinding himself. I remember a scene from a Joan Crawford film called *Autumn Leaves*, where Cliff Robertson plays a writer who's having an affair with an older woman and she gets furious with him and takes the typewriter and smashes his hands. It's a pure writer's fantasy.

The other screenplay I wrote which got made around this period was *Old Boyfriends*; Joan Tewkesbury made it in 1979. That was a script which had a sex-change operation, as *Light of Day* later did. It was originally called 'Old Girlfriends', about a man who went back and looked up his old girlfriends. It didn't really work, and I realized that if I turned round the sexes it would be less prosaic, more interesting.

I had a production credit on the film because I helped set it up, and I mistakenly thought at the time that I shouldn't direct it, because I, as a man, couldn't really penetrate the female psyche sufficiently and so on. There weren't many opportunities for women directors at the time and I saw myself as being able to alleviate the situation, so I supported Joan. In retrospect I wish I had directed it.

KJ: *Why?*
PS: I think I was yielding to a kind of insecurity by saying that I shouldn't do it. I think I *did* know how to direct it, and that I could have done a better job, or at least a more piercing job. I don't think that it has enough of an author's edge. I would have pushed things more and made them more edgy, more spooky, more scary, with characters that are more mesmerizing and more obsessive.

KJ: *So the finished film was like a sentimental journey, where you wanted it to be a painful reworking of the past?*
PS: Yes, and I wanted the characters to be grander. You know, everything I've done has been informed by biblical characters. That's our mythology. Even the latest script I've written, *Forever Mine*, which is an attempt at a kind of popular romantic thriller, has all kinds of echoes of Joseph and his brothers.

KJ: *What else were you writing at this period?*
PS: There was *Quebecois*, which was a disguised remake of a Japanese gangster film set in Montreal, about the battle between two crime families, one French–Canadian and the other Italian–American. It focuses on two brothers in the French family, one of whom is an adopted American who

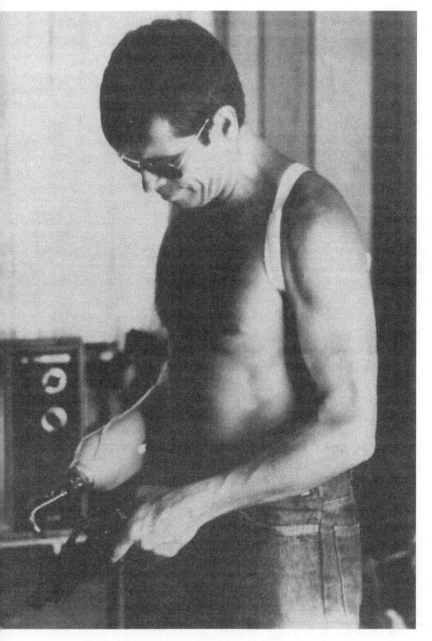

15 *Rolling Thunder* (John Flynn, 1977): William Devane as
Charles Rane.

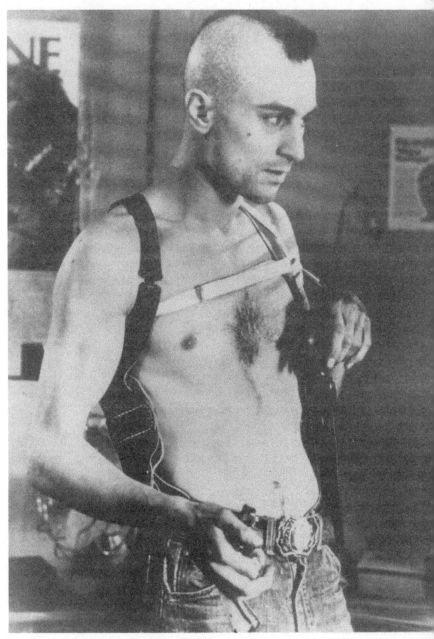

16 *Taxi Driver* (Martin Scorsese, 1975): Robert De Niro as Travis Bickle:
'A man and his room'. (1)

ends up taking over the family because the rightful heir is involved in the Quebecois revolution. So it's sort of America versus Canada, French versus Italian, and brother versus brother, all lined up. I think the reason it didn't get made was that I miscalculated and wrote it just as the gangster trend was coming to an end. I would still like to see it made.

Then there was *The Havana Colony*, all about the fall of Havana, which I wrote for Paramount, but both that and *Quebecois* were bought by Warner Brothers. *Havana Colony* has since been rewritten by other writers; in fact, I had occasion to reread it for the first time in years the other week, because Sydney Pollack is making it and he had never in fact read my original. I think it holds up well, but Sydney's script is based upon Judy Rascoe's version.

Close Encounters and *Covert People*

KJ: *Is it true that you were also involved in writing the first draft of* Close Encounters of the Third Kind *for Spielberg?*
PS: Yes. That came out of the group that spent their weekends at the Phillipses' beach house. Steven had told Michael and Julia that he wanted to do something about flying saucers, so they put us together and I wrote the first draft, but Steven and I had a falling out along strictly ideological lines, which was quite an instructive disagreement – it says a lot about him and it says a lot about me.

My script centred on the idea of a modern-day St Paul, a guy named Paul VanOwen, whose job for the government is to ridicule and debunk flying saucers. But then one day, like St Paul, he has his road to Damascus – he has an encounter. Then he goes to the government; he's going to blow the lid off the whole thing, but instead the government offer him unlimited funds to pursue contact clandestinely, so he spends the next fifteen years trying to do that. But eventually he discovers that the key to making contact isn't out there in the universe, but implanted inside him.

About the only thing that was left of all that when Steven finally made the film was the idea of the archetypal site, the mountain that's planted in his mind, and some of the ending. What I had done was to write this character with resonances of Lear and St Paul, a kind of Shakespearean tragic hero, and Steve just could not get behind that, and it became clear that our collaboration had to end.

It came down to this. I said, 'I refuse to send off to another world, as the first example of earth's intelligence, a man who wants to go and set up a

McDonald's franchise,' and Steven said, 'That's exactly the guy I want to send.' Steven's Capra-like infatuation with the common man was diametrically opposed to my religious infatuation with the redeeming hero – I wanted a biblical character to carry the message to the outer spheres, I wanted to form missions again. Fortunately, Steven was smart enough to realize that I was an intractable character and he was right to make the film that he was comfortable with.

KJ: *Did you retain a credit on the final version?*
PS: No, at Steven's request I withdrew from the credit arbitration, which is something I've come to regret in later years, because I had points tied to credit. So I gave up maybe a couple of million dollars that way, but that's the way it happens.

Then in 1978, shortly after *Blue Collar*, I wrote a script that was never made, called *Covert People*, which was a kind of disguised remake of the old *film noir*, *D.O.A.* I wrote that after I wrote the critical essay on *film noir*; there were a number of films I had unearthed in that piece and brought to attention – *Out of the Past* was one and *D.O.A.* was another.

KJ: *Did the script of* Taxi Driver *owe anything to your viewings of* films noirs?
PS: Not too much – the darkness of *film noir* attracted me, but *Taxi Driver* really comes, as I say, out of French existential fiction. The darkness of *film noir* is much more socially motivated than it is in *Taxi Driver*: you have these heroes who've got a dirty deal; they've come back from the war and their wife has gone and they don't have a job . . .

KJ: *But you could say much the same of Travis, who's a Vietnam veteran.*
PS: Well, I didn't really make him a Vietnam vet, that's part of the subtext. It's assumed that he has some kind of searing memory and that he's had some familiarity with weapons, but it's not meant to be a story about Vietnam and Vietnam is never discussed. There's a reference on his jacket to 'King Kong Company', which could be a reference either to the Vietcong or to the movie. It's something which is just left to be inferred. *Covert People* was about three government employees, two men and a woman, and the woman is moving from one man to the other. One of the men discovers that he is dying and the diagnosis is that he has been poisoned, so he tries to track down the killer. What emerges is that all three of them have been involved in clandestine operations – they each had overt and covert jobs – and that his friends had devised the poison for another purpose and then given it to him unwittingly.

KJ: *Was that not made because it was felt to be too dark?*
PS: I guess so. Either too dark or too difficult – the buzz words of my problems in getting films made. Maybe just not very good.

KJ: *In interviews around 1979 you also made reference to a film about Hank Williams.*
PS: Yes, that was written and I did a lot of research on it. I wouldn't want to make it today even if someone offered me the chance, because I've done my film about a suicidal artist in *Mishima* and I did my film about music in *Light of Day*.

KJ: *Was there anything else about the topic that especially interested you?*
PS: He was a real momma's boy; he couldn't resolve his feelings towards women except in terms of momma idolatry, so that was an interesting kind of pathology. Then there was the fact of his being so emotionally loose, not in charge of his emotional life at all – the opposite of Mishima, who was very securely tied to the deck in terms of his own inner calculations.

KJ: *You make him sound a little like Travis.*
PS: There was definitely that element to it. *Hank Williams* was going to be structured in an unusual way. I have problems with conventional biographical films; I just can't bear to see movies about real events that falsify them. All the forays I've made into biography have ended up having peculiar styles: on *Hank Williams* it was called 'Six Scenes from the Life of Hank Williams', like *Mishima* was 'A Life in Four Chapters' – it just took six separate months from a five-year period and focused on the things that happened in those months. *Raging Bull* also had that odd structure, and *Patty Hearst*, even though I didn't write it, has an odd structure. I've more or less decided to stay away from biography in future because I find that I always impose these structures so that I don't have to fabricate events – the fabrication occurs in the structure rather than in the episodes.

Mosquito Coast, Gershwin and Others

KJ: *Apart from* The Last Temptation of Christ, *the only screenplay you've worked on that came from a novel was* The Mosquito Coast, *wasn't it?*
PS: Yes. That was to pay for the whole *Mishima* episode. I went for a couple of years without earning any money because of *Mishima*, so I wrote

The Mosquito Coast just before I left for Japan in late 1983 and I wrote a screenplay about George Gershwin as soon as I got back in 1984.

KJ: *So Mosquito Coast was a commission rather than something you had a burning desire to write?*
PS: Well, I loved the book and I loved the character of the father – a terrifically self-destructive character – so they were congenial areas for me.

KJ: *Could you have written a screenplay from a book that you had little or no interest in, or must there always be some element that fits in with your private interests?*
PS: Yes, there has to be something, some door into the material that will open for you. The big problem with *Mosquito Coast* was one of condensation; it had such sweep in terms of the events that it was impossible to get it all into a two-hour format. But I was dead set on being faithful to the book. I don't think the finished film really worked in the way the book did, which was, rather like *Taxi Driver*, to have a character who's initially charming and attractive and who suckers you in, so that by the time you realize how mad your guide is you're already out in the wilderness with him.
   One of the problems was the casting of the lead role. It was written with Jack Nicolson in mind; he was the only actor I could imagine who would have that kind of absolute charm. But for one reason or another Jack became unavailable and so they went with Harrison Ford, who doesn't have that reptilian charm. He doesn't sucker you in the first fifteen minutes and so the movie is in effect over, because he's only going to become less and less likeable.

KJ: *There's something of a representation of American virtue gone sour in the Harrison Ford character, like a cross between Ben Franklin and a frontiersman. Is the idea of examining the American psyche one that's of interest to you?*
PS: Yes, but only in the sense that every national is interested in local mythology. That side of the film is really all Paul Theroux's vision, and I saw the script as being in service to Theroux. The truth is that, in a way, it's actually easier to write original scripts than to adapt books, because when you write an adaptation you have two employers, the person who's paying you and the author of the book, both of whom militate against your own creativity and make writing a slower and more difficult process. When you write an original you're only constrained by your own imagination and how fast you can work; there aren't so many script conferences.

17 *Mosquito Coast* (Peter Weir, 1986): Harrison Ford as Allie Fox.

KJ: *Was* Gershwin *also a commissioned script?*
PS: Yes. It was a project that came from Scorsese and De Niro, who both have a love for musicals that I don't really share. The great problem with that screenplay is that you have a central character whose life really didn't have a great deal of drama. He wanted music and fame and money and women, and he got all four and then died at the age of thirty-nine. It wasn't a tortured life – it was an all-American success story. Again, I just couldn't see inventing some kind of ersatz drama, so I had to create the drama structurally.

What I did was to come up with nine approximately chronological thematic chapters with titles like 'Women', 'Classical', 'Hollywood', 'Psychoanalysis' and so on, and then in each of those chapters, which were about ten minutes long and shot in black and white, we'd shoot forward in time following that theme. At the end of each chapter there would be a musical section in different formats by different artists, a Gershwin song which would encapsulate that theme. So after 'Women' it would be 'I Just Can't Get Started' and after 'Psychoanalysis' it was 'How Long Has This Been Going On?'

It was a very adventurous structure and I think it's a very good script, but by the nature of the material it's a very expensive piece, at least $25 million or so, and, as Hollywood learned from *Pennies from Heaven*, you don't make these experimental films at that price.[1] Because you need music rights, you need Warner Brothers who owns them, and Warners isn't about to make a $25 million *Mishima* or another *Pennies from Heaven*. On the other hand, they're not going to relinquish the script because that means relinquishing the possibility of their making the more conventional Gershwin film they would like to make.

KJ: *Did you already know Gershwin's music well, or did it need a lot of research?*
PS: I did a lot of research. One of the benefits of this occupation is that you really do get to play in someone else's sand-box. You get to immerse yourself in the world of Detroit auto workers or pornography or Japanese culture; it gives you a chance to pour into those fields.

KJ: *Did you write anything else around this time?*
PS: There was a Vietnam script called *Round Eyes* which I wrote for Alan Ladd, who still wants to make it, but I think its time has come and gone. It's about a man who goes to Vietnam to find his brother's daughter, who's an Asian, and then falls in love with his brother's ex-wife and then finds out his brother is still alive. Shades of *The Third Man*.

Raging Bull and *The Last Temptation of Christ*

PS: Mardik Martin's draft of *Raging Bull* was a script that Scorsese and De Niro had but they just weren't happy with it. They couldn't get a go on it, so when Bob came by late in 1978, while I was shooting *Hardcore*, I went straight from shooting *Hardcore* into writing *Raging Bull*, editing my film by day and writing by night.

My main contribution to it was the character of Joey La Motta. Jake didn't like his brother much, so he wasn't in the first draft and there was no drama there. I did some research, met Joe and he struck me as much more interesting. You had these two young boxers, the Fighting La Mottas, and one was sort of shy while the other one had a lot of social tools, so Joey quit fighting and managed his brother. The only thing Jake was good at was taking a beating, he wasn't a terrific boxer but he could take a beating and meanwhile Joey was off managing and getting all the girls. So injecting that sibling relationship into the script made it a financeable film.

KJ: *Was the flashback structure also yours?*
PS: I think so.

KJ: *What was the main point of that structure as far as you were concerned – the fact that La Motta found a new way to be a performer, a public figure?*
PS: I think Marty was more attracted to that element than I was. I was very much attracted to the notion of his hands. La Motta felt that his hands were small and ineffectual, that they weren't really boxer's hands, and the climax of my script was a scene which Marty and Bob chose not to do, or rather did in a different fashion.

It is the prison scene. Jake is in the cell and he's trying to masturbate and is unsuccessful, because every time he tries to conjure up an image of a woman he's known, he also remembers how badly he's treated her, so he's not able to maintain an erection. Finally he takes it out on his hands; he blames his hands and smashes them against the wall. I'm not sure why, but they were uncomfortable shooting this and so it became 'I am not an animal' instead.

KJ: *You've said that your characters are drawn from the Bible in one way or another; is that true of your Jake La Motta?*
PS: Not so much with him, because you're dealing with a real person. But there's obviously a pseudo-religious masochism to it – regeneration by

18 *Raging Bull* (Martin Scorsese, 1980): Robert De Niro as Jake
La Motta.

blood, ritual beating – and that aspect of it certainly appealed to both Marty and me.

KJ: *Scorsese has spoken of it as a film about redemption.*
PS: Yes, but redemption through physical pain, like the Stations of the Cross, one torment after another. Not redemption by having a view of salvation or by grace, but just redemption by death and suffering, which is the darker side of the Christian message.

KJ: *It ends with a quotation from the Bible: 'I was blind, and now I see.' Was that in your script?*
PS: That's purely Marty. I had no idea it was going to be there, and when I saw it I was absolutely baffled. I don't think it's true of La Motta either in real life or in the movie; I think he's the same dumb lug at the end as he is at the beginning, and I think Marty is just imposing salvation on his subject by fiat. I've never really got from him a terribly credible reason for why he did it; he just seemed to feel that it was right.

KJ: *In the film La Motta is jealous almost to the point of insanity. Is that true of life, or did you introduce that theme?*
PS: It's put in a bit. Some of it is to do with that kind of hidden sexual bond between brothers. The sexuality of the siblings expresses itself by Jake being convinced that his brother has cheated him.

KJ: *The other strange thing about Jake's sexuality is his habit of remaining celibate before big fights so as not to sap his energy. That may be a common athlete's myth, but it also aligns him with your other pent-up, celibate characters.*
PS: Yes, that's the Deadly Sperm Backup. Marty and I call it the DSB. I don't know whether we coined it or just heard it, but the idea comes up again in *The Last Temptation*, where Jesus comes outside and one of the characters says, 'That's what happens when you don't sleep with women – your sperm goes up to your brain and makes you crazy.'

KJ: *Could you find any affinities between your character and La Motta's that helped you write it?*
PS: Not really. I would not have done this on my own, and I don't think Marty would have, either, but it was Bob's passion. Marty is fond of saying that *Taxi Driver* is my film and *Raging Bull* is De Niro's and *The Last Temptation of Christ* is his.

KJ: *The script looks very loosely structured at first, but then you start to notice all sorts of connections and parallels being set up between situations and lines.*

PS: One of my vices as a writer, and I really don't think it's necessarily a good thing, is a kind of undue parallelism, a kind of book-end mentality that wants to have everything balanced and neatly structured. One of the reasons *Taxi Driver* is so good is that it appears random, but every scene logically leads to the next and it all fits in.

When I was a critic I was very fond of the semi-colon; I loved that parallel structure of one long sentence, semi-colon, another long sentence. Pauline Kael once described my style as the revenge of the semi-colon. I have to watch out for scripts becoming just a little too neatly structured. That's partly a product of my particular college education, focused heavily on good English and correct prose. As I said, my favourite writers in college were the Victorians.

KJ: *It doesn't seem to have inhibited your ability to write demotic dialogue, or to portray characters like La Motta who are next to inarticulate.*

PS: This goes back really to the fork in the road between criticism and fiction. I found myself writing and directing the kind of movie I would not have approved of as a critic. The two processes are diametrically opposed. Criticism is essentially a cadaverous business: you perform an autopsy on something and try to determine how and why it lived. Screenwriting and film-making are much more embryonic – something is growing and you have to nourish it and not pass judgement on it until it is born. So all the thought processes that are valid for criticism are often counter-productive in fiction writing. You have to whack yourself on the head and say, 'Don't get so literal. Not everything has to fit.'

KJ: *Do you have any special technique for avoiding that kind of self-censorship?*

PS: I used to write at night and I used to write drunk. I wrote drunk for fifteen years, but now I'm too old – I can't do it any more, it takes too long to recover. My latest script, *Forever Mine*, is the first I've written sober. There's not really that much difference; it's just that when you're sober your critical faculties start to get in the way, but when you're drunk you get grandiose and emotional and start to go with the flow.

KJ: *How do you feel about* Raging Bull *now?*

PS: I think it's a terrific movie, but it's just not that close to me personally because La Motta is not the kind of character I would have imagined on my own. Christ is the kind of character I would have imagined.

KJ: *Which you had a chance to do next . . .*
PS: Well, if you've been fooling around with redemptive themes in various surrogate guises, tackling the prototype is pretty irresistible.

KJ: *What was the history of your involvement with the film?*
PS: Barbara Hershey gave Marty a copy of the book during the shooting of *Boxcar Bertha*, and he'd wanted to do it ever since. He first mentioned it to me around the time of *Taxi Driver*, but he wasn't able to raise the money to secure the rights. Then in 1980 or 1981 he finally bought the rights and I wrote the script in the summer and fall of 1981.

KJ: *Why was Scorsese intent on using the Kazantzakis novel rather than going straight to the Gospels?*
PS: The greatness of the book is its metaphorical leap into this imagined temptation; that's what separates it from the Bible and makes it a commentary upon it. If I could have come up with a similar kind of inspiration I would have loved to do something like that myself – if I had written a Christ film from the Bible I would have had to come up with something similar to keep it fresh, some hook. The great hook of *The Last Temptation* is the idea of the reluctant God, the person whom God is imposing himself on – that's pure Kazantzakis.

KJ: *How did you go about adapting such a difficult book?*
PS: As soon as I read it I knew that it had to open with narration, and with a description of a migraine. And as soon as I knew that, I knew the tone – there is this kid with these vicious headaches and he just doesn't know what to make of them.

It's a 600-page novel and a 100-page script, so I had to throw out a lot, and then I added new scenes as well. Essentially what I did was to make a long list of everything that happens in the novel, every single event, and then put a check mark beside the events that related to things I was interested in – how they related to the struggle 'What does God want of me?'; or how they related to the central triangle of the film, which is Jesus, Judas and Magdalene – and just focus on those elements.

I just lifted out all the scenes that had the most checks on them and chose maybe thirty-five scenes that stood out as being focused on where I wanted to go. Then I wove them together and said goodbye to everything else in the book, cutting it down to about seventy or eighty pages.

KJ: *At the end of* Transcendental Style *you contrast religious films which have over-sparse means with those that have over-abundant means, such as Charlton Heston as Moses. Was the problem of over-abundant means something which crossed your mind?*

PS: The Last Temptation of Christ is not a religious or transcendental film in that way. It's really much more a psychological film about the inner torments of the spiritual life; it's not trying to create a holy feeling. That's what the book is like, that's what Marty wanted and that's the script I wrote. It's a tortured human struggle about a common man possessed by God and fighting it. God is a demon in that way.

KJ: *Is the idiom of the characters yours?*

PS: Yes. That's just a case where you have to bite the bullet. You can't do it in King James English and you can't do it in Aramaic, which would be the only way to make it realistic. You have to assume that these people are conversing in a normal fashion and in order to make it sound as if you're hearing these conversations for the first time you have to use a fresh, idiomatic dialogue. People will recoil at that because it violates all they've read and heard over the years, but that's just unfortunate – there's no other solution.

KJ: *Did the script go through many rewrites?*

PS: Yes, Jay Cocks rewrote it repeatedly, but nothing really changed with the exception of one or two scenes which were dropped and the scene where Saul kills Mary Magdalene which was changed because Marty just felt you couldn't show a pregnant woman being killed, so now she dies sort of miraculously.

KJ: *Apart from Kazantzakis, were there any other sources for the ideas about spiritual struggle and torment? Some of it seems like another return to Bresson.*

PS: Yes, it's obviously that in the narration. The one scene I did add that wasn't in the book was the one where Christ takes out his own heart. It just hit me and I loved the scene and Marty loved it, and then someone pointed out to me – I hadn't thought of it at the time – that that is the emblem of Calvin College, the heart in the hand.

KJ: *Did you and Scorsese have theological discussions when you were preparing the film?*

PS: Marty and I never really collaborated over a desk; we really don't work that way. I understand how he thinks and feels and I talk with him and try to find out where he is coming from, but then I go off and write and when I come back he accepts it or not. What he doesn't accept he changes on his own. I don't bother him when he directs and he doesn't bother me when I write.

KJ: *At what point did you become aware of the fundamentalist rage that was about to come down on you?*
PS: I really didn't think there was going to be that much trouble. I come from a background where theological debate is a staple, and considered conducive to faith rather than detrimental to it. It was fundamentalist, but it was intellectually oriented rather than faith oriented, which is the inheritance of John Calvin: Christianity is basically logic. Most of the people who protested came from another aspect of Christianity where it's practically all faith. What happened with the film was that the Evangelical Right pre-empted the debate. They got out there early and started characterizing the film in an inaccurate way. The Right had fallen on hard times and this was a great way to call on their support and raise money. They framed the debate by saying that Hollywood is attacking our Lord and we are defending our Lord. Well, you know, the coffers of Christianity spring open when they hear that argument, and the mainstream of Christianity has to side with the fundamentalists when the debate is couched in those terms. The film was rushed into the theatres to put an end to the propaganda.

But none of us thought that it was going to be a big problem until about 1983 when the Right started marshalling their forces when they heard that the movie was under way.

KJ: *Does the theological debate in the film come straight from Kazantzakis, or is it one that's of some older vintage?*
PS: There are two elements in the book. One is a kind of Nietzschean superman struggle, and the other is more Eastern, more mystical. Because of my background, I skewed it towards the Nietzschean and Calvinist and away from the mystical. The struggle to be God, the struggle with one's own sense of divinity is an *Übermensch* problem. In the film you can see the progression from Greek Orthodox to Dutch Calvinist to Roman Catholic, and I think that layer-cake aspect of Christian theology is one of the things that's interesting about the film.

KJ: *Does any one strand predominate?*
PS: We hit on all three, but the end of the film is a kind of superman triumph – calling yourself back to the Cross by force of will – and the

19 *The Last Temptation of Christ* (Martin Scorsese, 1988): Willem Dafoe as Jesus of Nazareth.

emphasis is definitely on the man who wills himself back to the Cross rather than on the God who puts him back.

KJ: *But the film never questions the reality of divinity or the fact that Christ's call is a real one.*
PS: No. One of the pleasing aspects of the whole controversy was how the whole debate became refocused on one of the early debates of the Church. The two major heresies which emerged in the early Christian Church were the Arian heresy, from Arius, which essentially said that Jesus was a man who pretended to be God; and the other was the Docetan heresy, which said that Jesus was really God who, like a very clever actor, pretended to be a man. So they called a council and branded both philosophies as heresy; but in fact the Church has tended anyway to go on its merry Docetan way, being much more comfortable with the idea of God pretending to be man than man pretending to be God. *The Last Temptation of Christ* may err on the side of Arianism, but it does little to counteract the 2,000 years of erring on the other side, and it was pleasant to see this debate from the early Church splashed all over the front pages.

KJ: *What was your reaction to all the arguments?*
PS: The picture was a provocation and I enjoy debate and argument. It would be very hypocritical to say that you don't enjoy it when you incite it.

KJ: *Did the debates hurt the film or your career, or was it successful as a result of them?*
PS: I think that because of all the publicity people assumed that the film would do better, but it's a three-hour film about the nature of Jesus; it was always a speciality-audience film. The publicity and the censorship probably ended up balancing each other out and in the end about the same number of people saw it as would have done otherwise. Most of the people who were protesting don't go to films anyway.

KJ: *Is there anything about the film that you're particularly pleased with?*
PS: I think Willem Dafoe did a terrific job. Invariably, when you write a script you write some scenes that are marginal and usually don't end up in the film, even if you direct it yourself, but you have to write them just in case the actor rises to the occasion and they work after all. They're usually the very bald scenes where the character discusses the theme of the movie and more often than not they end up hitting the floor. What I was most pleased with is that Dafoe managed to pull all those speeches off. When I

watched the film for the first time I half expected them not to be there, but they were and I was extremely pleased by that.

KJ: *Looking back over the three films you've written for Scorsese, what – apart from the redemptive theme you've already mentioned – do you think gives them a common thread?*
PS: They're all of the same cloth: they're about lonely, self-deluded, sexually inactive people.

KJ: *What is it about celibacy that makes it such a fascinating subject for you?*
PS: It certainly reflects the upbringing I had, which was very puritan and taught that sex was for procreation, not for pleasure. It all comes from St Paul – marry if you must, but marry to have children, not for pleasure. Now our Church, like other little pockets of conservatism, has become progressively integrated into the rest of America. I'm sure it's not taught that way any more.

Note

1 Though it received some enthusiastic reviews for its lavish recreations of classic MGM musicals and its mordant wit, this 1981 American adaptation of Dennis Potter's BBC television series (directed by Herbert Ross and starring Steve Martin in the role originally taken by Bob Hoskins) proved to be a box-office failure.

CHAPTER 5

The Director: *Blue Collar* to *The Comfort of Strangers*

Blue Collar

JACKSON: *When did you first realize that it was possible to become a director?*
SCHRADER: Well, there was a group of us – kind of top-gun, fresh new writers who wanted to direct, like John Milius and Walter Hill – and the strategy we all used was to build your price up sufficiently high as a writer and then give a script away so that you could direct it. The very first script I wrote, *Pipeliner*, I also wanted to direct, so I had my eye on being a director fairly early on. A screenwriter is not really a writer; his words do not appear on the screen. What he does is to draft out blueprints that are executed by a team. So if you want to be in control of what you are doing as a writer you either have to become a novelist like Gore Vidal or John Gregory Dunne or you have to get into directing. Being a screenwriter is in the end rather unsatisfying for an artist. It's very satisfying commercially and it's a pleasant lifestyle, but in the end you don't really feel you have anything that represents you.

I went about *Blue Collar* in a very methodical way. I wrote it as an ensemble piece so I could get three hot young actors who would work for minimum, and with whom I could make deals independently, and I followed the Don Siegel maxim of taking the plots from three movies and putting them into one.

KJ: *Where did the main plot idea come from?*
PS: That's complicated. What happened was I was speaking at the Writers' Guild in 1977 and a man named Sydney Glass came up to me afterwards and asked me if he could talk about an idea, so I said yes. He came by my place and said he wanted to write a script about his father, who was a black auto worker in Detroit. And in my conversation with him I started spinning out this story, and said, you know, there's a much more interesting story here than a defeated man who commits suicide, and that's about a man who commits metaphorical suicide by stealing from the

union, the organization which is supposed to protect him. Then I started thinking about it later that day, and I knew when he left the room that he would never write it; he just wasn't picking up on the idea at all. So I called my brother Leonard and said, 'I just gave a wonderful idea to somebody and he's not going to write it, so let's us write it.'

KJ: *Why call in your brother rather than write it alone?*
PS: I was writing something else at the time – maybe it was *Havana Colony* – and I didn't have the time to write two scripts simultaneously, so I would be writing one more or less during the day and the other in tandem at night; it's easier to do that when you have a partner. So we wrote it, and then just as I was about to start shooting this guy went to the black caucus at the Writers' Guild and said I had stolen his idea. Now, I had registered the idea as soon as I came up with it, and he hadn't written a word, but there was a highly politicized atmosphere at that time and the Guild said that they would not clear the rights to the script until this was resolved, so I had to sit down and make a deal with them.

KJ: *What was it that you especially liked about the main idea?*
PS: Just the self-destructiveness of the metaphor about people who would attack the organization that was supposed to defend them. And how that kind of dead-end mentality is fostered and engendered by the ruling class in order to keep the working class at odds with itself.

KJ: *Though there is no representative of the ruling class in the film.*
PS: The union officials are seen as the ruling class. I believe that all organizations of that sort end up being undemocratic, they end up being clubs, and I guess this really comes from my feelings about the Church. People ask me about the way I broke into Hollywood and say, 'How did you do it?', because they see Hollywood as a kind of monolithic structure. I usually reply that when you've been raised in an environment which seeks to control your private thoughts, dealing with an environment that only wants to control your physical deeds is relatively easy. Hollywood doesn't really care what you believe; all they want you to do is to behave in a certain way in order to make money.

I've always felt uncomfortable in clubs of any sort, including my own Guilds, the Writers' and the Directors'. I've been at odds with them all along. I'm a big advocate of that kind of capitalist 'make your own way' ethic: if a person has ingenuity, he can survive in this world without falling under the influence of clubs. But the capacity of the human psyche for forming that kind of country-club mentality is tried and true; it doesn't

20 *Blue Collar* (1977): Richard Pryor as Zeke Brown.

matter whether it's the Teamsters or Fidel Castro – in the end certain people are gonna run it and certain people ain't. The advantage of the West is that you have more room and that to a certain extent you're encouraged to try to outwit the system.

KJ: *Union politics and working-class problems aren't on the face of it very appealing subjects for financiers. How did you get the backing?*
PS: I sold it on the caper aspect most of all. But another problem came up with the casting: I knew it would have to have black characters, and I wanted to do something about the petty struggles and the physical needs that make up day-to-day life and not simplify my black characters or on the other hand be too soft or affectionate towards them. Now, you couldn't have two whites and one black, because he would have to assume the Sidney Poitier role, the decent black guy; otherwise it would be two nice whites and a black villain. So to make your main character complex, there had to be a second black guy to bounce off from, so it wouldn't be racist, which was why it had to be an ensemble piece.

KJ: *So Richard Pryor was never meant to be the star?*
PS: No. A lot of the difficulties on the film came out of the fact that I had approached Richard and Harvey Keitel and Yaphet Kotto separately and led each of them to believe that they were the star of the movie, because that's what it took to get them involved.

You were basically introducing three bulls into a china shop and asking them to get along, and you can't really blame the bulls when things start getting wrecked. Very early on, by the second or third day of production, Richard became convinced that he was playing the black sidekick to Harvey's Terry Molloy, and Harvey became convinced that he was playing Ed McMann to Richard's Johnny Carson, and Yaphet was convinced that they were both trying to ace him out, and things got very heavy.

We were shooting in auto plants in Detroit and Kalamazoo in the middle of a heatwave and pretty much what was happening on-screen started happening off-screen. Not a day went by without some sort of confrontation. Right after you said 'Cut', a fight would start. After about three weeks in, I was in the middle of the set and all of a sudden I started crying and I just couldn't stop, something I'd never done before. The AD grabbed me and took me outside and walked me around the block and I said, 'This is not working. The movie is never going to get finished and I'm never going to work again.' But he calmed me down and walked me back in and I guess everyone realized I wasn't as much the iron man as I had been appearing. Richard looked at me and said, 'You pussy – are you gonna be a man or not on this movie?', and I said, 'OK, Richard, I'm sorry. It won't happen again.'

KJ: *Did things improve from that point on?*
PS: No, there were other problems. Part of it was to do with Richard's style of acting. Being primarily versed in stand-up comedy he had a creative life of between three and four takes. The first one would be good, the second would be real good, the third would be terrific and the fourth would probably start to fall off. Whereas Harvey, with his theatrical training, very self-analytical, would work on the meaning of the scene in the early takes and then after ten takes he'd be terrific. Well, there's virtually no way you can film those two men together, so you'd have to rehearse Harvey with a stand-in and then bring Richard in without any rehearsal.

The other thing that Richard would do when he felt his performance going flat was to improvise and change the dialogue just like he would have done in front of a live audience, and he would never tell me or anyone what he was going to do. In one case I had a two-shot of Richard and Harvey where Richard just started flying, and of course Harvey tried to top him, and as soon as that happened Richard just sort of took off and became brilliant.

Harvey broke a take once because he felt himself being knocked out of shot. I had to grab Harvey and get him down on the floor and yell at him, 'Don't you ever break shot!', because Richard was right behind me trying to get at him.

So the shooting strategy became very limited: 'I know I may only have one take with these actors, so what's the best one?', and you'd work out the minimum coverage you needed and that's all you got. Sometimes if they were in a good mood you could actually try something a little different, but by the time we shot the last scene, the one with all three of them on the sofa after the party, they hadn't been talking to each other for a long time, and I had fallen into a prolonged pattern of script negotiations which usually began the night before and went on into the morning of shooting, talking to each of them until they were all happy with the others' improvisations.

Now the day before the sofa scene Richard had hit Yaphet with a chair on-camera, so I knew it was going to be tough. We lit the scene with extras, put their names on the sofa with pieces of tape, and the crew were all warned. The three of them came into the room in silence, there was no discussion, I said 'Action' and we did the first take, which ran to about four or five minutes – much too long. So I said, 'OK, that's very good, but it's

21 *Blue Collar*: The final set-up of the shoot: Yaphet Kotto, Harvey Keitel, Richard Pryor.

too long for us. We're going to go right again. No one move, no one talk, let's just do it a little faster. Action.' We did that take on the same reel of film and that was two and a half minutes. I said, 'Cut', and Richard got up, went downstairs, got in his car and drove home. End of movie.

KJ: *All this must have given you a completely different perspective on the job of being a director than the one you'd envisaged when you were a critic.*

PS: It did. I said afterwards that if this was what movie-making was like I didn't want to do this any more. On that film, I very quickly learned to confine myself to talent management, to making sure the actors stayed in character and the storyline remained coherent. I handed over shot selection and lighting and blocking essentially to my crew. I didn't have time to explore those areas.

KJ: *Did you have a strong sense of what its visual style ought to be before shooting started?*

PS: I had a stronger sense, I'll tell you, but then the locations themselves indicate visual style to a large degree. When you're shooting in a factory you don't have to dance around much; it's not like having to shoot in offices and motel rooms where the environment is so sterile that you have to be imaginative.

KJ: *But some of the sequences are very strikingly done – Kotto's murder with paint-sprays, for example, or the credit sequence.*

PS: Yes, well, some of the effect of that opening came out in post-production, when my composer Jack Nitzsche was working on that musical line from the Bo Diddley song, which in turn is from a Muddy Waters song. But I love that sense in a movie as it starts that's like the cranking a roller-coaster makes as it approaches the top, that sense of exhilaration, and I love to induce that. Also, I think opening sequences lend a film a very strong sense of authorship. One of the things an audience wants most in the opening moments of a film is the sense that someone is in control. I remember watching the opening of *Deliverance*,[1] just seeing that car going up and hearing the voices and saying, 'This guy knows what he's doing. I can just sit back and enjoy the movie.'

KJ: *One of the strange things about* Blue Collar *is that although there's not an inordinate amount of physical violence, it feels like a violent film.*

PS: Yes, it does. At that time people were always saying to me, 'Oh, you make such violent films,' and I'd say, 'No, they're psychologically violent, but they aren't really that physically violent.' In my whole career I've killed about as many people as, say, Walter Hill kills in half an hour, so the sensation of violence comes from something quite different, which is my sense of claustrophobia.

KJ: *Literal claustrophobia?*
PS: Yes, I've had a big problem with this all my life. Finally, in my late twenties, through psychoanalysis, I got over the most severe symptoms, like being unable to ride in an elevator – these days I'll take the elevator up, but I'll still walk downstairs. So part of the psychological violence in the films is to do with people who feel themselves penned up and strike out irrationally, flailing at their condition in a self-destructive way, in the same way a person locked in a closet will smash his head into the door and knock himself out. In fact, I had an episode like that when I was an undergraduate, when I snuck into the heating system with a friend to set off a smoke bomb. The janitor saw us go in and locked the door behind us, and I had a terrible claustrophobic attack. My friend picked up a two-by-four and was going to knock me out because I was so crazy, but eventually in my panic I knocked the door out of its cement casing. Obviously these feelings have their historic, sexual origins, but growing up in a restrictive environment doesn't help.

KJ: *Did the claustrophobia also have a social dimension?*
PS: Yes. Even though I was a middle-class kid, the fact that we lived in a poor part of town gave me the sense that rich people aren't going to give you anything, you're gonna have to take it. That Animals song, 'We've Gotta Get Out of This Place', was a real strong song for me, and a real strong feeling for me.

KJ: *When the film came out a lot of people made the assumption that you must be a Marxist, and you seemed to go out of your way to undeceive them.*
PS: Yes. There is an American publication, a leftish publication, called *Cineaste* which heralded me as the new Marxist hope. Well, I didn't mind the praise, but I knew I wasn't going to live up to it, so I tried to show them that this wasn't where I was headed. I wasn't the new Haskell Wexler.

KJ: *So how would you describe the politics of* Blue Collar *today?*
PS: Its politics are the politics of resentment and claustrophobia, the feeling of being manipulated and not in control of your life.

Hardcore

KJ: *That sense of emotional violence is also strongly present in the later parts of* Hardcore, *which also has a strange and extremist moral stance, as if the only two options which existed were the extreme rectitude of the George C. Scott character or the extreme depravity of the pornographers. There is no middle ground.*

PS: Yes, that's a kind of adolescent hyperbole I'm not very happy with. It's certainly a movie I could neither write nor direct today.

KJ: *You've outgrown those notions?*

PS: Or those urges.

KJ: *Perhaps the most surprising thing about it on first viewing is that you expect the father, Jake VanDorn, to be revealed as some sort of a hypocrite, and then it gradually dawns on you that the film is generally endorsing his point of view.*

PS: Yes. My favourite line in the film is where he says, 'I don't care what's happening in the world, I don't care who's on Johnny Carson, I really don't care,' and that's an attitude I really respect. I've made two more or less autobiographical films – *Hardcore*, which is about my father, and *Light of Day*, which is about my mother – and I think they both may have failed commercially because they're a little too personal.

There's also a delicious line in *Hardcore* that's taken from one of my uncles, which is at the beginning, at the Christmas party. The kids are sitting around watching some innocuous TV special and the uncle walks in and turns off the set – this is something that actually happened to me – and he says, 'Do you know who makes television? All the kids who couldn't get along here go out to Hollywood and make TV and they send it back here. Well, I didn't like them when they were here and I don't like them now they're out there.' And this struck me as absolutely true. That's what we all do, you know: misfits from small towns across America go out to Hollywood, make TV and movies and pump it back into our parents' homes and try to make them feel guilty.

KJ: *But the paradox of* Hardcore *is that you're using the means of the misfit kids to endorse the values of your father.*

PS: Or trying to. I wish I had succeeded more.

22 Shooting *Hardcore* (1978): Schrader with George C. Scott (Jake VanDorn).

KJ: *Where do you think it fails?*

PS: I think I succumbed to the sort of glorified, prurient nature of the sexual underworld. The second half has a kind of kid-in-a-candy-shop feeling that I'm uncomfortable with. Since I didn't participate in the sexual liberation of the sixties, though I participated in the political liberation and the drug liberation, my sexual freedom took this rather aberrant form of an obsession with people who lived the forbidden life. Where the film becomes untrue to itself is when you feel the director's prurience and not the character's.

KJ: *How did the story evolve? Is it true that Warren Beatty was going to play the lead at one time?*

PS: Yes. Another thing that dissatisfies me about the film is that I changed the ending and never really got it to work. I wrote it as a father–daughter story and then Warren got involved and felt he was too young to play a father so the character had to be a wife. That was a good lesson in some ways, spending every morning going through that relentless process of his, the way he wears you down, and swearing at the end of it that I would never write at the behest of an actor again.

Anyway, Warren dropped out and the project moved to Columbia, who had George C. Scott, but by that time the ending had already changed. Originally I had the daughter being killed in a car accident, or in some way completely unrelated to pornography, so the father goes on this kind of journey through hell seeking to redeem his daughter, finds out that she has been killed in some mundane way and then has to go home and live with what he's learned. But the studio felt that it had to have a more upbeat ending, to do with the redemption of the child, so I changed it, though neither I nor George was ever really satisfied by it.

KJ: *You describe his trip as a 'journey through hell'. Does Calvinism have a highly defined notion of what hell is like?*

PS: Well, it's certainly no fun. I remember my mother once telling me what hell is like, and I can't imagine a more vivid image. She took my finger, took a pin and pricked me. She said, 'Now you know how that felt? The moment the pin went in your finger?' I said, 'Yes.' She said, 'That's what hell's like all the time.'

KJ: *But is there a strong tradition of visual representations of hell?*

PS: You mean fire and brimstone and things like that? No, it's generally a very intellectual idea of hell, defined as the eternal absence of God.

23 *Hardcore*: 'A journey through Hell': Jake VanDorn alone in the porno district of Los Angeles.

KJ: *Is there still a part of you which believes in that hell?*
PS: No, it doesn't make any sense.

KJ: *But there's one scene in* Hardcore *where George C. Scott outlines the harsher tenets of Dutch Calvinism by explaining what the acronym* TULIP *stands for,[2] and it seems as if the film sympathizes with him at that point.*
PS: Yes, it's a scene I'm greatly fond of, but . . . no, it doesn't really make sense to me any more.

KJ: *As a child, did you ever believe that you were one of the elect?*
PS: Oh, I *knew* I was one of the elect.

KJ: *Just by virtue of belonging to the Church?*
PS: This gets into a very complex theological area. Calvinism has this dreadful predestination problem, which is also described in the film, because if God is omniscient then the elect have to be known; there have to be people who are in and out, and if that's the case then why should you bother to be good? Calvinism sort of solves that by saying that unless you accept the fact that you're in the elect then you're not in the elect. And this is where they come up with the notion of the unforgivable sin . . .

KJ: *Which is being debated at the Christmas dinner at the beginning . . .*
PS: Right, and the unforgivable sin is the sin against grace. There are two types of grace: universal grace, in which everything participates and which makes the trees grow; and specific grace, which is the blood of Jesus. If you reject grace then that is the unforgivable sin. I remember worrying as a child that I might commit it and end up in that place where they're always sticking pins in your fingers.

KJ: *On the subject of religious mysteries, isn't there a cryptic meaning in Jake VanDorn's name?*
PS: Yes. Dorn means 'thorn' – originally he was going to be called Zondervall, which means 'fall of man' in Dutch – but the key word in that name was Jake, because of Jacob wrestling with the Devil, a very powerful image for me and one which I used in thinking about *The Last Temptation of Christ*. Wrestling all night with the Devil and finding out in the morning that he was the Angel of God.

KJ: *Did you often give your characters symbolic names?*
PS: Yes, and I still try to. Travis Bickle I think was a very good name, and

24 *Taxi Driver*: Travis Bickle alone in the porno district of New York.

25 John Wayne as Ethan Edwards alone in the final shot of John Ford's *The Searchers* (1956): 'The price of vengeance is that you have no home.'

that came from the romantic, soft sound of Travis, meaning 'travel', and the hard, unpleasant sound of Bickle, which I took from a little radio show about a couple who always argue called *The Bickersons*.

KJ: *When the CIA man asks him for his name, Travis calls himself 'Henry Krinkle'.*
PS: That's for comic reasons, and because, as Walter Matthau says, K is funny.

KJ: *Julian Kay, in* American Gigolo, *isn't a funny name.*
PS: He was originally going to be Julian Cole – Julian from *Le Rouge et le Noir* and Cole from 'cold', and then it turned out there was a man in Westwood called Julian Cole so I changed the name to Kay, from Kafka's Joseph K.

KJ: *Apart from literary and biblical references, your films also allude to or draw on other films. One of the films behind* Hardcore, *and also* Taxi Driver, *is John Ford's* The Searchers.[3] *Could you explain why that is such an important film for you and for other directors of your generation?*
PS: A couple of reasons. One is the frailty of the great American hero, the psychological instability of the pioneer. Another one I like even more is *Naked Spur*, where Jimmy Stewart actually starts crying as he gets on his horse – taking the great iconographic hero and breaking the icon down. That was always the appeal of *The Searchers*.

Another appeal, besides the enormous technical expertise of the film, is that it's the kind of big romantic movie that intellectual film-makers can respond to, in the same way that *Lawrence of Arabia* will always mean more than *Gone With the Wind*, because you have a character you can identify with, and the John Wayne character in *The Searchers* is one all film-makers can identify with. Wayne is playing with his persona; he hardly ever plays the outsider, but this is a man who is deprived of the pleasures of hearth and home because he has blood on his hands. At the end of the movie he walks away and the door closes on him; he has returned the lost child to the home but he can't enter. It also has resonances of Moses, who struggled through the desert and was not allowed to enter the Promised Land – it has great traditional resonances.

KJ: *It's also a film about vengeance, which is something you seem to have been preoccupied with in your early years.*
PS: Yes, and the price of vengeance is that you have no home. And that's very appealing in a complex way because there's a truth in it; when you

indulge in these extreme forms of behaviour you have to pay a price, and even though you're acting at society's behest, that doesn't mean they'll forgive you for it.

KJ: *But the implication of the revised ending of* Hardcore *is that Jake VanDorn will manage to return home.*

PS: Yes, I suppose that if I'd really been true to *The Searchers* then he wouldn't have been able to, that the idealized world which is summoned up in that hymn, 'Precious Memories', which I use as the title music for the film will have been lost to him because of his immersion in a world of violence. In the original ending the Peter Boyle character says, 'What do I do now?', and Jake says something to the effect of, 'Well, you go home, try to forget it.' 'How is that possible?' 'That's your problem.'

KJ: *You shot the opening of* Hardcore *in Grand Rapids, so it was a kind of homecoming for you too. Did you experience nostalgia or less pleasant sensations?*

PS: Well, I'm still very much a son of Grand Rapids; I'm still intensely moral in the sense that I believe that actions do have consequences and that, while that doesn't mean it's wrong to behave badly at times, it does mean you will have to pay the price. Yes, there was an element of nostalgia about going back. I used a number of my family and my college friends. My mother is in the family-reunion scene, and an old friend is playing the piano, singing one of the old Calvin College songs from the fifties – 'C is for the countless things she taught me . . .' – and so on.

KJ: *How did your mother react to being in a film called* Hardcore?

PS: No one in Grand Rapids really knew what the movie was about at the time, and it wasn't called *Hardcore* then – it was called 'Pilgrim'. My mother died before the film came out, and my father's sole critique on my work came a year or so later, when he admitted that he had seen the film.

KJ: *What did he say?*

PS: He said that he was glad my mother wasn't alive to see it.

KJ: *He didn't recognize himself in Jake?*

PS: I don't think so. I think he just saw it as an attack on him and on everything he believed in. But then he was also involved in the opposition to *The Last Temptation of Christ*.

KJ: *After all the troubles on* Blue Collar, Hardcore *must have been a comparatively painless experience.*

PS: In fact, it was also a difficult experience. George C. Scott was unhappy at the time. He had directed a couple of films which hadn't done well and he was resentful about that. Also, he had a drinking problem.

One night we were shooting in San Francisco, in the Tenderloin area. It was about midnight, and we were planning to wrap that part of the shoot, fly to San Diego the next day and start work again on Monday. All George had to do in the scene was enter a bar and look around, and I knew I could light that section very quickly, whereas the other sections would take an hour or two. Now normally I would have shot him first, but I checked with the AD and said, 'Can we let George sit in his trailer for two or three hours?' and everyone said, 'Sure, he's a professional.' But then, when the time came for his scene, I started sending emissaries to his trailer and he just wouldn't come out. So finally I went to see him myself and he was sitting at the back of his trailer with an empty bottle of vodka in front of him and he was drunk and he was pissed off.

I walked in and said, 'Hi, George,' and he said, 'This movie's a piece of shit.' So I started to reason with him, but he said, 'This is shit. You're a terrific writer, but you're a terrible director. You should not be directing.' So I said, 'Yes, George, I see you're right. I've made a terrible mistake, but now I have to finish the job, so will you come and help me?' He says, 'I'll come on one condition.' 'What is it, George?' 'You have to promise me you'll never direct again.'

So I got down on my knees and promised and he got up and did his one-minute shot, then we finished the main part of the shoot. Then there was a hiatus and we went back to Michigan to shoot a spring scene just for a couple of days. We're sitting in the bar of the hotel and George is at the bar and I'm at a table and all of a sudden I hear this booming voice, 'Schrader!' I walk over and he's got *Variety* in his hands and there's an announcement that I'm going to do *American Gigolo* with John Travolta. He said, 'Schrader, you promised me you would never direct again.' I said, 'George, what can I say? I lied.'

American Gigolo

PS: *American Gigolo* was the third script I had stacked up ready to direct. I wanted to build a career and I wanted to have at least three shots from the gun before they took it away from me, so during 1978 I was shooting *Hardcore* at the time *Blue Collar* opened and I was shooting *Gigolo* shortly after *Hardcore* opened.

KJ: *Unlike the first two films, it doesn't have any reference to the world of your childhood.*

PS: No. One important thing to remember about film-making, or about any artistic enterprise, is that it is for the most part problem solving. It's not necessarily ideologically oriented, or shouldn't be. You are confronted with certain problems and you try to devise an appropriate solution – it goes back to what Charles Eames said about measuring people's asses.

The idea for *Gigolo* came to me at a time when I was teaching at UCLA, and I was just speculating in the class about what a character in a student's script might be doing. I said, 'Is he a banker, is he a lawyer, is he a cop, is he a gigolo . . . what kind of a man is he?' And later that day I was on the couch at my shrink's office and we were talking about the inability to express love, and all of a sudden I thought, 'That's it – there's the metaphor, there's the theme.' The theme is the inability to express love, the metaphor is a gigolo. Well, once a theme and a metaphor hit, that's really it; plot and execution are relatively easy after that.

The hardest thing is finding a theme which has personal power for you and a metaphor that has social resonance. When you're trying to write you spend a lot of time wandering around hoping for these two to meet. Arthur Koestler wrote a book called *The Act of Creation* where he says that all great ideas are always a sort of Hegelian mix, and Charles Darwin was a mixture of anthropology and mathematics. He brought two things together that previously seemed to have no connection and you got Darwinism.

Anyway, I hit on this theme and I realized that the character of the gigolo was essentially a character of surfaces; therefore the movie had to be about surfaces, and you had to create a new kind of Los Angeles to reflect this new kind of protagonist. Well, what better way to do this than to bring in outsiders for whom there is no old Los Angeles? So I went to what I called my new Axis powers, from Munich and Milan, and I got the visual style from Armani and Scarfiotti and the music from Giorgio Moroder from Germany. The imposition of these very European sensibilities started to create the kind of new LA I wanted; I pretty much sat at Nando Scarfiotti's knee in the same way I had sat at Eames's knee years before and let him teach me about visual thinking.

KJ: *Gigolo is your first film with a very distinct visual identity.*

PS: Yes. I played around with it in *Hardcore* but not very well. I ended up trying to use gels to create style but that's not how you do it; since then I've tried to stay away from gels. I prefer to make colour in the set and in the wardrobe, rather than rely on gels.

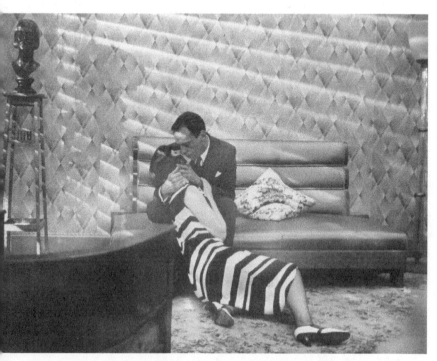

26 *The Conformist* (Bernard Bertolucci, 1969): Stefania Sandrelli and Jean-Louis Trintignant.

KJ: *Was it Scarfiotti's work on* The Conformist *that led you to seek him out?*

PS: Yes, *The Conformist* was a very important film for my generation, because it was a film that reintroduced the concept of high style. Movies used to have high style in the thirties and forties and then gradually, through the fifties and sixties, they became more realistic, less production-designed, and *The Conformist* became a real sort of rallying cry. It's influenced a lot of people – Scorsese, Coppola – to create films of high style, and now it's finally reached its conclusion in things like *Miami Vice*. You can trace *Miami Vice* right the way back to *The Conformist*, because Michael Mann, who's a friend of mine, was very impressed by the work Scarfiotti did on both *Gigolo* and *Scarface*, and that's what he's tried to emulate.

Anyway, I sent Nando the script and explained what I wanted and he rose to the bait. I think the whole sexual chic of the film appealed to him.

KJ: *When you say 'sexual chic', do you think of it as an erotic film or as a cold film where the eroticism is displaced from bodies and on to things?*

PS: The latter. Even the sex scenes are very cold; the sex scene with Richard Gere and Lauren Hutton is actually Godardian; all the images in it are from *Two or Three Things I Know About Her*. The trick of the film – and I guess if I ever try to do anything resembling transcendental style this might be it – is to try to create an essentially cold film in which a burst of emotion transforms it at the end, which is why I had the audacity to take the end of Bresson's *Pickpocket* and put it in there.

KJ: *There's another direct reference to Bresson, isn't there?*

PS: Yes, the barber-shop scene, which is taken from *Pickpocket*, which in turn is taken from *Crime and Punishment*, with its moral debate between the Inquisitor and the criminal. The criminal says that some people are above the law and the Inquisitor says, 'But how do they know who they are?' The criminal says, 'They ask themselves.'

KJ: *That seems to have some affinities with Calvinist notions about accepting that you are one of the elect.*

PS: Yes, I think so.

KJ: *Do you think that* Gigolo *would have been a very different film if you had used John Travolta as originally planned?*

PS: That's hypothetical. I don't know. It's easy for people to say, 'Oh you were so lucky to get Gere,' but you just don't know. It would have been a different film.

кj: *I take it that the film is meant to be ambiguous until very near the end about whether or not Julian is innocent?*
ps: Yes, I was trying to keep that ambiguity. Julian is a lounge lizard and you're never quite sure about him, but I had to pull back a little bit: I didn't want to make him too unlikeable.

кj: *Audiences, especially male audiences, respond strongly to the scene where Julian lays out his shirts and ties . . .*
ps: The artist at his palette . . .

кj: *. . . but are you supposed to find that narcissism appealing, something to participate in vicariously, or are you meant to find it off-putting?*
ps: Well, I certainly participated. Let me explain this a little. If I chart out my life, I came to Hollywood as an overweight kid from the Midwest who always wore undershirts and too many clothes. Gradually I succumbed to the physical culture of Los Angeles, which I think is one of the best things the place ever did for me. I lost a lot of weight and I became interested in presenting the proper LA image. This is a business based on looks and style, and if you don't have either of those things it's just an encumbrance in trying to sell yourself. If some schlump comes in they're going to think it's a schlump movie, whereas if someone walks in who's the hippest thing this week, they'll be impressed and think, 'Well, he's on top of it.' So that's one of the feelings that went into *Gigolo*.

The other was to do with the fact that I came from a background in which physical contact was rare, and in my family was exacerbated to the point at which my father actually shook when he held you. So when I came to LA I was very uncomfortable with that kind of kissy/holdy feeling, but then I started moving in gay circles and going to gay discos and I found a way into physical contact, because it was harmless. I mean I could go dancing stripped to the waist, hugging and holding men, and feel completely released and liberated because I knew nothing would come of it; I knew in the end I was not going to have a sexual contact.

A lot of people have asked me why I have this strong concern for and even love for gays, and why my best friends over the last ten years have been gay, and whether it means I'm really in the closet, but it's really because of that liberation: I couldn't get there through the heterosexual door so I went through the other door and then came back round.

27 *American Gigolo*: Richard Gere as Julian Kay: 'A man and his room'. (2)

KJ: *Gigolo seems to have been aimed as much at a gay audience as a straight one – there are a lot of gay characters, there's an air of sexual ambiguity that matches the ambiguity of the character, and Gere's good looks have something slightly androgynous about them in the film.*

PS: Well, you know, a certain amount of androgyny is desirable in movie actors. All the great stars work both sides of the line; they have to be appealing to both men and women sexually. This goes back to what I was saying about Parker Tyler, and it includes actors you don't usually think of as androgynous. If you look at the way John Wayne walks, he walks just like Jack Benny with that swishy little gait, like he was holding something up his ass. I think all actors are aware of this. But one of the ironies of the film was that though the circle I was moving in when I made it was seventy-five per cent gay, and the movie does have that gay feeling you mention, when *Gigolo* came out it was viciously attacked in the gay press, largely because the two villains are gay. At the time I thought it was just an interesting idea; I didn't see it in political terms at all and was very hurt by all the criticism, but now, in retrospect, I can see the justice of those arguments more clearly than I could at the time.

KJ: *One of the scenes in the film which seems to be about that sense of narcissism and physical culture is the scene where Julian works out while learning Swedish for his next trick. But it's also like the scenes of purification which happen in your other films – Travis Bickle holding his hand over the flames, Mishima at the gym . . .*

PS: That's Bresson again, and before Bresson it's Dostoevsky, Camus and Sartre. It's the existential hero – what I like to call 'a man and his room' stories. You have these two characters, the man and his room – I love the kind of movies that are about those two. *Pickpocket* is like that, *Diary of a Country Priest* is, *A Man Escaped* is. In fact I have a new idea which I haven't written yet about an older character in his forties – another man and his room movie.

KJ: *Apart from the idea of loneliness and reclusiveness, there is also some notion of subduing the body.*

PS: Calvin wrote that the body is the prison-house of the soul, and that it is a hindrance to spiritual life which has to be overcome – the idea of the monastic life is to do just that. That kind of notion still survives in my films in these intense, solitary lives. I've lived alone for long periods of time myself; I'm not a person who really demands or needs constant companionship. I take vacations alone, I've lived alone. I don't really mind my own company.

The other way in which the monastic idea is created is in the design of Julian's room. My idea of a well-decorated room is four white walls with a little cross over a cot. If you analyse Julian's room there's no physical decoration at all; it's all structural decoration, and the on-going motif is whether or not to hang a painting. He has a whole stack of paintings and he can't decide whether to hang one.

KJ: *One of the other things that made* Gigolo *successful was its music – the theme song 'Call Me' by Blondie was a hit and, as you suggested before, Moroder was someone you turned to for help in making Los Angeles seem new. Could you explain your principles in using particular composers and scores?*

PS: Conventional movie music does not really appeal to me. For the most part, music in movies is simply a reinforcement or a reflection upon emotion; scores have a tendency to run behind the movie like a mirror reflecting it – happy, sad, suspenseful and so forth, and they don't really have a life of their own. It's as if the audience doesn't have the intelligence to realize the kind of scene they're watching, and I've always found that insulting. So I've tried to find music which had a life of its own, which meant going into music that wasn't yet in the vernacular of films. For the first two I used Jack Nitzsche, who had just come out of rock and roll, working with Phil Spector and the Rolling Stones, but by the time *Gigolo* came along that sound was already in the mainstream, so I turned to Giorgio Moroder. Then for *Mishima* I had the odd concept of an operatic score, so I went on to Philip Glass. *Light of Day* had to be a return to rock and roll because that was its subject, but for *Patty Hearst* I went back to the Glass type of score and got a young composer called Scott Johnson.

KJ: *But the point generally is to have music that exists in some kind of tension with the image rather than simply telling you what the image is about?*

PS: Right.

KJ: *You explained that the film began with the metaphor of a man who's incapable of expressing love. Do you think that metaphor is realized in the finished film, or did it become somewhat clouded by your other interests in narcissism and so forth?*

PS: It may have been. It's the story of a character whose life is predicated on not surrendering to women, but on serving them and therefore standing distant from them. Bresson's films end with moments of grace – just as at the end of *Pickpocket* the main character accepts the grace of Jeanne, so at

28 *Pickpocket*: The final scene.
29 *American Gigolo* (1979): The final scene: Richard Gere,
Lauren Hutton.

the end of *Gigolo* Julian accepts the gift that this woman has given by sacrificing her social position.

KJ: *Do you think of that as a spiritual grace, or is it a grace you construe in secular, emotional terms?*
PS: It's the acceptance of unconditional goodness, which is the same as spiritual grace. You accept the idea that Christ died for you and you did nothing to deserve this; it's a gift and you just have to be open enough to accept it in order to become whole. When it's the case of someone offering their love, you just have to swallow your ego and accept the fact that someone loves you even though you don't deserve their love.

KJ: *When* Gigolo *was finished, did you feel that you'd finally made a film that bore your personal signature?*
PS: I felt that I had arrived as a director; I felt confident about moving the camera and placing the camera. I *saw* the movie for the first time; I saw the whole notion of visual thinking that had first been suggested to me by Eames – it now properly made sense to me.

But then when I wrote my next script, 'Born in the USA' – which I eventually made as *Light of Day* – I found that I couldn't get it out at the time, so when the opportunity came in 1979 to do *Cat People*, which was not a script I had written, I decided to do it in order not to do a personal film. One of the reasons 'Born in the USA' was running into difficulties was that it was just too personal, so I said, 'OK, I'm going to do a genre film, a horror film, a special-effects film that will not be about me, and that will be a very salutary exercise.' Well, in truth, when I look back on it, I see *Cat People* as being almost the most personal film I've done.

Cat People

KJ: *How did that transformation from a genre piece to a personal film come about?*
PS: Mainly in the way we evolved the character of the zookeeper played by John Heard as a sort of pursuer of a Beatrice figure. He's a man who lives with animals because he doesn't like humans very much. And then his Beatrice appears and his greatest fantasy has come true, because Beatrice is an animal. Well, as we developed the character he evolved more and more along the lines of myself, and then during the actual shooting of the film I became involved with Nastassia Kinski and became obsessed with her. So

the story of the film started to become very personal, so much so that I wasn't really aware of how perverse it was getting. I remember on the opening night going with a producer, Jerry Bruckheimer, to the cinema, and we were sitting in the back row with a group of girls in front of us. And it came to that scene where he is tying her to the bed to the strains of this liturgic, primitive music; it was shot as a religious ceremony but it was a zoophiliac bondage scene, and I remember this girl in front of me going, 'Oh my God,' and I turned to Jerry and said, 'I think we went a little too far here.'

KJ: *Was the Beatrice idea in the original script?*
PS: It's the opposite side of the coin from the 'We've Gotta Get Out of This Place' feeling, an idealized version of what the shining goal is, and that may take the form of the redemptive moment or, in sexual terms, the form of Beatrice, the female equivalent of Christ.

KJ: *There's actually a point in* Cat People *where the zookeeper listens to a tape of a translation of* La Vita Nuova. *When did you come across Dante? At Calvin?*
PS: No, it was later. At Calvin I took a course on Milton, but I was more attracted to Dante because I liked the idea of that sort of romantic obsession. Beatrice was always a more compelling figure to me than Milton's Satan, even though Satan is one of the great figures in literature. But *Taxi Driver* has the Beatrice theme, *Obsession* has it, and, of course, it's one of the reasons I like *Vertigo* so much. The image of Beatrice also appears in *Cat People* in the form of a sculpture, a bust of her which you see at one point; I kept it after we finished the film and it's still in my study.

KJ: *What other changes did you make to the script?*
PS: The original had a very conventional ending. There was a big dark house and the monster was killed and the house was burned down. So the big change I made was that he doesn't kill the monster; he makes love to her and puts her in a shrine and lives with her.

KJ: *Am I right in thinking you don't care for horror films very much?*
PS: I like existential horror. I think the greatest metaphor in the cinema is in *The Exorcist*, where you get God and the Devil in the same room arguing over the body of a little girl. There's not a more pristine debate imaginable – it's literally Satan and Jehovah arguing over who will possess this girl. I mean *that's* a horror film, that is truly great. In the same way,

30 *Cat People*: John Heard as Oliver, Annette O'Toole as Alice.

31 *Cat People* (1981): Nastassia Kinski as Irena, the Beatrice figure.

Rosemary's Baby has deep spiritual connotations. I like those kind of horror films.

KJ: *Did you try to make it that kind of horror film, or try to adapt your own concerns to the disciplines of the genre?*
PS: The *Newsweek* review said it was a movie for the Jung at heart, and I guess that's pretty much what I wanted: the idea of myth and the kind of primal images that are embedded in our genes. The only moment in the film I really regret is in the autopsy scene, where the man's arm lashes out from the cat's belly. That was a little too genre for me, but in a film like that you have to have certain of those elements.

KJ: *Does that interest in myth make you, like lots of other film-makers, an admirer of* The Hero With a Thousand Faces?[4]
PS: I am an admirer, though I'm a Freudian as well, and I vacillate between the two. But at one time I was a big reader of Joseph Campbell and I'd like to do another mythic kind of film, though it depends on the right circumstances. As we're talking certain kinds of themes emerge; I move between *Kammerspiel* films like *Hardcore* and *Light of Day*, suicidal glory films like *Mishima*, existential man in his room stories like *Taxi Driver* and *Gigolo*, and Beatrice films like *Obsession* and this new script, *Forever Mine*.

KJ: *The fantasy aspects of* Cat People, *the transformations and the timeless other world of the cat myth, are reminiscent of Cocteau in some ways.*
PS: Well, when you shoot any film there are always a couple of tapes you lug along with you and you play them in your office continually with the sound off. On *Gigolo*, besides *The Conformist*, it was *L'Éclisse*;[5] there was something about those angles and that sensibility. And on *Cat People* the tapes I took along were *Beauty and the Beast* and *Orpheus*, which are obviously nonpareil landmarks in the history of movies. There will never be another Cocteau.

KJ: Cat People *was your second film with the 'new Axis' of Scarfiotti and Moroder, but the effect of the collaboration is very different this time –* Gigolo *is shiny and cold, but this film is heavy and sensual.*
PS: That's partly just the difference between LA and New Orleans, which is the most unAmerican town in America; five different flags have flown over it and it's the most Latin city in the States. I tried to reflect that in the casting, to have a gumbo kind of cast to tune in with New Orleans's gumbo-pot of races and nations.

32 Schrader directing *Cat People*.

The film owes a lot to Nando Scarfiotti; in fact, I tried to get him a co-possessory credit on the film because he was having problems with the union and couldn't get his proper credit as production designer. *Cat People* is very colour co-ordinated, in salmon reds and chartreuse greens, right from the opening where you have those green letters coming over red sand.

KJ: *Did you look much at the original* Cat People, *or did you stay as far away from it as you could?*
PS: To tell you the truth, I don't think much of the film. It was interesting in its use of shadows and so forth, but I didn't find it very good and I was perturbed that people were trying to compare the two. In retrospect, I wish I'd changed the title because then there wouldn't have been the comparisons.

KJ: *But there are a couple of small quotations from it, aren't there, like the swimming pool scene . . .*
PS: And the scene where Nastassia is in the bar talking to her friend and the woman comes up and says, 'Mi hermana . . .' Yes, that's a little tip of the hat to the original.

KJ: Cat People *had all the elements of a hit movie – fantasy, horror, sex, even a theme song by David Bowie. Was it in fact successful?*
PS: No. *Gigolo* was very successful, but *Cat People* wasn't. It really fell between two stools: it was an attempt to have things both ways, which is to have a classy film and a horror film. Well, the horror audience went and said, 'Hey, this doesn't look like a horror film, it's not for us', and the sophisticated audience went and said, 'Hey, this is just a horror film.' So it wasn't really satisfying to the audience.

Mishima

KJ: *How did you first become interested in Yukio Mishima?*[6]
PS: My brother was in Japan at the time of the suicide. I had heard a little bit about Mishima before; I think my brother had once met him at a cocktail function. But the suicide captured the world's imagination, of course, and it certainly captured mine. My brother told me a little more about him and then I started delving into the subject. We wanted to do it almost from that time on because Mishima was the sort of character I'd

like to have created if he hadn't already existed. He has all the power of fiction, in fact he *is* a fictional creature because he is a character created by a great writer.

KJ: *It was the life and death rather than his writings which first drew you?*
PS: I do believe that the life is his final work and I believe that Mishima saw it that way too. He saw all his output as a whole, from the tacky semi-nude photographs to the Chinese poetry to the Dostoevskian novels to his private army – it was all Mishima. And the public, particularly the Japanese public, wanted to slice it up into bits that they could appreciate and he refused to let them. He said, 'If you accept me, you have to accept the high and the low; it's all part of my output.'

KJ: *So you were interested in his attempt to be a sort of modern Renaissance man?*
PS: That, but also the fact that he was the most Western of all Japanese writers. He courted the West and tried to emulate Western styles. I would certainly never have thought of doing another Japanese writer. Plus, of course, the fact that the great dilemma he faced was a Western dilemma too: for the modern writer, when does life supersede writing, when are words insufficient?

He was the first man really to formulate a problem which has been bedevilling writers ever since the advent of television, which is that writers are now a lot better known as performers in the media than for their writing. Mishima got wise to that change very early, and not only did he get wise to it, he brought it to its fully logical and hideous conclusion: he wrote the first chapter and the last chapter, he opened up the issue for debate and then he closed it.

KJ: *These are obviously problems that you face as well – the need to be Paul Schrader the interviewee as well as Schrader the director.*
PS: Yes, and there's also the desire to be a fictional creature yourself. I don't have it as badly as a number of others do, but it's certainly there. I'm sure something like it has always infected artists: Wagner was a shameless showboat, but today the reach of global media has made it possible for a 'Wagner' to become better known than his music.

KJ: *Is there an additional appeal in the Japanese aspects of Mishima's story, though? It seems as if you have a strong affinity for Japanese culture – you wrote about Ozu, your first sold script was* The Yakuza . . .

33 *Mishima* (1985): Ken Ogata as Yukio Mishima: 'A man and his room'. (3)

PS: I think the affinity is this, and it's the same one my brother experienced when he lived in Japan: Japan is a very codified little moral universe with very strict rules which govern all forms of behaviour and decorum. It's not unusual for a person to flee one prison only to find that same prison in another place. So all the confining aspects of the culture of Grand Rapids, which my brother and I rebelled against but then came to miss, we found again in Japan, but since we were strangers in a strange land we didn't feel so hidebound by them.

KJ: *We've been talking about the autobiographical content of your screenplays, and Mishima is striking in that regard because he's the first of your characters, apart from the zookeeper in* Cat People, *who's really an intellectual. He's certainly the first who's an artist.*
PS: And he's middle-aged. *Mishima* satiated the urge I had to do a film about a suicidal artist which had begun with Hank Williams; once I did *Mishima* I no longer had the desire to do *Hank* because Williams was the uneducated, unself-aware native artist and Mishima was the opposite. I was much happier dealing with the question in Mishima's terms, because I do not think that the suicidal impulse in the arts is a product of ignorance or immaturity. I think it's a part of the artistic process.

KJ: *Do you think of it as a terrible failing, or is there a side of you which is attracted to these suicidal urges?*
PS: Well, there is. Mishima said somewhere that life is a line of poetry written in one's own blood, and he had intended, after he had disembowelled himself, to take a brush and write one last *kanji*. He didn't have the strength to do it, but that would have been the writer's farewell and it is not unlike Christology – Christ taking on the sins of the world through His agony and transforming the world that way.

Long before I made *Mishima*, people would criticize me for *Taxi Driver*, saying that I glorified the impulse of suicide through the personage of an ignorant man, and I would say, 'No, the suicidal impulse has nothing to do with lack of education; it's to do with the artistic impulse to transform the world.' The best example I could think of would always be Mishima. I think the great difference between *Taxi Driver* and *Mishima* is exemplified in a line from *The Yakuza*, where one of the characters says that when someone in the West cracks up they open the windows and shoot at people outside, whereas a Japanese who cracks up will close the windows and shoot himself. In that way the Japanese response is the more proper because the act of transformation and aggression is directed at its proper source.

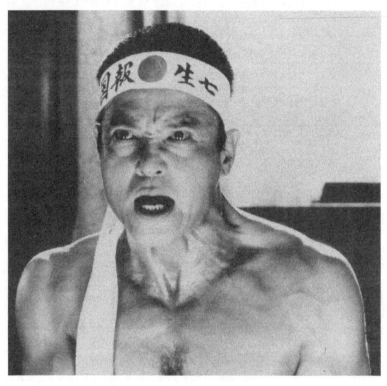

34 *Mishima*: Yukio Mishima's *Seppuku*.

KJ: *When you came to plan* Mishima, *did you have the idea of echoing the styles and methods of the Japanese cinema?*
PS: The sections of the film which show the last day of Mishima's life are essentially done in a kind of Costa-Gavras style. But the black-and-white material does echo the Golden Age of the Japanese cinema, the films of Ozu, Naruse and Mizoguchi.[7] Of course the dramatized sequences of the novels are the new Japan, as seen through the eyes of our production designer, Eiko Ishioka.

KJ: *Those sections have some very unusual colours. Did you use a special type of stock?*
PS: No, it's all done in the lighting and the sets. Eiko only did the sets for the novel sections; another designer did the realistic sets. I wanted there to be a very clean break. Each of the three novel sections is colour-coded to make the film a little more comprehensible, because it is such a jigsaw of a film. The first novel is gold and green; the second novel is pink and grey; and the third one is *shu* – a kind of orange that they use in temples – *shu* and black.

KJ: *How did you determine which of the passages you were going to dramatize? Was it a case of reading through the entire Mishima œuvre and seeing what caught your attention, or did you set out knowing roughly what you wanted?*
PS: Again, this is a matter of problem solving. You find passages that have a chronological progression so that they fit in with the life: you had to have an early, a middle and a late book, and you had to have passages which fit into the separate themes, so that the last one, which is about Mishima the revolutionary, leads you to that section of 'Runaway Horses' from *The Sea of Fertility*; and for the early obsession with beauty you have the famous novel *Golden Pavilion*.

The middle section was a little rough, though. I had wanted to use *Forbidden Colours*, which is Mishima's only overtly homosexual novel, but part of his widow's post-mortem business is to whitewash the bibliography. She has tried to play down the anti-social aspects of her husband's work, the politics and the homosexuality; she really hates *Forbidden Colours*, though I think it's a terrific book and I thought I could eventually beat her down about it. In the end, it became a deal-breaker: she agreed to give me the rights to the other novels if I agreed not to do *Forbidden Colours*. So what I did was to resort to another novel, *Kyoko's House*, which I think she had assumed I would not know about because it's never been translated into English. And in the story of the actor I found the same kind of sexual ambivalence and narcissism I had wanted from *Forbidden Colours*.

KJ: *Did you have a model in mind for this kind of interweaving of biography and fiction, or did the form simply evolve from the nature of the things you wanted to demonstrate about Mishima?*
PS: No, there wasn't a model. I became aware of this one day during the shooting, when the Japanese AD, who was the crew member closest to the movie, said that I was the only person who understood how the movie was working, and that if I were to be incapacitated there'd be no way to finish it because no one else had the plan in their head.

KJ: *Did you always intend the film to have an operatic feeling?*
PS: I think that may have come from Phil Glass, whom I approached when we were still at the script stage. Phil has written a number of biographical operas – Einstein, Gandhi, Akhnaten – and I asked him to approach Mishima in the same way. So he delved into Mishima's work and the biographies and the drafts of the script, and wrote a score without seeing any of the film, one that could be played as an independent work. I then took that work and sort of deconstructed it, repeating sections, extending and condensing, and cut the whole movie to that; I then presented him with the score in a pastiche version that he had to recompose to the images.

KJ: *How strongly did you direct him in the early stages?*
PS: Beyond saying that I needed a martial theme for the last day and then a sickly nostalgia theme for the earlier stuff, I really tried to stay out of it as much as possible. On other scores I've worked on I have been involved more closely and dictated the score to a large degree. The way you do that is to create a guide track, editing the film to a pre-existing piece of music you feel is right, and then you hand it to your composer and say, 'This is what I want the music to sound like,' and he will then homogenize your guide tracks. In that way you've more or less ghosted a score. But I did not want to ghost the score to *Mishima* and I did not want to inhibit Phil. I said, 'I'll make the boat and I'll people it, but you've got to make the river.'

KJ: *How did you go about financing such an ambitious and apparently uncommercial film?*
PS: It was really something of a con job. First of all, as I said, I had to get the widow's support and that took quite a few years, trips back and forth and the kind of courtship that the Japanese require. Shortly before shooting

35 *Mishima*: The rebel cadets in *Runaway Horses*.

began it became apparent to her that a lot of her comments were not being adhered to, so she threw up her arms and we directed her attention to the contract, where she'd already signed away those rights. That's when she turned on the film, but by that time we were already in motion. I think we were successful in raising money because people simply didn't think we would get away with the project, and by the time they realized that we really were going to make it it was too late to stop us; so they concentrated instead on stopping the release of the film, which they did.

Half the money in the film came from Warners and half came from Fuji and Toho. It was a very strange story. Our Japanese producer, Mata Yamamoto, is very internationally oriented and he wanted to make an international film – the Japanese have this sort of inferiority complex which is that they make all the hardware for the international market, but they can't make the software, the films and television programmes. So our producer backed the film himself up to about $1 million of his own money. Well, when the pressure that the widow was exercising through the old-boy network started coming down on the film, this man was in trouble. The pressure was only gentle, but in Japan gentle pressure usually works. These fellows came to see the producer and said, 'We know that we promised to give you this money, but the situation has changed.' He went back to them and said, 'You have to finance me. I'm practically a million dollars in debt on this one, and if you pull out I'll be bankrupt and will have to do what is necessary to protect my family.' In Japan that phrase is a kind of code: if a man commits suicide over a business debt, his family and his kids get to keep their house and savings and do not assume those debts. Now, if he had committed suicide, there would have been repercussions throughout Japanese business. Someone at Fuji and at Toho would have had to resign and so on, and no one wanted to be put in that embarrassing position. So apparently they came to him one night and gave him $2.5 million in cash, and said, 'We did not give you this money'; and still to this day they deny that they gave him any money, though if the film is ever released in Japan they still own it.

Once we had that $2.5 million, I prevailed on Lucas and Coppola, who were very flush at the time in their power and their reputations, to induce Warners to put up the other half, but I don't think anybody who invested money in that film ever expected to get it back. So while making the movie I had a very peculiar luxury, which was that of making a film that no one ever expected to make a dime. On the other hand, that entailed enormous pressure and responsibility, because there was no way you could turn round and say, 'Hey, look, I tried to make a buck, I failed, too bad.' The only criterion I could hold the film up to was that of excellence.

KJ: *Will the film never be shown in Japan because of the way you treated the subject, or simply because Mishima is still too much of a scandal?*
PS: He's too much of a scandal. Japan is a consensus society, and no matter how many times you say that, you can't say it enough. When Mishima died people said, 'Give us fifteen years and we'll tell you what we think about him,' but it's been more than fifteen years now and they still don't know what to say. Mishima has become a non-subject – a fascinating one. People read about him but there is no official viewpoint, so that if you're at a dinner party and his name comes up there's just silence.

Now, that atmosphere of cultural discomfort is amplified by the fact that one of the precepts of the Japanese psyche is that outsiders really cannot understand them; up until a hundred years ago they did not even believe that it was possible for a Westerner to speak Japanese. So if they don't understand Mishima, how can a foreigner possibly hope to? And then into that environment you inject this right-wing pressure that comes from the widow, and the fact that it's an American – whom the Right hate because of the MacArthur-imposed constitution – who is presuming to make a film about their icon. It's almost as if you tried to go to the Near East to shoot a film about Muhammad.

KJ: *Were there threats of violence?*
PS: We had some threats during the filming, and also there were rumours that if the film were ever shown in Japan there would be bombings. At one time I thought I might be in danger and for a while I took to wearing a knife-proof vest when I was working outside on the streets, but then it was explained to me that foreigners, like drunks and babies, were not really responsible for their actions and that if anyone was going to be attacked it would be the Japanese for letting me do this. Our cast and crew were very much hand-picked, not only for their talents but also for their courage and independence.

KJ: *Ken Ogata's performance captures very well that partly Western sense of charm that Mishima's biographers talk about.*
PS: Yes, but one of the unfortunate things about casting Ogata is that he lacks Mishima's bisexuality. Ogata's image and persona are very much those of a somewhat lower-middle- or working-class heterosexual and, try as he might, that is still how he is perceived. We searched long and far trying to find an actor who had that sexual ambiguity and we just couldn't. We succeeded much better in the casting of Kenji Sawada as the actor in the middle novel. He's a rock star, a kind of Mick Jagger in Japan.

KJ: *The directly homosexual elements in* Mishima *are quite underplayed, though.*
PS: There's one little scene in a gay bar where he's dancing with a young man, so it's explicit to that degree, and though it's not the centrepiece that the gay press would have liked to have seen, it's certainly not ignored as some critics have said.

KJ: *Was that what they wanted?*
PS: Yes, because Mishima is also part of the gay pantheon, but that wasn't the reason I wanted to make the film. I wanted to explore the art–life dilemma; the homosexuality fed into that, but it wasn't a necessary component of it. The same dilemma could have existed in a heterosexual. I felt that underplaying the homosexual aspects didn't undermine the piece, though I had problems introducing even as much as I did. I had to document every bit of that movie. I did interviews with all sorts of witnesses and there is nothing in the biographical sections that isn't well documented – there is *no* fiction in that part of the film.

KJ: *Did you end up feeling sympathy for Mishima's political beliefs?*
PS: I've got into arguments with a lot of people about this, but I genuinely believe that it was all theatre – well, that's not fair: say seventy-five per cent theatre. He did have a fixation on the Emperor and he did have a very strong sexual fixation on militarism, but his interests were primarily ritualistic and artistic. When it came down to hard-core politics he wasn't really that interested. It was all dressing up, D'Annunzio style.

KJ: *You've expressed dissatisfaction about the way some of your films have turned out. Do you feel that about* Mishima?
PS: No, it's the film I'd stand by; as a writer it's *Taxi Driver*, but as a director it's *Mishima*. There's an element of perverse joy in it – just the fact that no one had done anything like that before and no one thought I could do it. Preminger said directors always love their bastard children most and there's an element of the fact that it's just so implausible I actually got it done.
  But though I don't generally look at my films again, I can still watch the end of *Mishima*, and when he becomes one with his three creations I still get chilled by that. I think it's just terrific.

KJ: *Did it give you the sense of having done something you'd find it hard to live up to?*

36 *Mishima*: Ken Ogata as Yukio Mishima.

PS: Yes, but the relative pain of that pales beside the sense of liberation that you've done something that you're proud of. There's no sense worse than the feeling that you're never quite going to do that one thing you want to put on your tombstone.

Light of Day

PS: As I mentioned before, *Light of Day* was originally called 'Born in the USA'. I wrote it right after *American Gigolo* but I just couldn't get it going, and then I realized that the obstacle to it was that the brother–brother configuration I had in it was just a little too familiar, a little too *East of Eden*-y, too like Cain and Abel, and when I changed it to a brother–sister relationship it had a new spin.

KJ: *What involvement did Bruce Springsteen have in the project? He has a song called 'Born in the USA' and he wrote the title track for* Light of Day . . .
PS: When I first wrote the script, 1979, Bruce was flirting with the idea of becoming an actor; in fact, he had been offered a million dollars by Twentieth Century-Fox to do any film he wanted. I went down to Jersey to discuss the script of 'Born in the USA' with him; we talked, and then I got word back from him that he had decided he didn't want to be involved in movies. He's a control freak, and the idea of submitting himself to someone else's fantasy was more than he could tolerate.

Then, when I was in Japan for *Mishima*, I came across this album called *Born in the USA*, and I thought 'Uh-huh, familiar.' I bought the album and he had been nice enough to credit me on the sleeve.

Anyway, Springsteen is a man of enormous integrity; he is exactly what he appears to be, and I knew that my day would come. Sure enough, one day the phone rang. We went and had dinner and he explained to me that what had happened was that the script had been lying around on his table and he just couldn't shake the title from his head. He apologized, and because he knew I was now making the film he said, 'You can have the song for free if you want, or I'll write you a new one for free.' I elected to take a new song, so he wrote 'Light of Day'.

KJ: *Was the film always going to be about rock and roll?*
PS: Yes. The first script was pretty much like the one we used, except that it was about two brothers.

KJ: *You've said that this film is the companion-piece to* Hardcore: *a film about your mother to match the film about your father. Does that make the Joan Jett character your surrogate?*

PS: I'm sort of split in half; part of me is in Joan and part is in Michael J. Fox, but the death scene between the mother and Joan as it appears in the film is more or less word for word what I went through with my mother.

KJ: *That must have been painful to film.*

PS: Well, you know, that's what you do for a living: you pick at your own wounds, and the deeper and more private the wound, the more special it is to you and possibly the more it can mean to someone else.

KJ: *Was there that same kind of reconciliation and forgiveness between you and your mother as there is in the film?*

PS: Yes. When my mother said, 'Promise me you will join me in heaven,' I said, 'Yes.' What else do you do?

KJ: *So in one sense the daughter's commitment to playing in rock-and-roll bands, which the mother disapproves of, is a displaced version of your commitment to making films, which your mother disapproved of?*

PS: Yes, yes. But one of the things I was trying to get across in *Light of Day* was rock and roll's function in everyday life. So many rock-and-roll movies revolve around the Cinderella myth of fame and wealth and girls, and what is missed in all those films is that rock and roll has a day-to-day practical function in the lives of thousands of people and thousands of little bands in thousands of little cities all over the world, and that all these little bands just go and kick it out on the weekends. They may have dreams of glory, but what it's really about is release. So I didn't want to make a movie about fantasy, I wanted to make a movie about the realities of rock and roll.

KJ: *The end of the film certainly catches that, with the freeze on Joan Jett's grinning face after they've performed the title song – despite her defeats and her mother's death, there's still a kind of release when she performs. How did you come to cast Joan Jett, who's a professional rock musician with not much acting experience, in such an important part?*

PS: What happened was that I got myself into one of those dreadful boxes. I had sworn that I would cast the girl's part first and then the brother, and I found this singer – not Joan Jett – who was not very well known and who had a soft kind of sensuality, but who also looked quite a lot like Michael J. Fox, who I knew was interested in doing the film. I thought, 'Oh, if she does it and Michael does it then the two of them are going to be terrific.' So we went ahead and cast Michael and then discovered that this girl had signed a contract to another film and wasn't available. I then had second thoughts about Michael because I still didn't want to cast the boy part first, but by this stage I was told that if I didn't use Michael we'd never get to make the film. So I ended up casting Joan on the basis of the script and not on the basis of her closeness to Michael, and it just never worked.

KJ: *She gives a strong performance.*
PS: It's a good performance, but there's a degree to which casting is predestination and that piece of casting just did not work: it didn't work on paper, it didn't work on screen. I remember going to my agent and talking about it. I said, 'Look, I think I can make this a good film but I don't think I can make it a successful film. I just don't think it's gonna work.' And he said, 'Well, if you don't make it this way you're not going to do it at all, and how will you ever know?' So I went ahead and did it, and of course as you're shooting you convince yourself that you're pulling things off, but my original qualms were right: it's just stillborn in the casting. That's not to say Michael didn't do a good job; it's just that audiences did not want to see him in a subordinate, working-class, non-humorous role, period.

KJ: *There are three different strands of rock represented in the film: the sort of small-town Springsteen music of the Barbusters; the heavy metal of the band that Joan Jett runs off to join; and a kind of effete synthesizer band. Did you have to research that world, or was rock music something you still have an interest in?*
PS: I'm still interested. Everyone of my generation was informed by rock, because it was our liberation. Springsteen said something wonderful when Bob Dylan was inaugurated into the Rock and Roll Hall of Fame; he said that Elvis freed our bodies, but Dylan freed our minds. Everyone has one figure in their lives whom they finally have to bend the knee to, who's their Number One, and for me Bob Dylan is that Number One.

KJ: *You made a rock video with him, didn't you?*
PS: Yes. We went to Tokyo to do that, the year after we finished shooting *Mishima*. The video didn't really work out, but I still have enormous respect for him, even though it soon became clear to me that we live in two different worlds. I'm a linear thinker, Bob is a poetic thinker. I think 1, 2, 3, 4, A, B, C; he thinks 1, A, Blue, Green, D. One night in Tokyo I started pontificating about his use of associative imagery and he took umbrage, because he did not see it as associative; he thought it was absolutely clear and lucid.

37 *Light of Day* (1987): Joan Jett and Michael J. Fox.

KJ: *Do you think one of the reasons for the failure of* Light of Day *was its attempt to do at least three things at once – to return to the kind of working-class frustrations of* Blue Collar, *to investigate rock music and to be an autobiographical statement about your relationship with your mother?*

PS: It may have been that. Being ambitious doesn't necessarily mean you will fail, but when it doesn't succeed then you look like a fool, because you've tried more than you should have. I don't dwell on failures; once they're done they're done. Even when I introduce my films at film festivals I don't watch them again. The problem is that all you see is the bad.

On the rare occasions I look at one of my films I can tell you exactly how I felt on the day of every scene, because so much of directing is spontaneous; you approach the day with certain plans, but then these are thrown awry and what you end up with on screen is the cumulative product of thousands of decisions made on the spur of the moment. You're making these decisions like a Gatling gun. That's the reason why a director cannot work under the influence of alcohol or any other kind of drug: the job just demands absolute mental clarity at all times and the decisions are irrevocable. You can write drunk or stoned and the next day look at it and say, 'Hey, that's thirty per cent terrific – now I'll make it sixty per cent terrific,' but you can't do that as a director.

KJ: *But the comparative visual anonymity of* Light of Day *doesn't seem like the product of miscalculation; it seems to have been deliberate.*

PS: Well, this is a *Kammerspiel*, about unflashy people who live unflashy lives, and I did not want an incongruous visual style. John Bailey, who's been my cinematographer on four films, was working with me on the film and every day we were finding ourselves in situations where I was saying, 'Look at this shot. We start slowly across the ceiling reading the graffiti, then we come down and everyone thinks they're upside down and then they realize they're right-side up. Wouldn't that be a terrific shot?' And John would say, 'Yes, it would have been a terrific shot for *Mishima*, but we're not making that movie.'

I learned a lesson from *Light of Day*, which was that I had been growing film by film in my visual intelligence. I had progressed from being a person with a literary vision to being someone with a visual vision, and with that film I tried to back off, I tried to suppress my new literacy. I would never again make a film with that kind of meat-and-potatoes style. I mean, there are scenes in a film that you would shoot in a meat-and-potatoes style because it's the only real way to do that scene, but I would never conceive of another film with the approach I used on *Light of Day*.

Patty Hearst

KJ: *The last thing one could call* Patty Hearst *is visually anonymous – the first half-hour or so of her captivity is shot in an extraordinary style of half-light punctuated with painful moments of brightness. Was that style implicit in Nick Kazan's screenplay, or was it something you developed yourself?*

PS: I developed it myself, though there was something in the script that tried to keep the SLA[8] anonymous for the first forty-five minutes. My first reaction was incredulity – OK, great, you can do that in a script, but how do you make a movie where the SLA aren't seen? But then I decided to take him at his word, and so for the first forty-five minutes you don't see them.

Once you lock into something like that the other decisions come fast and furious; the slow part is the locking in. The definitive problem with *Patty Hearst* – and this is the reason that other directors turned the project down – is that it deals with a passive protagonist. Movies are about people who *do* things. The number one fantasy of the cinema is that we can do something – we are relatively impotent in our own lives so we go to movies to watch people who are in control of their lives. *Patty Hearst* violates the cardinal rule of cinema.

Atlantic, who financed the film, didn't see this problem; they just looked at it from the outside and saw kidnapping, bank robberies, shoot-outs. What they didn't see is that the main character has little or nothing to do with this; she's just a voyeur, an observer. So I hit upon the solution of abusing her in the same way that the SLA abused her, which in turn means that the film should abuse the audience. If you abuse a character enough, eventually you get into the concentration-camp-guard syndrome – you don't care about the victim any more because you see only their degradation; they've become a non-person. So I set out to create a style that abused the audience.

Those who are critical of me like to say, 'Schrader's wilfully perverse. He assaults his audience because he doesn't want to make people feel good.' But you never set out as a principle to abuse an audience; on the contrary, you want to entertain them. But if you're confronted with a problem and the only workable solution is this, then you execute it. Maybe the perversity comes of deciding to execute the project rather than just walk away from it.

KJ: *Some of the earlier sequences are based on Patty Hearst's memories, fantasies and fears, particularly her claustrophobic dread of being buried*

38 *Patty Hearst* (1988): Natasha Richardson as the captive heiress: 'The solution was to abuse her in the same way the SLA abused her.'

alive. *Does this have some bearing on the film's portrayal of the SLA as a group whose politics were largely based on self-aggrandizing or paranoid fantasy?*

PS: Yes. The SLA liked to pretend that they were a huge movement, but in fact they were a tiny cult. In my mind I associated them with another cult that came out of Oakland at the very same time – James Jones's sect. In the case of Jones you had a white messiah with a black flock which degenerated into a suicide cult; here you had Cinque, a black messiah with his white following which did the same. I felt this at the time the events were happening. The SLA certainly had no connection with any Left politics I ever had.

KJ: *There's a good deal of black humour in the way the film treats the SLA zealots, particularly the married couple, Teko and Yolanda, who are constantly squabbling with each other; they're almost like a Mr and Mrs Travis Bickle.*

PS: Yes, but without the luxury of taking their point of view. I would actually have been willing to make that film from Cinque's point of view, and I think it would have been a very exciting, incendiary film, ending with this operatic orgy of suicidal glory with the house burning down and everyone throwing their arms out yelling 'Cinque!' I suspect in fact that's how I would have written it if I had initiated the project, but there would have been no pleasure in writing that because it would never have been made.

The script as presented to me was entirely from Patty's point of view, and I just said, 'OK, that's valid. Let's look at the world through this person's eyes. Let's not wink at the audience; let's just follow it through and let it take us someplace interesting.'

KJ: *The film seems entirely sympathetic to her . . .*

PS: That's the conceit: I took her point of view, period. As I say, in personal terms I could just as easily have taken the opposite viewpoint, but I think there's something to be said for following just one point of view, especially if it's an unpopular one. I know people could easily say, 'Well, here's a guy who starts off making *Blue Collar* in the defence of the underdog and ends up making *Patty Hearst* in defence of the overdog,' but that was just something I had to swallow. In a way, Patty Hearst is sort of the reverse of Travis Bickle because Travis is an underdog who militates against the world and Patty is an overdog against whom the world militates. I had very mixed feelings about her during the case and during the film-making, and I still do.

39 *Patty Hearst*: surreal lighting effects inside the SLA safehouse.

KJ: *The film is very good at conveying her feelings of disorientation and the uncertainty or plasticity of character that accompanied them.*

PS: In one sense there seems to me no doubt that she did become a revolutionary, but was she Patty Hearst when that happened, or was she someone else? It's a genuine conundrum and I realized very early on that there is no solution. If you ask the question 'Did she or didn't she?', the answer is yes and no, all the time.

Incidentally, I don't think it takes fifty-seven days of solitary to change someone's personality; about ten days is all it takes. The government has done research into this and concluded that you can't really expect even a trained combat soldier to endure more than about eight or ten days under those conditions. The proper way to prepare a soldier for that kind of treatment is to inculcate him with certain residual values that he will retain while he submits his mind and body, and prepare him not to feel bad about submitting, so that when the conditions of duress are alleviated there's still a personality left.

KJ: *You've said that* Cat People, *the only other film you've made from a script you didn't write, proved to be one of your most personal, and many of the scenes in* Patty Hearst *seem to dovetail with your other obsessions – there's the claustrophobia, the Bressonian ending . . .*

PS: Oddly enough, when I was first given the script I didn't want to read it because I assumed it would be some sort of exploitative TV drama, but then I looked at it and thought, 'Oh . . . Oh . . .' There was a purely pragmatic reason for making the film, which was that the depression brought about by the failure of *Light of Day* was rather crushing, because it was both a personal failure and a career failure. So I was very anxious to get back in the saddle, and this was a film that they would green light just as soon as a director said 'Yes.' I agreed to do it for a very low fee and on a very small budget, but those economic restrictions eventually became freedoms, because as my perception of the film became more and more idiosyncratic and less commercial, and the pressure was put on me to do something more conventional, I was able to say, 'Look, I'm doing this film for no money on a short budget; under these conditions I am going to make the film I want. Give me a decent salary, give me three more weeks of shooting and I'll make your movie and I'll make my movie and then you can choose, but under these conditions I'm going to make mine.'

KJ: *Presumably there was also hostility to the idea of casting a British actress, Natasha Richardson?*

PS: Yes, also because she was more or less unknown in America at the time.

But I'd seen her in *Gothic* and I auditioned her and I just couldn't imagine any other actress enduring that passive role for more than forty-five minutes. I couldn't burn Natasha out; in the film's second hour she still has something to give, and at the very end of the movie when she speaks to her father you *really* want to hear what she has to say. There was also her physical similarity to Patty, but the real thing was that enormous sense she has of a secret reserve; she has something special that she will divulge to you in her own good time. It's the same quality her mother has.

KJ: *Do you think that Patty Hearst is your most fully fleshed woman character?*
PS: I would think so, yes. The Joan Jett thing was a little too much of an ideology on two legs; she expounds a principle at the expense of character complexity. And Nastassia in *Cat People* is a male creation. But Natasha's part was really a female creation. And that's entirely down to her – credit where credit's due.

KJ: *What does the real Patty Hearst think of the film?*
PS: In my experience, people who have films made about them usually turn on the films, but she loved it and came to Cannes to help promote it. Ironically, the first time I showed it to her there was one scene she really hated. She said, 'All you wanted to do is make me look like a rich bitch who deserved everything that happened to me.' And you know what that scene was? It was the last scene. She had no difficulty being put upon mercilessly for two hours, but the one scene in the movie where she stands on her own feet, she hated. What that reveals is, I think, her ability to survive and her ability to assume a subservient, daughter's role – she's far more comfortable being the victim than being independent, which is probably how she got through the ordeal. I said to her, 'Patty, I cannot make a film where a character is constantly put on and never gets the chance to say her own piece, and these are all things that you have said; you said them in your book; you've said them to me.' She saw the point, but she's still uncomfortable with it.

KJ: *I suppose it must have struck you early on that there's another well-known film about a member of the Hearst family . . .*
PS: Yes, and that was always something to be assiduously avoided. Patty says in her book that the members of the San Francisco SLA wanted to go and see *Citizen Kane* and she refused, because she didn't want to be arrested walking out of that film. And I wasn't going to get arrested for copying that film.

40 *Patty Hearst*: 'The *Mishima* shot'.
41 *Mishima*: 'Those little glowing rooms simulate the writer's vision.'

KJ: *One of the most unusual scenes in the film comes when the lawyers are discussing Patty's case and you shoot them from above so that it becomes clear that the room they're in is a small lit stage and they're otherwise surrounded by darkness. It's very like certain shots in* Mishima, *such as in the 'Runaway Horses' section where the military conspirators are arrested.*

PS: In fact, when we were shooting *Patty Hearst* we used to refer to that as the *Mishima* shot. The reason I did it in *Mishima* was that I wanted to create a sense of the author's eye and of these events existing in limbo. Those little glowing rooms simulate the writer's vision. In *Patty Hearst* there is only one scene in which she is not a participant; every other scene is from her point of view. But it's important at some stage to get a sense of how the outside world viewed her, so I struck upon the idea of using the little glowing room again, where all these men – importantly, men – are walking around determining her fate. I liked the device a lot in *Mishima* and I was a little surprised that no one had knocked me off on it, so I decided to knock myself off.

KJ: *How was the film received in the US?*

PS: It got very good reviews, but it came and went quickly. There are a number of reasons for that: it was an art-house film dumped into a mass-audience circuit, with a releasing pattern predicated on television advertising, and Atlantic hated the film by this time and took no television advertising. This is like the kind of whining every director does when his film fails – 'Gee, it wasn't my fault, it wasn't the audience's fault, it was that damn studio.' The truth of its failure may lie closer to that problem of having a passive protagonist, and to the unconventional stylistic manner in which I treated her. It could have been a nice little respectable film, but the company that financed it didn't have the luxury of releasing a nice little respectable film. Shortly afterwards they were bought out by a children's video company, which seems only poetic.

The Comfort of Strangers

KJ: *In February 1989 you were preparing a film based on your screenplay* Forever Mine. *What became of that?*

PS: My actor fell out. I was after another actor, but I was not very confident about getting him, and I felt that the studio was going to be quickly cooling on the project. By coincidence my agent called me the same week and said how would you like to do a Harold Pinter script in Italy? I told him to send

42 Schrader and his cinematographer, Dante Spinotti, on location for *The Comfort of Strangers*.

it by, I read it, liked it immediately and realized it was just the type of thing that I could do quite well. So then I went to Columbia and said, 'I hope you don't mind terribly if I do another film first,' and they were very gracious and said, 'Of course, Paul.'

KJ: *Why did you feel* The Comfort of Strangers⁹ *was the sort of subject you could do well?*

PS: Because of the moral complexity in language and behaviour. Pinter's characters are always saying one thing and meaning something slightly different. There are layers of nuance and innuendo and seemingly inexplicable actions and events which are in fact very explicable in a non-prosaic fashion. I'm very attracted to the idea of a psychological life running just under the surface of normal life and motivating the normal life in subtle ways: it goes back to why does Travis take the girl to the porno movie? It seemingly doesn't make sense, but of course it does make sense. This script is full of that kind of complexity. It also offered the opportunity to do something which had quite a glamorous polish on it, a stylistic sheen, and I hadn't really made anything stylish for a while. I was eager to do it again, not only for myself but also for those people in the industry who may have forgotten that I was capable of making this type of film.

KJ: *Both the Ian McEwan novel and the Pinter script have very definite identities. How do they become a Schrader film?*

PS: Well, the first thing they become is an American film, which I think was the reason the script was offered to me. At one point Pinter had wanted a British director, but the feeling of the Italians was that if you combine this screenplay with a British director and a British cast it starts to have the stately distance that is the hallmark of what is conveniently called BBC drama. One of the nice things about the Pinter–Losey collaborations¹⁰ was that they had very British scripts but very American direction. Americans – this is very glib, but I think true – are basically more impatient. They want to get the show going, they want to move along, they like to move a little faster on their feet as artists. So that kind of American energy and restlessness when properly combined with this very understated British writing can be a dynamic collaboration.

KJ: *How have you evolved a visual style for the film?*

PS: I had to decide what to do with Venice because there is a sort of postcard Venice that flashes through everyone's mind as soon as the name is mentioned. So, number one, I needed to get around that so that you couldn't just close your eyes and see the movie before you got into the cinema. That Venice is one primarily of white stone and white light and water. The second consideration was that the peculiarity of the story seemed more properly set in a more exotic environment. It's the kind of story that, if someone told you this had happened in Paris or Rome, you'd say, 'That sounds bizarre,' but if they said it had happened to them in Tangiers or Cairo you'd say, 'Yes, of course, that kind of thing would happen there.' The solution was easy enough because it was right at hand, which was just to turn Venice slightly on its axis and point it towards the East, where in fact it pointed for most of its history. Today it is regarded as an Italian city, but for most of its vital life it was the link to the Orient. It was much more closely linked to Byzantium, to Constantinople, than it was to Rome.

So it was a simple matter to choose those locations in Venice which had the hallmark of Byzantine culture in colour and in architecture, and then to carry that scheme on into the lighting so that it has the feel of Istanbul or Cairo. The major set, the Palazzo, which we built at the Pathé Studios here in Rome, is decorated as if it had been redone several hundred years ago by a man who was in the Levantine trade.

KJ: *So one of the main reasons for shooting at the Pathé Studios was to control the visual style?*
PS: Yes. Also, in Venice all the grand palazzos are protected or are museums, and you really can't shoot in them. We shot outside in the courtyard of the Palazzo Barbaro, but we weren't allowed to shoot inside and it wasn't even up to the owner. It was a question of the stability of the building. The Historical Commission wouldn't have allowed us.

KJ: *What were the principal changes Pinter made when writing the screenplay? Did you add any further changes of your own?*
PS: Harold made a couple of interesting and I think essential changes. The McEwan novel is a terrific book but I think a little one-dimensional. It has a theme and it rides the theme hard and singlemindedly. Its theme is essentially that no amount of civilization can paper over the animosity between men and women. I am not sure that the theme is entirely correct and, secondly, I don't know if it's enough to sustain a complex drama; it needs some other theme running through it. What Harold did is that he took the character of Robert and he used him to bookend the film. The film begins by hearing Robert's voice and it ends with Robert speaking to the police. By elevating the character of Robert in this way he introduced a second theme which lies right underneath McEwan's theme – the persistence of childhood and the inability to shake off childhood experiences.

That's much more Robert's character. He's a man who lives in the past. And so whenever McEwan's theme gets a little thin the new theme starts to grow up from underneath it and that makes a delicious combination.

KJ: *There's a hint in the novel from Robert's wife that his memories of his father's sadism may be exaggerated or even pure fantasy. Has that element been removed?*
PS: Harold had taken that line out of the script and I suggested he put it back in because I don't want completely to disregard that possibility. The way Chris Walken is playing it, there is a lot of ambiguity about the character. Chris is using an accent which is a little bit here and there: it's a little British, it gets a little German, a little Italian . . . it moves around. This is a guy who has bounced around a lot and he may not be entirely forthcoming about facts in his life.

KJ: *How did you go about casting the film?*
PS: You had to have four real actors, you just couldn't rely on screen personalities who looked right and had box-office viability. You needed people who had stage abilities, the capacity to read any given line in a number of ways with equal validity and to play the nuances in and out of a scene. The other consideration was that it was June and we had to start shooting in September. So it was a case of the best actors available at the time.

For the part of Mary, Natasha Richardson jumped immediately to mind because I had worked with her and I knew her ability and I also knew that she wanted to play a more glamorous role. I had to make amends for what I had done to her in *Patty Hearst* in terms of the resolutely unglamorous way she is portrayed in that film. Rupert Everett was obvious for the character of Colin because Colin is an extremely handsome man, somewhat narcissistic, who essentially is the battleground over which the drama takes place. For Caroline I was thinking either of Mary Beth Hurt, my wife, or Helen Mirren. I talked it over with Mary Beth and we decided it was probably better for us not to work together.

For Robert there was one critical change I had to make from the book. The character of Robert is described there in a much more sleazy manner: open shirt, gold chain with a razor blade . . . it's just not credible on screen that Mary and Colin are going to take off with this guy. Chris Walken was right at the top of my list for the part. I'd known him for some time and I knew he wanted to do a part like this and he has the right theatrical skills. The way he plays Robert is as a real Venetian gentleman who dresses in a forties white double-breasted suit and has all the hauteur of aristocracy and

43 *The Comfort of Strangers* (1990): Natasha Richardson as Mary, Christopher Walken as Robert, Rupert Everett as Colin.

the congeniality of an established family man. He doesn't appear to be a
hustler. The number one issue on the agenda was for Chris just to play the
charm, play the charm and let everything else come behind. As Chris told
me, he was shooting a film this summer and they shot some light up
underneath him and he said to the director, 'I don't need to be made to look
evil. I can do that on my own.'

KJ: *We've discussed the ways in which your films often progress towards
a transcendental moment. Will that be true of* The Comfort of
Strangers?
PS: No, I think it's more of an exploration of personality, behaviour and
morality. Pinter has been very attentive to this project and I think he feels
quite possessive about it, rightly so. It's the kind of piece he might well have
written as an original – it has a lot of character similarities, it has action
similarities to his plays. Venice has always been important in his plays, one
of the characters is very much like one in *Betrayal*, there's a bit of action in
it which is right out of *The Birthday Party* and so on. So he's more
possessive of it than he would be of *The Handmaid's Tale* or *The French
Lieutenant's Woman* which are not really Pinter pieces, whereas *The
Servant* is also very much a Pinter thing. Part of my job in this is to be true to
his qualities. Pinter is not a big one for transcendence, he's not even a big
one for resolution, so any attempt of mine to run in that direction would go
against the strength of the piece.

KJ: *At what stage do you work out the way in which each scene is going to
be shot?*
PS: Certain shots occur to you fairly early on and sometimes you actually
shoot them, but usually it comes out of geography, out of your locations
and your sets. It's awfully hard to see a shot in the abstract; you don't really
see the shots until you see the space. You've chosen your location for a
certain shot, and the actors get there and they block it in such a way that
you can't get your shot and then you either have to talk them into
reblocking it or you have to bag the shot.

KJ: *You let your actors do their own blocking?*
PS: Oh yes, yes, I mean you have to let them find their way around the space
and see what's comfortable. You tell them how you see it, one person here,
the other there and you say, 'Now let's play around . . .' and they do it one
way and you ask them to do it another way and you try to take the best of
what they're doing and get into the kind of plans you had made before-
hand. Venice of course was very demanding in this way, because you had to

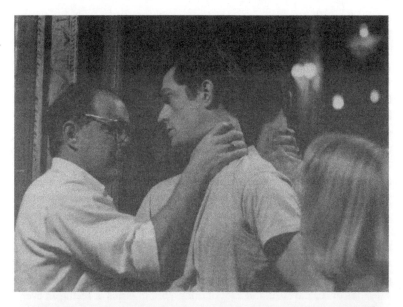

44 *The Comfort of Strangers*: Schrader demonstrating how Colin should
be strangled . . .
45 . . . and Christopher Walken acting on the instruction.

establish your lighting pattern months in advance because you have to light from people's houses and you have to get permission from them.

KJ: *So many of your decisions are made on the day?*
PS: Yes. I was interested in reading in *Scorsese on Scorsese* that Marty said he began storyboarding after being fired from a film because he was doing insufficient coverage and he was determined not to make that mistake again. I've never storyboarded. I tried it once or twice but I always found that once you get into the space you always see something more interesting than you had planned. And I have a suspicion that although Scorsese says he storyboards, in fact he moves and lives with the moment. Otherwise you're not alive. You can't really storyboard anything except action sequences.

KJ: *Is it that ability to live in the moment which makes a director a director?*
PS: Well, there are many sides to being a director – you have to be a big poppa and you have to be a financial conniver and you have to be a salesman and a narrator and a lot of things, but in terms of seeing an event and finding the dramatic presentation of it, that really is a kind of seat-of-the-pants operation. I really do believe in this notion of the 'floating rectangle'. There are certain characters in a scene, two people are talking, and then there's another character, he's off-screen and he's holding the floating rectangle. How he moves this rectangle determines a lot about that scene. You can pretend that you don't exist and just set your rectangle down and do master, two-shot, over, over, single, single. But that still is a statement – in that case, that the rectangle isn't very important for that scene. Some scenes you do shoot that way because you don't want the audience to be terribly aware of the rectangle. Other scenes just demand it.

KJ: *Some directors say that the part of their job they enjoy most is editing. Is that your experience?*
PS: There's a maxim of Truffaut's: 'When I'm writing I like directing best, when I'm directing I like editing best, when I'm editing I like writing best.' I think most directors would agree with that. But I actually do like directing. I can be away from it a little longer than some others perhaps, but I wouldn't be happy to let more than two years go by without directing. It has a few irreplaceable pleasures. One is the communal pleasure of being in charge of an artistic group, or troupe. Your own little gypsy band, and all the communal warmth that comes from arriving on the set in the morning and saying hello to people and knowing about their personal lives. Having

that extended family is very pleasurable, particularly for someone who has been a writer in the past. It's a very welcome antidote to the solitude of writing. And then there's this kind of on-the-spot rush that you get from directing which you usually have first thing in the morning when the actors are out there and they start blocking the scene and then for fifteen or twenty minutes you're suddenly alive. They're moving around, you're moving around, you watch the scene from one side, you watch it from another, you crawl right between them and watch it, you watch it from a distance, you walk this way and that way and you have them do it over and over again and you see all kinds of different things. Suddenly after four or five rehearsals like this you step back and it comes to mind and you say, 'OK, this is it. We do this shot, which cuts to this shot, which cuts to that shot . . . eight set-ups.' And then the rest of the day you monitor those decisions which were made in the heat of the moment in one creative burst. That's the most exhilarating part of the day for a director.

More and more I find that I cut in the camera. I shoot the cuts and I don't shoot a master a lot of times. The first rule of directing is always shoot a master, but often if you get involved in some very interesting blocking, then there is no master, people are not in the place where you can actually have a master. The only reason to do the master is to have something you can show the editor. As you make more and more films you grow confident enough just to shoot the coverage. You don't even bother to shoot dialogue from an angle when you're not going to be at that angle, and therefore you wed yourself to an editing pattern. This is something I said the other day. I shot one rather interesting move and then I did some coverage, but I never covered the area of the move. The script supervisor said to me, 'The actors never did the dialogue that you did during that rather peculiar move.' And I said, 'I know, I want to be married to it, I don't want to have the choice of not using it. I don't want to have the option of being cowardly in the editing room.'

Notes

1   John Boorman's *Deliverance* (1972): a violent, nightmarish adaptation of James Dickey's novel about four Atlanta businessmen who go off for a weekend's canoeing trip in the Appalachians.

2   As George C. Scott explains in *Hardcore*, TULIP is 'an acronym . . . T stands for total depravity: all men, through original sin, are totally evil and incapable of good: "All my works are as filthy rags in the sight of the Lord." U stands for unconditional election: God has chosen a limited number of people to be saved, the elect, and he's chosen them from the beginning of time. L is for limited atonement: only a certain number of people can be atoned and go to heaven. I is for irresistible grace: God's grace cannot be resisted or

denied. And P is for the perseverance of the saints: once you're in grace, you cannot fall from the numbers of the elect.'

3 Ford's *The Searchers* (1956) stars John Wayne as Ethan Edwards, a Confederate veteran who sets off on an obsessive search for his young niece (Natalie Wood) after she is abducted by Comanches. Among the many films to allude to *The Searchers* are George Lucas's *Star Wars* (1977) and Martin Scorsese's *Mean Streets* (1973).

4 *The Hero with a Thousand Faces* (1949) is probably the most widely read of many works on comparative mythology by the scholar Joseph Campbell (1904–1987). It has had an unsual degree of influence on Schrader's generation of film-makers, notably George Miller (*Mad Max II*, 1981) and George Lucas (who produced Ron Howard's *Willow*, 1988).

5 Michelangelo Antonioni's *L'Éclisse* (*The Eclipse*) (1962) is the third of a trilogy which begins with *L'Avventura* (1960) and *La Notte* (1961). The film stars Monica Vitti as Vittoria, who leaves her lover Riccardo (Francisco Rabal) and begins a short-lived affair with Piero (Alain Delon). Schrader's reference is to Antonioni's austere portrayal of Roman streets and buildings, as well as to his cool treatment of these characters, who have generally been described as 'alienated'.

6 Even before his ritual suicide, in 1970 at the age of 45, Mishima was the most celebrated of all modern Japanese writers. His work, which included fifteen novels, thirty-three plays and many other books, earned him comparisons in the West with Sartre, Proust and Gide. Mishima himself considered that his final tetralogy, *The Sea of Fertility* (1970), which includes the novel *Runaway Horses*, was his masterpiece.

7 Although Mikio Naruse (1905–1969) began his career as a director in the 1920s, he is still best known in the West for the films he made during the 1950s, including *Okasan* (*Mother*) (1953) and *Ukigumo* (*Floating Clouds*) (1955). Kenji Mizoguchi (1898–1956) is considered by some critics to be the greatest of Japanese directors, despite the fact that only a handful of his many films have ever been shown commercially in the West. Among his finest works are *Ugetsu Monogatari* (1953) and *Sansho Dayu* (1954).

8 The Symbionese Liberation Army was, as Schrader's film shows, in fact no more than a handful of self-styled 'revolutionaries'. A full account of Patty Hearst's kidnapping can be found in her book *Every Secret Thing* (by Patricia Campbell Hearst with Alvin Moscow, Methuen, London, 1982; reprinted as *Patty Hearst*, Corgi Avon, London, 1988); this volume was the basis of Nick Kazan's screenplay. See also Filmography.

9 Ian McEwan's *The Comfort of Strangers* (Jonathan Cape, London, 1981; Picador, London, 1982): see Filmography for further details.

10 Harold Pinter and Joseph Losey collaborated on three films: *The Servant* (1963), from a novel by Robin Maugham, *Accident* (1966) and *The Go-Between* (1971), from L. P. Hartley's novels. Pinter also took small acting parts in the first two films.

CHAPTER 6

Intermission: Stage Plays and Other Considerations

SCHRADER: *Berlinale*[1] is a stage-play I wrote about the Berlin Film Festival; it's sort of a *Noises Off*-type comedy about the machinations of a festival jury. The hero is a director who accepts an invitation to be on the jury at the very last minute because his new film has flopped. When he gets there, he finds out that competition is boiling down to an American film which has been highly praised and a Russian film that he doesn't like. One of the other jury members is an old friend of his, an ex-friend from the days when they were both critics, and he's a champion of the American film. But the director hasn't seen the American film and doesn't want to see it because he knows it's a personal attack on him produced by his ex-wife. It goes on from there.

JACKSON: *Comedy is a new departure for you. Did you write it because you think of yourself as being too serious?*
PS: Yes. Comic relief is really all I'd written before, but I was surprised how easy I found it to write straight comedy. The trick of it is that comedy is much more character-oriented than story-oriented.

KJ: *The clashes between the director and his old critic friend in* Berlinale *offer an occasion for some scathing observations about the state of film criticism at the moment. Does that reflect just a moment of ill-temper, or do you tend to believe that criticism is in a bad way?*
PS: Yes, I do, and it's not necessarily the critics' fault. People aren't really reading so much any more and they certainly don't read serious criticism. If the audiences were there then the critics would emerge again, but it's very hard for them today to create a reading public for themselves, so they just end up either as consumer guides or as TV entertainers.

Criticism has lost its mandate, and I suppose in one sense you could trace that back to the structuralist criticism fad, which was when criticism really moved off the streets and into the academies; but in fact that movement was only reflective of the fact that it was dying on the streets.

KJ: *But when you wrote criticism you believed that you were actually changing the kind of films that were going to be made?*
PS: Yes, and I think we were.

KJ: *At another point in* Berlinale *there's an interesting argument in which the director defends the present Hollywood system, which might seem surprising given some of your experiences.*
PS: Well, I've just come back from a festival of my own films at Dartmouth where I ended up doing the same thing I do whenever I go to these festivals in New Delhi or Havana or Dublin, which is to wax very eloquent defending the supply-side economics of Hollywood – that bad doesn't drive out good, that in fact good comes from bad, and the more bad movies are made the more likely it is that good movies will be made, and that to try to dictate quality is stifling.

The greatest thing about movies is that they are a truly popular art, and you can't dictate to a popular art; you just have to let it live in all its perverse permutations.

So I go off on all these polemical tangents and then invariably someone from the audience says, 'Well then, how come your own films aren't Hollywood?' And I say, 'Well, I've always tried to be a Hollywood director.' When I go back to LA and talk to my old friends who are now in the studios, I say to them, 'Hey, I'm just like you – I'm a Hollywood director. All I want to do is entertain people and make a few bucks,' and they say, 'No, you're not a Hollywood director,' and I say, 'Yes, I am, believe me!'

KJ: *Just a little disingenuousness there?*
PS: Maybe, yes. And obviously that's reflected in the films I've done, that unease with being either too corrupt or too pure. Trying somehow to be both at the same time.

KJ: *Another aspect of that* Berlinale *speech is that it comes in the context of an argument about Hollywood's domination of the world's cinemas.*
PS: Yes, where you get into that damned imperialist, colonialist argument which I think is just a bunch of hooey. My response to that is that it's a gross misreading of the role America plays in world cinema. There really isn't an American national cinema. American cinema from the get-go was always an international cinema, founded by Russian and German Jews to create goy entertainment for the world, and today it is still intentionally international.

Whenever you have a story conference you're always talking about a film for the world markets; you're never talking about a purely domestic film. Americans even make films that they know will not fare that well domestically, like the Chuck Norris films, because they will do well internationally. Of course, American films are made in the lingua franca of cinema, English, so that whenever people in the various national cinemas get to the point where they want to become international directors, a Peter Weir or a Wim Wenders or a Bernardo Bertolucci, they leave their countries and come to America, where the international films are made.

KJ: *That touches on an area which is raised by the screenplay for* Gershwin, *which is the thought that though Gershwin derived his musical inspiration from a variety of national backgrounds, the synthesis is a music that is purely American. Do you feel that your own films, which have looked to France and Italy and Japan for their inspiration, have done something similar?*

PS: Well, yes, and that's really the strength of American culture in general: its readiness to assimilate different cultures and races and produce something new and different. You go to certain parts of Europe and you think, 'No wonder their movies are so dull – they don't have any blacks and they don't have any Jews.' Blacks and Jews are the people who have given American culture its energy, and the new impulse in America is that we are progressively becoming a Hispanic nation. I think the great challenge and great excitement now is to try to incorporate the Hispanic sensibility into our own. Hollywood has always been a little uncomfortable with that particular market, but I think there's now really an intention to try to bring it in.

KJ: Berlinale *isn't your first play; you also worked on a play about psychoanalysis. What was the history of that?*

PS: A long one. It took a whole year of my life around 1982. I was trying to write it for the National Theatre in Britain, at the suggestion of Peter Hall. So I did research, I went to graduate classes in psychoanalytic theory at New York University. It was going to be about this Russian woman, Sabina Spielrein, a schizophrenic, who had been a patient of Jung's and had helped him formulate the theory of the *anima*. Jung had an affair with her and she had a breakdown, and then she went on to Vienna and became a disciple of Freud's, and then went back to Russia to do her own therapeutic work, but ended up being killed in a pogrom.

The play is really about the dialogue between Freud and Jung as seen through the vessel of this woman. It's such a great story that it took me a long time to realize that it just wasn't working. I kept struggling with it over and over again, but I couldn't find anything new or original to say. It usually just ended up being some sort of defence of feminism or a simple account of the origin of psychoanalysis, and those themes just weren't fresh enough.

KJ: *Will you ever finish it?*
PS: I don't know. I have my rough draft and I have all my research, so you never can tell. All I have to do is one day figure out what it is I'm trying to say. I wrote out a list of twenty-one possible themes for the play on a sheet of paper and I couldn't get behind any of them.

The play came about because someone had given me Spielrein's book, *The Secret Symmetry*, and I was very attracted to it, but decided that it had to be done as a play rather than a movie because it's so talky, all about letters and conversations. Peter Hall liked the rough draft and was ready to take it into workshops, but I just didn't think it worked, and though I'm arrogant enough to go, as a screenwriter, into the National Theatre and take on everyone if I'm confident about what I've done, when I'm not confident it's like stepping into a shit-storm. That community is not going to want to accept you, and why go through all that pain and agony and lack of money if you're not absolutely confident about what you've done?

KJ: *You obviously have an interest in Freud, and you've referred to being in analysis, but some of your critical writings and early interviews are rather hostile to Freudian readings, such as the attempt by* Cahiers du Cinéma *to see an Oedipal theme in* Hardcore.
PS: I guess it's because I think things like that are subtext, and the moment you allow it to become text then you're not really doing what you're supposed to be doing. Movies should reflect the truth of things like psychoanalysis on a parallel track, not on the same track, because the moment you're on the same track then you're illustrating dogma rather than exploring truth. And for a film-maker there is no dogma so sacred that it must be adhered to. If you're going to do a film with a Freudian context then you have to have the freedom to come to an unFreudian conclusion.

KJ: Berlinale *is also full of praise and disparagement for any number of contemporary directors, whether directly named or under thin disguises. You've explained that the directors who meant most to you as a critic were Bresson and Renoir and so on, but who are the directors who have been important to you since becoming a film-maker yourself?*
PS: I've already mentioned Bertolucci in the context of *American Gigolo*, and obviously he has been the major influence. I've stolen from *The*

Conformist repeatedly, not only in *Gigolo* but in *Cat People*, where the camera is at an angle and as someone opens an animal cage it skews back; that's a scene from *The Conformist* where Trintignant goes to his mother's house. Then shortly afterwards in that scene there's a low shot where the camera is moving and all the leaves are whirling up; I used that shot in *Mishima*, in the 'Temple of the Golden Pavilion' section where you see all the red leaves.

There are other films I've stolen from, like Nic Roeg's *Performance*, which is very invigorating visually – if you ever need something to steal, that's a good one to check up on. There's a scene in the middle section of *Mishima* where the girl puts a mirror on the boy's chest and reflects her own breast – that's taken from *Performance*. Then there's *Vertigo*, the green-light scene where the hero recognizes that the two Kim Novaks are the same, and *L'Éclisse*, which I've liked to steal from because it's so strong architecturally. And, of course, there's Welles.

KJ: *What would you say these sources had in common, if anything?*
PS: The underlying thing of it all, which for my generation starts with Bertolucci, is the idea of the unmotivated camera. By and large, in the first half of the history of movies the camera moved as action or character dictated; it moved to follow a character, it moved to lead with an action, and so on. But starting with Bertolucci we see a really strong case of the unmotivated camera, the camera moved on its own. If Trintignant was walking away from you in the hallway, the camera might be pulling back rather than following him, and if he was in one room the camera might move over to the next room and wait for him to come rather than move when he did.

I remember in *Taxi Driver* there's a scene where De Niro's on the phone and Marty pans away from him, dollies a little bit towards the door and then the conversation continues off-screen until it comes back again. I asked Marty why he did that and he said, 'Oh, it was just too painful to watch him – I wanted to look someplace else.' That's the unmotivated camera, and I think for a lot of Americans the first time they really understood how deliciously that can work was in *The Conformist*.

KJ: *What is your present perspective on the generation, your generation, of film-makers who learned from Bertolucci?*
PS: There's a general sense of disillusion. We came up full of piss and vinegar and politicization, and we really felt that we were going to create a new brand of movies. Now, if you look at the film-makers of my generation – Walter Hill, Phil Kaufman, John Milius, George Lucas, Spielberg – by and

46 *The Conformist*: whirling leaves outside the house of
Trintignant's mother.

47 *Mishima*: leaves outside the Temple of the Golden Pavilion.

large you see a kind of middle age creeping in, a kind of establishment attitude and a lack of eagerness to take risks and challenge and upset.

You start to bemoan that and you say, 'Why have so many directors lowered the banner?', but then you look at the films of the generation that has followed us and you see even greater timidity and even more craven sensibilities. So as disillusioned as I sometimes feel, I still think that my generation was a damn sight more interesting than the one that's come up after it.

KJ: The Last Temptation of Christ *and* Patty Hearst *don't strike me as timid films.*
PS: No, I guess not. The fires aren't burning as high as they were, but the coals still glow.

KJ: *And many of the masters of world cinema were masters at an advanced age – Ozu, Bresson and Dreyer are good examples – so there can't be anything wrong about middle age* per se *for a director.*
PS: No, but this is a case of becoming the backbone of an industry. You're Movie Brats, Inc.; this attitude is more prevalent among executives and agents than it is among directors. You will often catch them saying – implicitly if not explicitly – 'I paid my dues in my young years: now I'm going to get rich.'

KJ: *Do you think there will be another wave of Movie Brats?*
PS: I'm not sure. Ours was the first film-school generation, the first generation that came up cognizant of film history and where we stood in relation to it. Previous generations had come up from television, or journalism, or theatre, and for them it was bringing another discipline to film, but for my generation it was standing in the tradition of what had gone before.

But a major change has happened. When I was a film student it was still possible to encompass what was thought of as all film history in your study; you could actually learn all world cinema. It's not possible for a student to do that today; there's just too much that has gone before, and he would have to study for ten years just to arrive at the point I was at after three years. There are so many more national cinemas, like the Chinese, to study, and there have simply been so many more films. For a young student today, *Bonnie and Clyde* is as far away as, say, *Casablanca* was for me when I was a student.

KJ: *Do you think there was a weakness in the fact that your generation had not come from other disciplines?*

PS: There is definitely a downside, even in the best of us like Spielberg and Scorsese. You could certainly look at some of our films and say, 'These movies are just too self-referential. They are movies about movies and not movies about life.'

I experienced some of this when I went back to teach at UCLA. Colin Young was the first head of a film school to introduce an undergraduate film programme, but two or three years later he came to regret this because the quality of the graduates started dropping enormously. The problem was that he was getting a generation of students who instead of being interested in existential philosophy were interested in Clarence Brown movies.

KJ: *So you think that your own background in theology and literature was a positive advantage?*
PS: Absolutely, and whenever I get a chance I persuade students who are interested in films to stay away from film majors and take a hard-core undergraduate major in a traditional liberal-arts subject, because in the end nothing will stand you in better stead for making films. You can learn about films later, but you're never going to have a chance to read the classics or psychology or philosophy the way you would in college, because that is where the mould is cut. If you don't cut the mould with a liberal education you are a less interesting person, and a less interesting film-maker.

KJ: *Throughout this interview you've been very clear-minded, methodical and analytical about what you have done and why. Do you think that on the whole those powers of analysis have been your great strength, or are they things which have inhibited you?*
PS: I enjoy being analytical; I'm analytical about myself and about others, but when you write a script you really try to set that aside. When I write a new script these days I try not to be analytical, and when I direct it I try not to be analytical, and only when that is all over will I be able to look back and analyse what I've done. It goes back to what we were saying about the dichotomy between a creative sensibility and a critical sensibility. You have to ride your instincts, you've got to get the critic outside the room and close the door.

Notes

1 History has turned the page on *Berlinale*; I doubt if it will ever be staged. The play's underlying metaphor is the Berlin Wall – enough said. PS, March 1990.

48 Paul Schrader on the set of *The Comfort of Strangers*, 1989.

CHAPTER 7

The Screenwriter, resumed: *Manhattanville* a.k.a. *City Hall* to *Bringing Out The Dead*

SCHRADER: *Manhattanville* was a screenplay I wrote with Nick Pileggi. The idea began with a man called Ken Lipper, who used to be Deputy Mayor of New York, and then became an extremely wealthy financial manager, who is still interested in the movie business. He had written a script about his experiences at City Hall, and Nick and I took it from there. The version he and I wrote was about how the Deputy Mayor connives to bring down the Mayor, who's kind of a secondary character. I was going to direct it, with Alec Baldwin and Marlon Brando, and I had several meetings with Brando before it all collapsed: Brando fell out, and then Baldwin fell out because Brando fell out, and then it moved on.

Brando and I had met in passing before, and I'd had a series of phone conversations with him around about 1980 through a woman called Lucy Saroyan, who was in *Blue Collar* and who knew Marlon. He called me from Tahiti because he wanted me to do a rewrite of H.G. Wells's *Invisible Man*. We talked and I said, 'I don't think it's such a good idea.' I couldn't figure out why he wanted to do it. But he called back a couple of times. Finally, I got it. He was going to do two days' work: he would be in the opening and in the ending, and the rest would all be voice-over, and he was going to get $5 million for it. Like that famous story on *Superman*, where he tried to convince Richard Donner that Superman's father should just be a voice coming out of a suitcase . . .

So, Nick Pileggi and I go to meet Brando at his house in Los Angeles for *Manhattanville*. Nick knew a lot of wiseguys from New York, and a number of them had introduced themselves to Brando over the years, because of *The Godfather* – they would come up to his trailer and try and get an introduction. All these guys were sort of blurred in Brando's head, but he could do imitations of them, and Nick could immediately say, 'Oh, that's so-and-so, he died', or 'He's off in prison in Pennsylvania.' And I'm sitting there saying, 'This is so cool – Nick Pileggi and Marlon Brando are playing 'Name That Gangster.' That was a high point.

Out of that meeting came the notion that the Mayor, who Marlon would play, should be a bongo aficionado, and have part-ownership of a bongo club. I said to Nick, 'Well, okay. We can work that in.' Then there was another phone call where Brando wanted to have a parrot. Well ... okay, but a Mayor who plays bongos, and has a parrot? This is getting harder and harder to accommodate. And every time you accommodate him, it gets even worse. So then we have another meeting, at which point he says: 'Who cares about New York politics anyway? Let's just do the bongo club!' We're all sitting there with long faces. Ken Lipper, whose idea and life story this is, is horrified. Finally, the producer, Ed Pressman, in his quiet voice, says 'I think we're sort of committed to a film about New York politics . . . ' After that, according to Ed, there was just one more phone call, where he tried to talk Brando back into it, and Brando said, 'Nah, I know people like Schrader, it would never have worked, they're always trying to tell you what to do.'

So it moved on – first, I think, to Barry Levinson and Dustin Hoffman; and then *that* fell out, and it moved on to Al Pacino, and Al brought in Harold Becker.

KJ: *Did you see the film when it eventually appeared as* City Hall?
PS: Yes, and it was seriously out of whack. It starts to fall between two stools, and you don't quite know what the movie is. What happened was that Al got attracted to the Mayor's role, the secondary role, and had it rewritten. But basically all that was done was that the Mayor's role was expanded, and he got a lot of speeches, and the Deputy Mayor, played by John Cusack, who had been the driving role, essentially had everything cut out from underneath him. And the dramatic mechanics of it didn't favour the Mayor as main character. So the film, I think, suffered a lot from being an Al Pacino film where Al didn't have a lot to do, except give speeches.

KJ: *How many other screenplays were you working on in the years before* Affliction *finally got made in 1997?*
PS: Let me just have a look at my filing cabinet . . . Okay, at around this time there were *Irresistible, By the Sea of Crystal,* and *The John Gotti Story.*

Also there was *Snow White*, which was meant to be a very grim

49 *City Hall* (1996): Al Pacino as Mayor Pappas.

version of Grimm. Somebody had written a first draft, and then it
was brought to me. I did a first version which was really too soft, so
then I wrote a very, *very* hard version, with a twelfth-century mentality, a lot of violence, and all the dwarves were physically and mentally
disturbed people. And in the end, the production company didn't
want to go with my script or with me: they figured they would only
get the hardcore R-rated audience, and wanted the Disney audience
as well as the adult audience. They ended up having Sigourney
Weaver play the main role, and it cost a lot of money and went
straight to video.

The John Gotti Story came from a non-fiction book that was
bought by Jon Peters, and I was paid well to adapt it. Peters . . . well,
I'm not the only one who will say this: you think after all these years
in the business that you can work with anybody, and then you meet
Jon Peters. The main problem was that he didn't always read the
books he bought. He knew that he wanted to make a film about John
Gotti, and he wanted Jack Nicholson to play the lead. Unfortunately,
the book he actually bought was about how the FBI caught Gotti by a
whole story of wire-taps and subterfuge. I did a lot of research with
the FBI and I wrote kind of a techie script, about how they did it. And
Peters was furious – he wanted to know where all the *Godfather*
scenes were, he wanted shoot-outs and all that. Now, Gotti was never
involved in a shoot-out, he never shot anybody. His *associates* did, but
Gotti spent most of his time on the phone or in court. But Peters blew
up with me for having screwed him over, and I pointed out to him that
if he had read the book he would understand that the script was
adapted from that.

Anyway, after me, they hired Joe Eszterhas, who was at the top of
his game. They paid him a fortune, and he ran into exactly the same
problem – the material they had was not the movie they wanted to
make, and the movie they wanted to make was not anywhere in John
Gotti's life. At one point, Peters was actually talking to me about
fictionalising Gotti's life, and I said, 'I don't think you can do that.
He's been in the newspapers every day for the last ten years. If you're
going to fictionalise, why don't you change the name?' But no. He
wanted Gotti's name, but he didn't want Gotti's life.

KJ: *So this thing has never been made?*
PS: No. Subsequently there have been two television movies, so that
burned up that territory. Ultimately, Gotti's life just wasn't that interesting. And now, of course, the gangster movie has moved into

parody, and things like *The Sopranos*. After De Niro does *Analyse This*, what else can you do with the genre?

At one point I was going to direct my script for *Quebecois*, but then I had a better idea, for a gangster movie set in New Orleans. It was called *The Fatness of the Earth*, which is from the Bible, Jacob and Esau, and this was a Jacob-Esau kind of story. I was going to do it with a friend of mine, David Marshall Grant, but we got about 30 pages in and I realised that the gangster genre was just death: I was trying to breathe life into a corpse. It had a very nice premise, but all the gangster stuff was just weighing it down, it just didn't want to be written. And I'm glad I walked away from *Quebecois* too, because that would have died for the same reason.

KJ: *The title of the next unproduced screenplay,* By the Sea of Crystal, *comes from a hymn, doesn't it?*
PS: Yeah. 'By the sea of crystal / Saints in glory stand / Myriad in number / Drawn from every land'. It's a hymn from our Church, the Reform Church. We used to have a radio show when I was a kid, the *Back to God Hour*, and every day at three my mother used to listen. The show always began with that hymn.

This was another script I wrote on spec. I've written a lot of scripts with protagonists that make them hard to finance – psychopaths, a gigolo, a drug dealer. But finally I came across one that really is unfinanceable, and that's a born-again Christian. The main character is a bad guy, a thug, who is converted and then goes undercover, and passes information that puts his former boss in jail. So the boss puts out a hit on him, and the guy's former confederates come after him. The whole script is summed up in a scene where the guy goes to his former boss in jail and tries to convince him that it will be counter-productive if he's killed. The boss says to him, 'I hear you went off and found Jesus Christ?' Then he looks hard and says, 'The day you met Jesus Christ was the day your troubles began . . . '

I have simply tried to give that script away: anyone who wants to make it can have it. Make it on video for $500,000 – I'll give it to you. I don't think *I* should make the movie, because I've got so tarred with this religious brush that if I go back in that area, I'm dead before I go to work.

KJ: *On to the next script, then:* Irresistible?
PS: That one came out of discussions with Gale Anne Hurd when we

were working together on *Witch Hunt*. Gale had the idea to do a female Jekyll and Hyde. The Jekyll character, a scientist who's into life-prolongation and genetics, is an unattractive woman. And when she turns into Hyde, she becomes beautiful, and much younger; so it's a double-flip on the original. In the end, though, we all walked away. The simple weight of the tackiness of the whole concept finally sunk it. It's one of those situations where you're all in the boat, bailing water, and you finally look at each other and say, 'No matter what we do, this boat's going down!' And even as I describe it now, it seems like a really cheesy idea. But it was written for Paramount and I got paid well for it, and that's the business we're in. In fact, I also wrote a script for Paramount on the life of Doris Duke, simply called *Doris Duke*.

KJ: *I'd better confess that I don't know who that is.*
PS: You know Duke University? That was founded by her father. The Dukes are one of the great, rich families that span American culture – oddball rich people. Doris Duke was famous for being rich, basically. And it's a script I sort of feel bad about. Mario Kassar visited me in Cannes, and he had four words for me: 'Doris Duke. Sharon Stone'. Sharon was a very powerful commercial force at that time, the job was very lucrative, I needed the work, and I convinced myself that I could do it. So I did a lot of research, much more than I would usually do. And my problem was that nothing really happened in this woman's life. A lot of *events* happened, but nothing of any real dramatic importance. She had a big affair with one of the Rothschilds, which was sort of interesting, but in the end it's just anecdotal. And her death was a bit of a scandal because there was a suggestion that she may have been poisoned, but there wasn't much of a story there, either. So I wrote this long script . . .

KJ: *And what did you make the point of the story?*
PS: That's it. There *is* no point. And I had told myself before this that I would write no more biographies, just never do it again. But because of my immediate need for cash – because the films I write and direct don't pay any bills – those four magical words blurred my perception. I thought I could pull it off; I couldn't. Finally I was back at Paramount on another situation, and I said to John Goldwyn, 'Before this meeting starts, I want to apologise. I lied to you guys. I said I could do *Doris Duke*. I couldn't, and I'm still kicking myself for wasting my time and your money.' And John said, '*Doris Duke*? What script was

that?' While I'd been agonising over my reputation, they'd completely forgotten and moved on.

KJ: *More recently, you did a rewrite on a project called* Suspect Zero?
PS: It's my humble contribution to the serial-killer genre. Tom Cruise's company had a script about a serial killer, which I completely revamped, and made into a serial-killer-of-serial-killers over the internet. I really thought it would get made, but there was a change of regime at the studio, and they were already making *The Bone Collector*, which at that time they thought was going to flop, and they didn't want to be doing two serial killer projects at the same time. And anyway, the genre had already run out of gas. By now, the whole thing has so much weight on it that you would need a superstar to bring it back to life: what with Tom Cruise's overheads, and the fees involved in four or five scripts, it's just sitting there costing money.

I also spent almost an entire year working on a script called *Magic Bullet*. I'm surprised that it didn't get made, and so are the people who financed it. It's about breast cancer, and I wrote it for a friend, Penny Marshall. I thought it would be interesting to do something for a woman, and in a genre I normally wouldn't work on, which is a kind of medical thriller. It was from a novel, an exposé of the medical establishment, written by a guy called Harry Stein whose brother was fairly high up in the medical world. It had a very feel-good, Penny Marshall mood, and it was very interesting working for a woman, because the comments that come back are really quite different: all of the kind of edgy, aggressive, male stuff she sort of ignores, then whenever you hit a warm, fuzzy section, she's all over it. But Penny went on to make *The Preacher's Wife* instead, because that had two superstars in it. And I don't think *Magic Bullet* will ever get made now, because advances in the field of breast cancer have been happening so quickly in the last five years that all the technical material is already antiquated.

These days, I'm writing a for-hire script at the rate of about one every year and a half, and a personal script about once a year. I'm also involved in more machinations, not only of raiding funds for production, but on these last couple of movies, trying to find a distributor for them too. There was as much work after *Affliction* was made as there was before; the same with *Forever Mine*. But after *Doris Duke*, the next script I wrote was nice, because I wrote it for money *and* love, *and* prestige. And that was *Bringing Out The Dead*.

KJ: *I had thought it unlikely that you'd ever work with Scorsese again.*
PS: So did I.

KJ: *Did you have a major falling-out?*
PS: Well, not really. But back in the 1980s, not long after *Last Temptation*, Marty had had an idea to redo *The Bad and the Beautiful*, based roughly on him, De Niro and myself: director, actor, writer – our days together as colleagues. I interviewed both of them about those times to come up with a treatment. Marty wanted to be the co-author of the script, which I had a problem with. I said, 'I've done three scripts for you, I'm not about to start being your co-writer.' And there were arguments with De Niro: he'd say, 'I would never do that!' and I'd say, 'But I was there when you did it!' So finally I said, 'Look, this is going to turn out one of two ways. Either it won't get made, and we'll become enemies; or it won't get made, and we'll stay friends. So let's just assume that the latter is true, and quit. We've done three films, they're good films, that's enough. Let's keep in touch, have dinner once a year or so.' Marty sort of saw that that was the case: basically the room had gotten too small for both our egos, and rather than make a big deal about it, we should just see that collaboration was not an effective course. So it was nothing more harmful than that.

And that's the way it went for about ten years. Then one day I got a call from Scott Rudin, who said, 'Scorsese has this book he'd like you to look at.' And that was ironic, because we were already due to have dinner together the following week. So we had dinner, at a restaurant, which is unusual for Marty, because he doesn't go out much any more. He told me, 'The only things I wear anymore are a bathrobe or a tuxedo.' But we talked about this and that, and for the whole dinner he never once mentioned *Bringing Out The Dead*. Finally, we're having coffee and I say, 'Marty, Scott Rudin called me about this book.' And Marty said, 'Oh yeah, I wanted to talk to you about that . . . ' He just couldn't bring himself to ask me, for fear of what I might say. Then he told me that Scott had said that I should write this, but he felt awkward about asking me. And when I read the book, I saw exactly why: because it was the kind of movie that I'd been writing on and off for a long time – a loner, a drifter, an existential man caught on the cusp of both inner and outer decay.

But the book adapted very easily into screenplay form, pretty much straight across. Joe Connolly, who wrote the book, had been a paramedic for five years, and if anything the book was excessively heavy in colourful details, and needed to be pared down. But I researched it a little by riding around on an ambulance, which was very entertaining. I just wanted to go around with these guys, so that their world didn't feel too alien to me.

KJ: *When I first looked at the screenplay, I found it a deeply compelling read: fast-moving, highly visual and very gripping.*
PS: It's because it's so linear that it reads well. Some scripts you get today, these deconstructed scripts, can be very good, but there was one I read recently where I had to read it twice – and the second time I had to take notes. Because the time frame was all over the place, the characters were popping in with one line of dialogue from one time frame and then cutting to another – it was like looking at a vase that's been broken into pieces and spread out over the floor. On the screen, we now have the visual knowledge to be able to experience that, but it's still awfully rough to read.

KJ: *Is the film's sense of black comedy also in Connolly's novel?*
PS: Yes. It was really more a question of selection than anything else. Because it is a fairly grisly world, I zeroed in on all the elements of comedy, made sure that they were pulled out and heightened. And the elements of the lead character's back story – how he grew up, the story about his ex-wife – those all got carved out. Those are the kinds of choices I can make because I've been doing this for almost twenty years. Whereas when I spoke to Joe Connolly afterwards, he said to me, 'It would have been impossible for me to go in and hack things out.'

KJ: *How about the spiritual material? Was that there in Connolly?*
PS: Excessively. Connolly was a Roman Catholic convert. And in fact, I thought I'd gotten most of it out. It was only when I saw the finished film that I realised there was so much left in, and I was surprised. I warned Marty, because of the work we've done together: 'We've got to weed this Roman Catholic stuff out. People are gonna nail us if we get too explicit here.' But I kept some of it in, and some of it snuck back in, and some of it I didn't even recognise – like a scene near the end which one critic identified as a reference to the wound in Christ's side on the cross. Well, *that* had never occurred to me. I don't know if it ever occurred to Marty. But you can see why people make that connection.

KJ: *What was the origin of the hallucinatory sequence where the dead start rising up from the street?*

50 *Bringing Out The Dead* (1999): Nicolas Cage as Frank Pierce.

PS: I think that in the book it's just a flashback. As it developed, it became more of a nightmarish dream, and when I wrote it, I wrote it as an extremely vivid hallucinatory nightmare. And then Marty started adding all the surreal elements, like the white horse, and the dead – that was all Scorsese.

I had a couple of arguments with Marty. The character was written as being in his twenties, and my first suggestion for the part was Edward Norton. My belief was that this is the kind of nervous breakdown you have in your twenties. By the time you're in your thirties, you've either learned how to do the job, or you've got another job. But this is a kid's condition. The guy seems to be too old to be going through that. And so it wasn't that I thought that Nic Cage was a bad actor, or a bad choice, I just didn't think he was the right age. But they needed Nic, because once he had agreed to work for a relatively low fee, Marty could just go ahead and make the movie he wanted to make, with a big budget from Paramount-Touchstone, and not be interfered with. It gave him freedom. But a hipper, cooler movie would probably have had more of a commercial chance.

Also I think the music should have been all techno and rap, instead of that music from the seventies and eighties – it would have made the film seem less old-fashioned. Because the film-making itself isn't old-fashioned: what's old-fashioned is the theme, the morality. That's something from Marty's and my generation. Young film-makers aren't really addressing that kind of theme, or that old, existentialist kind of character.

KJ: *Was the experience of collaborating with Scorsese again happy enough to have opened a door to further projects?*
PS: Well, I don't know. He did ask me to work on a book about the Second World War, by an Italian writer, Malaparte – which would have been a very expensive project, full of war imagery. And I told Marty that it would take a huge amount of work, and I just didn't see it getting made, and I didn't know how to do it. There was no real narrative there, I could see myself spending several years on it, and I'm just too old to do that.

KJ: *And, as you've said, you need to keep writing scripts at a fair rate to subsidise your own films.*
PS: Well, take *The Walker*, which is a script I wrote for myself to direct and have been trying to make for a few years now. The original budget had a fee for my services, then the budget went down, so I had

to throw my fee into the pot, and that meant I had to scramble to get a writing job. But when I'm doing that kind of for-hire gig, there has to be some engine on the project driving my salary – Penny Marshall, Sharon Stone, Martin Scorsese – because they're not just going to pay me sight unseen.

CHAPTER 8

The Director, resumed: *Light Sleeper* to *Exorcist: The Beginning*

The Comfort of Strangers revisited

KJ: *How did* The Comfort of Strangers *fare commercially?*

PS: It did well in Europe, and very well in London, particularly because it was British material, British actors – it felt more like a British film than an American film. Angelo Badelamenti won a BAFTA for best score. But in America it was seen very much as an art-house movie, and again – as has happened to me so often – I ran into a distributor who was going down. I've been working with marginal distributors for a while now, and it can be depressing, because all of a sudden they don't have the budget to release the film, or they're going out of business and they try to sell the film off to somebody else.

KJ: *What do you think of the film now?*

PS: I love it. It's so deliciously droll. There was a theme in the Ian McEwan book, that men and women are basically antagonistic, and no amount of socialisation can help. Then there was the Harold theme, which is that language affects the way we deal with reality. And I thought that those two themes were sufficient, that I didn't need to impose my own theme onto this. But about two weeks into the filming I realised I *had* imposed my own theme – the *Mishima* theme, which is that physical beauty is, in and of itself, dangerous: it's threatening, it's destructive. And I had come to this theme because the story was so tawdry that I wanted to make it seductive and attractive, to polish the apple until it absolutely shone, so that you would be enticed to take a bite of it and then find your mouth full of decay. The book is not nearly so luxurious, but in making this glorious exterior, I ended up in classic Mishima decadence: beauty itself drives people crazy.

So I was pretty pleased with the way *The Comfort of Strangers* came out, and I loved working with Pinter. That was just a hoot – Harold is definitely a major customer, and I still see him about once a year. Harold and I would have wonderful conversations. I remember one time getting into an argument about whether the end of a particular line should be a dash or an ellipsis. The argument was getting more and more intense, and then I thought, 'Wait a second. The actors are going to be *saying* this, there's not going to be a dash or an ellipsis on screen . . . '

I remember that the actors, all four of them, had been bugging me about things in the script they didn't like, but I like that elliptical way Harold writes, so I called him up and said, 'Would you come down and do rehearsals with us for a week?' And I said to the actors, 'We'll rehearse like a stage play, Harold will be in the room, I won't say anything. Then Harold will go back to London, and we'll rehearse it again as a movie, and at that point, I'll address all your questions and comments.' So Harold came down, and we just took the script and read it and read it. And at one point, Natasha Richardson said to Harold, 'This woman I'm playing has two children but no husband. Is he dead, are they divorced, what's the situation?' And Harold growled back, 'Natasha, I have never answered a question like that, and I'm not going to answer it now. Read the text!' The point being that if she reads it enough, she'll answer that question herself, and her answer will be a better answer, because she will have come up with it. After Harold went back to London, I said to the actors, 'Okay, let's talk any concerns you have.' And Chris looked at me and said, 'You know, I like the script the way it is. I think it's pretty good.' And the others said, 'Yeah . . . ' So we didn't make any changes.

kj: *A technical point we've never really discussed is how long you tend to have by way of a rehearsal period?*
ps: In that case, it was two weeks. Usually it's about four or five days. Sometimes it involves just reading the script, and discussing it, and sometimes it involves re-writing, so every day after rehearsals you go back and make changes. But with *The Comfort of Strangers*, the only change I made was before rehearsal. In the book, this couple stay in a hotel room for two days, making love. But there was nothing in the script: Harold doesn't write sex scenes, and I don't think he's ever really been comfortable writing them. But I said to him, 'We can't just say that they've been making love for two days, we need at least one scene of the two of them in that room, undressed.' I couldn't get him to address it, and finally I wrote out a short scene myself and faxed it to him. An hour later, it came back, rewritten. He realised that I'd

called his bluff, and that if he didn't come up with something quick I was going to put my own scene in.

It was a fun film to cast too. I fooled around with Al Pacino for a while, for the older male role, Robert. We had a reading, and I knew he was committed to do *Godfather III*, but he assured me he could do them both. So I phoned up Francis, and he said, 'No way. At the time you'll be wanting him for the film, he should be in rehearsals with me, and I'm not going to let him go.' Well, I knew that Chris Walken would be willing to do it, and I knew he would make a good film, so I phoned Pacino's agent and said, 'Look, if I don't hear from Al by five o'clock on Friday, I offer it to Chris.' Five o'clock came, no call, so I called up Walken's agent and made the deal. Then, come Sunday, I'm having a birthday party for my son, and the phone rings. It's Al. So I go upstairs, and I can look out of the window and see the birthday party. And Al wants to talk about the role. I let him go on for about ten minutes, and I say, 'Look, Al, I delivered an ultimatum of five o'clock on Friday, I didn't get a phone call, so I called Walken's agent and Walken is going to do the movie.' And Al said, 'Yeah, yeah, I know all that. I just wanted to talk about the character! He's so interesting, I just wanna talk about this guy!'

Anyway, Pacino asked me to send him everything I'd ever written that might possibly be right for him. So I sent him *Light Sleeper* and never heard anything. And then one day I run into him in an elevator, and he says, 'What are you doing?', and I say, 'Well, I'm working on this film about the mid-life crisis of a drug dealer.' And he said, 'Oh yeah, I read that script, really interesting, I want to talk to you about that . . . ' And I said, 'Al, I cast Willem Dafoe, I shot the movie, and now I'm editing it!' And he said, 'Oh, oh, okay . . . '

Light Sleeper

KJ: *There are some obvious echoes of* Taxi Driver *in the script for* Light Sleeper. *Were the similarities between the two films planned from the outset, or did they arise from the nature of the subject matter?*

PS: Well, the format of the script is the same as the format of *Taxi Driver*, in that it uses pseudo-chapters rather than scene numbers, but the deeper connection comes from the fact that this is a character that I have felt comfortable with in the past and hadn't written about in some time. As to the specific moments – well, you don't want to be too self-referential, but if it works, it works, and if you're ploughing the same row ten or fifteen years on, you're going to end up with the same roots being dug up. The character of John LeTour is, in my mind, another installment of the characters of Travis Bickle in *Taxi Driver* and Julian Kay in *American Gigolo*. These characters are really not so much people as souls, they drift around and things happen to them, they watch and they are acted upon. I don't really see this group of films as a trilogy, I just think that as I get older my views about this character and these themes change. So that when the character and myself were in our twenties, he was very hostile and paranoid and felt oppressed by the world, and was a cab driver. When he was in his thirties he was very narcissistic and self-involved, and he was a gigolo. Now he's forty and he's anxious and uncertain, and he delivers drugs. He hasn't made anything of his life, and he doesn't know what will become of him.

KJ: *So in that sense* Light Sleeper *is a film about a mid-life crisis?*
PS: Yes, in the very direct sense that it's about a man who doesn't know what to do next – his boss is about to leave and go into the cosmetics business and he has no marketable skills. He's been a dealer for ten, twelve years. Also, as a result of this situation he starts to worry: he consults a psychic and his worries grow to the point where they become distorted, and he starts to see events somewhat inaccurately; he starts to see a conspiracy. But I think that what we call a mid-life crisis is really just a life crisis, it's that period in your life when you realize that you are what you are going to be. All these characters I've written about are looking for a place to fit, but as they get older, the eagerness or the anger to make a place for themselves subsides.

KJ: *What were the circumstances of writing the script?*
PS: Well, another connection with Taxi *Driver* is the speed with which I wrote *Light Sleeper*. *Taxi Driver* was written non-stop, but I'm older now and have to keep family hours, so I couldn't write around the clock, but it was the same type of energy, and I finished the script in two weeks. It came to me pretty much as a piece; I saw it all, and I always knew what was going to come next. What happened was that I had a dream about this character sometime in September 1990, somebody I had known years before. I woke up at about four in the morning, and I knew from that moment that he wanted me to write about

him. By six I also knew I was definitely going to do just that. I hadn't written about this type of character in almost ten years. I'd been looking around for a personal, original piece to write and it hadn't been coming, so I had given up, and then it just came. So I set off to track down this man I had known.

KJ: *And did you find him?*
PS: Yes, and he helped me with research, but for reasons of discretion and professional courtesy I can't say much more than that.

KJ: *Portraying drugs and drug dealers without taking up an overtly censorious attitude is not likely to win a writer many fans these days. Did that worry you?*
PS: Just the opposite: that's what got me going. The idea of taking a would-be presidential assassin and making him a hero, or making a male prostitute a hero – that's absolutely invigorating, because it's the element of originality that can run against the grain and create sparks, give a character depth. It's tricky, too, because you have to make this character sympathetic without making him ersatz. I think that's quite possible, because these people who do these day-to-day evil and demeaning things are not actually evil themselves, and it's easy to identify with their daily routines.

KJ: *Was one of the impulses behind* Light Sleeper *a documentary ambition, the wish to show exactly what those routines are?*
PS: Yes, because these are interesting characters who haven't been in the movies before. When people think of drug dealers they have very broad stereotypical images – sort of Hispanics with Uzis – and this is a peculiar, middle-class family grouping.

KJ: *Yes, the relationship between Ann, John and Robert reads almost like a parody of life in a rather conventional, but mother-dominated, family. Was this invention, or something you had observed among dealers?*
PS: It was something I saw. Big Momma and her boys.

KJ: *Are there any points of similarity between the three different occupations of this protagonist of yours across the three films?*
PS: They're all sort of non-people. They appear in other people's lives to perform a service, and they're all terribly important to their clients when their clients don't have them, but the second they've done their

job they become non-people; they vanish before your eyes. And therefore they see life from the outside, they drift about, watch the high and the low, the educated and the vulgar, and they're sort of detached from it all. Really quite pure at an intellectual level. It's like the character in *Taxi Driver* says, 'I'll take anybody, it doesn't matter to me.' It's that kind of cold detachment that allows them to be part of the world but not really in it, and to be incorporeal in a way, like souls that are looking for a body to inhabit.

KJ: *One of the chapter headings in* Light Sleeper *is 'Confessor LeTour', and there is a sense in which all these three characters are like confessors or analysts – they're available for hire to people who need to talk, like the jealous husband played by Scorsese in* Taxi Driver.
PS: Though there's no communication. These are people who are in communication with themselves, but not with others.

KJ: *Why the more abstract title* Light Sleeper *rather than, say,* Dealer *or* Connection *or some other vocational label?*
PS: I would have preferred to have a vocational title, but there really was none that didn't stereotype the film in such a way that you couldn't ever get across the type of film you were dealing with. *Dealer* wasn't good, *Delivery Boy* wasn't good, *Drug Dealer* wasn't good. Drug dealers sometimes call themselves 'D.D.s' or 'D.D.ers,' but *D.D.er* isn't a good title either. So I took the title from the fact that this character has reached the point in his life where he can't really get through a night, and then there was a text from Corinthians that I remembered and that made an ideal epigraph.

KJ: *As soon as you'd written the script, you took it immediately to Willem Dafoe. Why was he your first choice?*
PS: I was so hot on the idea that I didn't even pitch it to anyone to get money. My agent even tried to dissuade me from writing it, because he felt it was an uncommercial subject, but I had very strong feelings about it. So now I had a script that I owned and could make right away, and it was a question of who was available. I had met Willem during *Last Temptation*, and was so impressed by what he did on the film, and I also thought he looked very much like my idea of LeTour – there's a certain pallor, a certain quality these dealers have. So I had dinner with Willem, found out that he was available, and he agreed to do the film the next day.

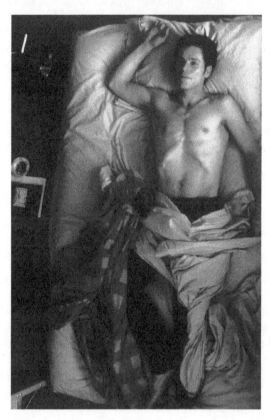

51 *Light Sleeper* (1992): Willem Dafoe as John LeTour.

KJ: *Did Dafoe's commitment make the film easier to finance?*

PS: No; and then I was told that it would make it easier to finance if I got someone of Susan Sarandon's caliber, so I set forth and got Susan Sarandon, and it *still* wasn't easy to finance. Eventually I did manage it, albeit with financial sacrifices by everyone involved in the production: Willem and Susan worked for a fraction of their usual salaries, I deferred my fees, and I cash-flowed preproduction out of my own pocket. But I don't consider my own sacrifices earth-shaking. Just because people get paid so much in movies, it doesn't mean that it's a greater sacrifice when they do what most artists do, which is finance their own art. Most novelists don't get paid more than a pittance until their books are published, and the same applies to a lot of painters and composers, but when a screenwriter says, 'I'll forego my fee,' he's treated like some kind of saint.

KJ: *But why were you so eager to get this particular film made?*

PS: I felt I knew it, it already existed in my head: the embryo was growing, and it got better the more I dealt with it and thought about it. And I guess it was a test to myself in a way, to see whether I could still work this territory.

KJ: *In the draft which was meant to be definitive at the time shooting began, a great deal of the script was taken up with quotations from two Bob Dylan albums,* Empire Burlesque *and* Oh Mercy, *which were going to provide the film's musical setting. What was the intention of that, and why did those songs go?*

PS: I wanted the film to have a ballad structure, with a chorus that kept coming in, so that there was a third voice for the main character. You had his dialogue voice, and then you had his diary voice, and then you had the balladeer's voice, which would throw a third perspective on this closed-off man. I liked a lot of the Dylan songs and thought that they were very apropos, with their apocalyptic, Biblical imagery and all that rabbinical soulfulness, so I put them in the script. It turned out that Bob did not want to cooperate fully – he would give certain songs under certain conditions, but not all the songs I wanted, and he was just difficult. So I went to a singer-songwriter named Michael Been, from a group called The Call, and they took a similar approach: six original songs, plus scoring, plus singing. Incidentally, Michael had a part in *The Last Temptation of Christ*, where he played the apostle John.

KJ: *It seems unusual to have music and lyrics quite so strongly and frequently signaled in a script.*

PS: It hasn't been done much. Lindsay Anderson tried it in *O Lucky Man!*, though I don't know whether those lyrics were ever in the script, and there he put the singer, Alan Price, on-screen, which was not something I wanted to do. *Pat Garrett and Billy the Kid* has this same quality, and I'm sure film buffs can point out other films in which a single voice has performed songs as a narrative thread. I wanted to have something musical which would underline the moments when the hero goes back to the road, back to the road, always cut to the road. In *Taxi Driver* it was the Tom Scott sax solo that brought you back, in *American Gigolo* it was the Giorgio Moroder music that brought you back, and here it's the chorus or verse of a ballad.

KJ: *One of the most noticeable things about the script is its habit of referring to or hinting at occult matters – psychics, numerology, Madame Blavatsky. Is this just atmospheric, a factual detail about the superstitions of drug dealers, or is it also thematic in some way?*

PS: Well, it originated in dealing with these people at a research level, and finding that all of them were involved in paranormal pursuits to some degree. Even if they didn't have psychic sessions or sign readings, card readings, palm readings, they were all very interested in the phenomenon of extra-physical powers. And I think it's because they all believe in this particular theory of luck. They think that they are able to read situations, to read the aura of a meeting and therefore know when to walk away and not get busted. They think it's a psychic power, psychic luck, that has kept them going. The idea of being 'in the groove of a situation,' as they put it, very quickly moves over to the question of whether you're in tune with your own self and with the psychic forces around you. It struck me that this whole notion of luck is very similar to the Christian notion of Providence, and that appealed to me very much.

KJ: *Your cinematographer on* Light Sleeper, *Ed Lachman, says that one of the things you did before the shoot began was to look at some early films by Antonioni. You've mentioned in the past that this is a common practice of yours, but that the kind of ideas you might take from these viewings don't necessarily end up on the screen. What has happened this time?*

PS: Antonioni is always good to look at because he loves to define situations by architecture. When you're getting ready to direct, you're just at the point where you're trying to think: 'What is the visual equivalent of this scene? What situation can I put these people in, how can I photograph them, so that what they are saying is redundant and I can actually cut out lines because I can *see* what they're saying?' So you turn to the filmmakers who are good on composition and architectural sentiment because that's the point that you are at in the evolution of the idea. I mean, you wouldn't watch an Antonioni film *before* you sat down to write a script.

KJ: *So a lot of this is to do with placing the character in an environment, and understanding him because of where he is and how he stands?*
PS: Yes, and having enough courage to make some bold statements visually. There isn't any direct reference to Antonioni in the finished film.

KJ: *In* Taxi Driver *you wrote one of the definitive films about New York, but this is the first film you've ever shot here. Was it just chance that you've avoided the city before, and was there any special reason for working here now?*
PS: *Taxi Driver* had to be set in New York, because it's the only American city where road transportation is really ruled by taxis, and it seemed natural to set *Gigolo* in L.A. because L.A. is that kind of moral world. 'Dial-a-Drug,' which is what this delivery service is called, is more New York. You can find it in any major city around the world, but in New York it's big and sophisticated because the market is big and sophisticated. In another city he might do his own driving, but in New York you need a driver because you can't park, and you have to pay someone to wait while you deliver. So you're in a very passive environment. In many ways, the difference between *Taxi Driver* and *Light Sleeper* is that in the first film the protagonist is in the front seat and in this film he's in the back seat.

KJ: *And the running joke about LeTour, Ann and Robert always ordering take-away food is a commentary on the kind of business they're engaged in themselves? They have to dial out for their needs, too.*
PS: They have to stay close to the phone.

KJ: *The time of* Light Sleeper *is a Labor Day weekend, in the middle of a sanitation strike. Why that date and that background?*
PS: No great significance; there's always a strike of some sort going on in the city, and some of them are more obvious and smelly and inconveniencing than others. Certainly a subway strike wouldn't be particularly inconveniencing for this man, but a sanitation strike is something he has to deal with because he's on the streets all the time.

KJ: *How did you arrive at the name 'LeTour,' which is fairly exotic?*
PS: I liked the idea of 'touring,' because he's on a tour and it's a tourist kind of part, and 'Tour,' or *tueur* is a French word meaning 'killer.' To make that pun work you needed a French prefix on it.

KJ: *Why did you decide to use the convention of chapter headings you've mentioned?*
PS: When you write a script you're writing it for a reader, not a viewer, and that's always a difference of approach. What you're trying to create in the reader's mind is this episodic world – another episode, another event, this happens, this happens, and then this happens . . . and there's a kind of hypnotic rhythm to it. And I find that giving scene numbers and a direct linear page count is not as hypnotic as giving chapter headings and white spaces.

KJ: *Was there something appealing about returning, after working on other kinds of scripts, to the type of structure in which your hero is in every single scene?*
PS: He's not only *in* every scene, a scene doesn't begin until he's in it and it doesn't last after he leaves it. You are not privy to the world about him. I like that sort of visual monopoly; it's like seeing life through a long tube, and you know that a thousand things are happening around but you can only see through the end of the tube. Everything is built on accretion of detail. The main character is passive; he lets the movie roll over him like waves on the beach. The waves will always come, but he will always be there. One of the things that Willem and I worked on was that he should never try to take a scene, never try to dominate it. Essentially, I said to him, 'You're always going to be there on-screen, these other people are going to come and go, so just give the scenes away one after another, because in the end your character will emerge from this passivity, it doesn't need to be stated.'

KJ: *There seems to be a note of redemption at the end of the film.*

PS: I'm not so sure I'd call it redemption; it's certainly a sense of 'the wind bloweth where it will.' *Light Sleeper* turned out very well, and it's the film that strikes me most personally – I still get moved at the very end. The thing that I regret about it is that in the end I couldn't get out of the dramatic box I had made except by returning to a kind of violence-oriented action. Todd McCarthy in *Variety* made that point, and it's an accurate criticism. But I just couldn't think of another way to do it.

KJ: *The feeling was that it was just too much of a genre conclusion?*

PS: Yeah. It was too easy, too convenient. One of the problems with these character studies is that, because they're not terribly directional, they need some kind of an event to wrap them up, and often that event seems imposed, because you haven't been operating on a traditional dramatic structure anyway. When I did the existential hero theme again, in a more recent script called *The Walker*, I managed to put that kind of wrap-up action into the person of another character, so I didn't have to have my main character with a gun in his hand.

KJ: *This might be the place then to discuss* The Walker, *which you have written for yourself to direct and which you intend to be the fourth and final part of a loose tetralogy, completing the character studies of* Taxi Driver, American Gigolo, *and* Light Sleeper. *The script is a portrait of another existential loner, this time in his fifties – a reasonably wealthy, urbane gay man who escorts grand Washington ladies to public functions.*

PS: It's a variation on the *Gigolo* character, finding him 25 years later, just as *Light Sleeper* took the *Taxi Driver* character down the road. In *Light Sleeper*, you put the *Taxi Driver* character in the back seat, and in *The Walker* you take the gigolo out of the bedroom and put him in a social function: so that what that character is selling now is companionship, fun, laughter.

KJ: *What prompted you to address such a character?*

PS: I had the idea shortly after *Light Sleeper*. I started thinking, '*Light Sleeper* is this character in his forties, so who is he in his fifties?' And at the time there was a man called Jerry Zipkin, who was Nancy Reagan's walker – a larger-than-life guy, homosexual, very funny, with a nasty sense of humour. He would be photographed with Betsy

Bloomingdale and Jackie Onassis. It was the publisher of *W* magazine, John Fairchild, who first called Zipkin a 'walker', and that was
when the term started being used for a man who could escort well-
known women in public. Nancy Reagan wanted to go to social events,
whereas Reagan had no desire to go to the opening of the opera or
whatever. And Jerry was funny, and he and Nancy would have a great
time, and so would the other people in the circle. The fact that he was
homosexual made it all okay, because there was never any question of
there being an affair. So I thought, 'Well, that's who the gigolo would
become – Jerry Zipkin.'

KJ: *Do these 'walkers' actually get paid for their services?*
PS: No, they like it. There is a kind of lower-class version who does get
paid, but the kind I'm writing about are independently wealthy, or
they're art dealers, or they have antique shops. And mostly they're
gay.
    When I first had the idea, I felt I was too young to write it, and
certainly too young to make it: I wanted about ten years to go by. So I
just held the idea in the back of my head, and finally, after *Forever
Mine*, it occurred to me that I was old enough, so I wrote it in the
summer of 1999.

KJ: *We've talked a lot about how this existential character generally
has some kind of symbolic relationship to where you are in your own
life. Is that true again of* The Walker, *or is the relationship now more
distant?*
PS: A little more distant, I'd say. *The Walker* has this notion of a
deeply superficial man whose superficiality is put to the test by circumstances, and he has to decide exactly how superficial he is. But as
you get older in life, there's a powerful temptation to be superficial,
there's a desire not to ask Big Questions. Because if you do, you're
likely to get the Big Answer, and no-one wants to hear that big
answer. Because the Big Question is 'What does it all mean?' and the
Answer is 'Nothing!' If you can avoid asking the question, you don't
have to hear the answer. But what happens in the script is that people
turn on the 'walker', and that becomes the challenge. He takes a
position to protect a woman with whom he has no real emotional
relationship, and then others turn on him, and the question becomes:
does he keep on protecting her because it's the right thing to do, or
does he just act the way the others do? And by continuing to protect
her, he explodes his carefully manicured world.

KJ: *In* American Gigolo, *the world of politics is glimpsed briefly but is mainly off-screen; whereas in* The Walker *it seems to be a lot closer to the foreground of the plot.*

PS: The only reason for that is because you need to set it in a city where you can be ostracised when it becomes apparent that you're homosexual. And Washington D.C. is the last city in this country where that can happen, because it's a city that's built on professional and mandated hypocrisy.

KJ: *I was struck by resonances with the career of Oscar Wilde, who is quoted a few times in the script: the apparently lightweight, superficial man who is suddenly shunned and thrown to the wolves, and then unexpectedly shows the full extent of his courage and integrity. Were you thinking of Wilde's story?*

PS: Thinking of it, but trying not to get too on-the-nose about it. Also, Oscar Wilde is the patron saint of all these 'walker' characters. The line goes from Wilde to Noel Coward to Truman Capote to Gore Vidal.

KJ: *There's a strong sub-plot in the script about the walker living under the shadow of his father – the father being a man of some distinction, the walker having achieved nothing much except a gracious way of life.*

PS: He's third generation, and sort of sees himself as the Black Sheep of the family.

KJ: *Though somebody tells him that he's really only the Grey Sheep . . .*

PS: Right. His form of protest against his father and his grandfather is to become inconsequential. This happens in a lot of important families – Franklin Roosevelt's son, Nelson Rockefeller's son, and so on. And he sort of enjoys that scandalous aspect.

I'm very much hoping that *The Walker* will get made. I now see the film as the closing of a certain thing that I've done, and that I'm good at. It doesn't mean that I'll quit making films after *The Walker* – I'm sure interesting things will come up. But I want to get it right; I don't want to feel like Francis Coppola did after *Godfather III*. When Robert Duvall refused to be in the movie, so that there couldn't be the big, logical confrontation between Tom Hagen and Michael Corleone, something went out of Francis, and it was not the culminating work that he had meant to do. I would like *The Walker* to wrap up this character, this man who has his roots in the existential tradition, a loner who drifts around, peeps into other people's worlds looking to get a life for himself. Then I would like to call it a day with that existential hero. One more crack, and then I'd like to put him to bed . . .

Witch Hunt

KJ: *After* Light Sleeper, *your next two films as director both have a comic spin, even if they're not really mainstream comedies. First of all, how did* Witch Hunt *come about?*
PS: I was becoming increasingly frustrated with my inability to get films made. *Light Sleeper* was only made in desperation, at the last second. *Affliction* went on for years, I couldn't get it financed, and essentially, both *Witch Hunt* and *Touch* were reactions to my inability to get *Affliction* financed. With *Witch Hunt*, I was offered a job, and the notion of just making a film − of not having to talk actors into being in it and working for nothing and letting me use their name, and then going on for years trying to raise finance, and then finally making a film where you don't know whether or not it's going to get distribution . . .

KJ: *Just listening to that litany makes me feel weary . . .*
PS: Yeah, and it still goes on. So when you then get a phone call and somebody says, 'Do you want to direct something for HBO? . . . ' And the budget was $8 million, two and a half million more than *Light Sleeper*, with a lot of special effects; and I'd never really done special effects before, so there was a learning aspect to it. And I just wanted to relax into a movie.

  Witch Hunt was the second of a series written by a man called Joseph Dougherty, and the first one, *Cast a Deadly Spell*, I had thought was sort of cool. It had a Forties feel, Fred Ward had played this private detective character, Lovecraft, and now they wanted to do a Fifties version. Fred Ward had wanted to play the lead role again, but in my mind he was so identified with the sort of Philip Marlowe *film noir* character, and I wanted someone who was more identifiable with the Beat Generation, someone who had more of a hep-cat feel. So that's how we ended up going to Dennis Hopper.

52 *Witch Hunt* (1994): Dennis Hopper as H. Philip Lovecraft.

KJ: *But in other ways, Hopper is cast against type as Lovecraft – he tends to play the baddie, the psycho, whereas Lovecraft is not only a good guy, but a fairly uncomplicated, unreflective good guy.*

PS: Dennis does some very interesting roles – he was cast as a kind of nebbish schoolteacher in one movie. I think the reason that he plays psychos so often is that that's what they'll pay him most for. At a press conference in Cannes, he once said, 'When I look at myself in the mirror in the morning, I don't see a psycho, but other people look at me and *they* do.' So there's a kind of fate to one's physiognomy.

KJ: *The detective's name is obviously derived from the American horror writer H.P. Lovecraft, who wrote a whole series of stories outlining a private mythology about Dark Gods waiting to take possession of the world. Cast a Deadly Spell made quite a few direct references to this mythos, but yours dropped it entirely.*

PS: I have the feeling that Joseph Dougherty and the producer, Gale Ann Hurd, took it all a lot more seriously than I did. What I'd liked about the first film was the playfulness of it. With this one, I liked a lot of the visual gags. I didn't care for all that giant-monster stuff and I didn't know what it was doing in there. So I just went for all the playful elements, and moved away from anything too heavy.

KJ: *Visually, the film is very distinct from a lot of your previous work. It's very brightly lit, with lots of strong, saturated colours: Lovecraft's office is turquoise, there are lots of gleaming David Hockney pools, lipstick is very bright red.*

PS: We were trying to get what in the 1950s they called 'The New Look', like Eames furniture. Colour-wise, the idea was to try to emulate the saturated colours of the period: *Leave Her to Heaven*, basically. Jean-Yves Escoffier was the cinematographer, and he had been sort of run out of France because of his connection to Leos Carax – they had made two films together, *Mauvais Sang* and *Les Amants du Pont Neuf*, and apparently *Les Amants* was just a scandal.

KJ: *Yes, it was like the* Heaven's Gate *of France. It cost, and lost, a vast fortune by French movie standards.*

PS: And the film-makers, including Jean-Yves, were seen as arrogant. So he was having a hard time working in France, and started looking for work in the US. I had loved his work on *Mauvais Sang*, and that's why I hired him. The irony is that Jean-Yves has now become a big Hollywood name, but he's not known for the *Witch Hunt* look at all – he's known for movies like *The Crow* and *Rounders*, dark, sketchy, second-generation-stock kind of things, those are his hallmark. But when I hired him he was known for working with a specialist German system, Kino Flo, that could be entirely lit with fluorescent light. The problem in the past was that you couldn't go all fluorescent because of the different colour temperatures – it would always look too blue. Well, this German system solved that problem. You can actually make a film all fluorescent now, or mix fluorescent and tungsten light, which when I started directing you just couldn't do, you had to choose. One of the reasons cinematography is so fast these days is that they just drop these little fluorescent tubes all over the place. So we filmed *Witch Hunt* in Kino Flo, and that look was in conjunction with the wardrobe, the sets, the cars. I had the luxury of some building on that film: there were so many special effects that you had to have some control over the world you were creating.

KJ: *It would be wrong to talk about a light comedy too earnestly, but there are a couple of quite sparky ideas in the film: for instance, that Hollywood stars are literally, rather than just figuratively, magical in their appeal. So a movie star takes off her charm amulet and suddenly becomes more ordinary-looking.*

PS: Right. And the whole deadpan idea of 'getting Magic out of Hollywood' is a delightful conceit – the idea that in order to keep going in the business, create stars and so on, you have to bring in sorcerers and magicians. There were references to HUAC in the original script, but again they were a little more heavy-handed – a little more earnest, trying to make some points. Gale Ann Hurd was behind the idea of making the film into a criticism of conservative attacks on the media. But I just couldn't take it that seriously, and every time I had a chance in the directing, I would make it more and more of a joke. Like casting Eric Bogosian . . .

KJ: *A funny touch: when the conservative 'Witch-Hunter General' played by Bogosian splits down the middle, and an id-like monster crawls out of his skin, that monster turns out to be the loud-mouthed, obnoxious Eric Bogosian everyone knows from his stand-up act.*

PS: Yeah, I liked that casting. In the original script it was an actual monster, a prosthetic creature. I also liked the casting of Lypsinka, the drag artist, because in the script the part wasn't a transvestite, just a woman.

KJ: *In general, the film's special effects seem to be more witty than frightening: written words flying through the air, a performer shattering into musical notes and then re-forming as a jazz musician ...*
PS: And the girl with the expanding chest. It's all coming back to me now ...

KJ: *There are some nice throwaway jokes too, like the running gag about Shakespeare being summoned through time and put to service as a Hollywood screenwriter.*
PS: The Shakespeare gag was in the script, but again the tone became more and more tongue-in-cheek, more playful. The original script was – I may be wrong – a bit more serious. It became wittier in the making.

KJ: *How about the* Big Sleep *joke, about the Packard in the bay?*
PS: Oh, that I added; and the shoot-out at the drive-in where they're watching *The Big Combo*.

KJ: Witch Hunt *went straight to video in the UK. Did it have a theatrical release anywhere?*
PS: I don't think so. And it didn't do much business as a video in the US either. There was some talk of doing a third instalment – I think the script was written, set in the sixties. But it never happened. I'd hate to think that it was because mine didn't do well, but I suppose that's the essential reason. Also, there was change of regime at HBO: a change for the better, in some ways, but they weren't interested in pursuing the series. I thought *Witch Hunt* would be fun, and – even though I haven't looked at the film since – I remember it as being fun. But no-one's ever heard of it. On my last film, somebody on the crew had seen a mention of it on my filmography, and asked if he could see it. So I loaned him a copy and he came back and said, 'Well, that was a lot of fun. How come no-one knows about it?'

Touch

PS: I had wanted to do an Elmore Leonard project, a genre movie, for a long time. So I tried to get the rights to *Rum Punch* while it was still in galleys, way before Tarantino got hold of it to make *Jackie Brown*. This was before the *Get Shorty* craze too. But it turned out that a producer of the older Hollywood generation had already bought *Rum Punch*, and he didn't want me to direct – I wasn't commercial enough. So I sent out the word through my agent that I would love to get my hands on an Elmore Leonard project. And I got a call from an independent producer in LA who had the rights to *Touch*, asked me if I was interested, and I was, although I realised that it would be very hard to set up. So I just wrote the script on spec. I had no intention of doing anything either spiritual or funny, my intention was to do something hip, like *Rum Punch*. It just so happened that the Leonard book I was offered had both a religious element and a comic element. I wasn't that happy about fooling around with religion again – though it didn't bother me that much, either – but I didn't see it as trying to make a statement.

To jump ahead a little to the end of the story: *Touch* was the only Elmore Leonard novel that was not commercially successful. He wrote it at the time he was making the transition from westerns to urban crime drama, and then his crime novels started selling well, so he used his leverage with the publishers to get *Touch* published. What hurt the book was the idea of taking that kind of hustler/scuzzball humour of Elmore Leonard – two goons with guns walking around saying, 'Where's my money?' – and mixing it with stigmata. And it couldn't be overcome even in the film. While writing it, directing it, editing it, I thought that I'd solved it, but once I started screening it, the reaction was 'This is a comedy. What's that guy doing in there with the bloody hands?' Or 'If this is a film about stigmata, why are people telling all these dirty jokes?' You could tell people what it was – a dark comedy about a stigmatic – and on the cards you'd still see, 'I didn't get it, what kind of movie is this?' It just didn't fit into any category.

Now – I have to be honest – that's what I liked about the chance of making it. Over the years, I tend to have been sent scripts and books that no-one else wanted to touch. *Patty Hearst* came to me because nobody could figure out how to shoot it, and *Touch* came to me because no one could figure out how to mix religiosity and vulgar humour. But it never bothered me. And perhaps one of my career difficulties is that I don't weigh the consequences that heavily. If it seems like it might be fun to do, and I think I can pull it off, I do it. And then when it fails, all of a sudden you see the consequences. Because, more than ever, Hollywood is a box-score community, and if your batting average is down or you're having a rough season, that's really all they look at.

KJ: *A line in the film that really jumps out as being almost self-referential is when the Christopher Walken character, talking about how you spin a news story on television, says, 'It all depends on the tone.' And that seemed to be the central problem: how to get the appropriate tone.*

PS: Which includes the idea of casting Chris. I happen to think that Chris has a very nice, light comic side, but, as I was saying about Dennis Hopper, it's just not what people want to see. You run against the audience's preconceptions and you're taking a big chance. For example, that's what killed Altman's *Buffalo Bill and the Indians* commercially – Paul Newman as a self-deprecating buffoon. That's it. Boom. The audience says, 'This is not our Paul Newman.'

KJ: *Another way in which an actor's physiognomy can affect the viewer's response is in creating ambiguity about a character's good intentions. The fact that Skeet Ulrich wore a goatee and had a faintly feral look led me to assume that he was duplicitous. So it came as a surprise when he turns out to be an innocent.*

PS: I made a joke when I was doing *Touch*, that it was a sort of anti-*Last Temptation of Christ*. The Kazantsakis Christ took himself very, *very* seriously. The Elmore Leonard Christ-figure doesn't take himself seriously at all. Skeet's every instinct was to go for the Christ symbol, rather than an ordinary guy with bleeding hands, and I think that's true for the audience too – they want to make something of it. And what I like about the Leonard novel is that it *doesn't* make anything of it. Another point about casting is that in the book, August Murray, the character I had played by Tom Arnold, was a really obnoxious little prick. While I was trying to put the film together – I was with Miramax, but we fell out – I had asked Tim Robbins to play Murray. I eventually lost him, but while we were discussing the script he said that he thought that the character ought not to be evil but just a big kid, a big doofus. That idea stuck with me. So I thought, 'Who is the biggest kid in show business? Tom Arnold!' And again, that was kind of perverse, because you're taking the ostensible villain of the piece and making him into a comic figure. So the movie doesn't really have a bad guy.

KJ: *The film begins with a television set showing a talk show – a slightly farcical interview with L L Cool J, who storms out in a huff – which hints at the idea that there's going to be a strand of comedy about the crassness of popular reportage.*

53 *Touch* (1997): Bridget Fonda as Lynn Marie,
Skeet Ulrich as Juvenal.

PS: That's much stronger in the novel, and at the time the book was written, around the 1970s, it was a more original idea – the whole talk show phenomenon was just beginning. But by the time I came to make the film, it was such an old, tired idea that I had to downplay it like crazy. Those kinds of statements – 'Religion is show-business', 'Politics is show-business' – don't even get a rise out of people any more.

KJ: *On the whole, and despite some absurdities such as the giant crucifixes, religion is handled fairly sympathetically in the movie. Is that true of the novel?*
PS: The film is pretty faithful to the book. Elmore Leonard was very happy with it, he felt that it had captured the tone.

KJ: *The film is set in the present day, and yet there are occasional hints of the 1950s about it, for example in the theme music – the little bass riff which comes up every time you have a shot of Christopher Walken's feet – and the bright look, as if something had unconsciously bled over from* Witch Hunt.
PS: The riff was from David Grohl, formerly the drummer for Nirvana, now of the Foo Fighters. With the look, *Pulp Fiction* had already come out, and I thought that I would try to do that kind of pop-cult thing. In fact, David and Sandy Wasco, who did the production design, had also designed *Pulp Fiction*. So it was the same kind of non-serious, flippant colour scheme, not so much straight 1950s as Pop, which is of the 1960s too.

Affliction

KJ: *How long was the whole process of bringing* Affliction *to the screen?*
PS: I picked up Russell Banks' book, which had just come out in trade paperback, at my local bookshop, and the very first line grabbed me: 'This is the story of my older brother's criminal behaviour and strange disappearance.' I kept reading, and very quickly I realised that I would have to buy the rights. I finished the book that same night, started asking around, and the rights were available, so I optioned it – not for very much money, it was my own money – and then I had to keep going back to Russell over the years, to keep that option alive. I

wrote a script, and the first person I thought of was Nick Nolte, and I sent it to him very early on. I would say that by the end of 1991, early 1992, he responded favourably. And then the battles began . . .

KJ: *It was another six years before you finally got to shoot it?*
PS: Yeah. The problem was that Nick wanted to get his usual salary, which at that time was about five or six million dollars. And you always start out that way, because you hope that you'll get lucky, and you don't want to say to the actor right off the bat, 'There's no way we're going to pay you this.' After we got turned down at that level of financing, Nick said that he would take less, but it never worked out – whenever it came back to the lawyer or the agent, he never really was with me.

So this went on, year in, year out, and at one point Willem Dafoe wanted to play the lead, but I didn't think that Willem was right, simply because the character does such unpleasant things, and you need to have an actor who has a very audience-friendly persona and face, the kind of actor for whom you wish the best. Nick is that, and Willem is not. So the whole thing went on and on, and finally it became possible when both Nick and I left ICM. Then, Nick finally realised what it would take to get the film made, and once he accepted a lower salary it became possible to get the film financed – not easy, it was still hard as hell, but it was *possible*.

Throughout all that time, Nick carried the book around with him and kept working on the character. I went into his hotel room during the shoot and the wall was just covered with his notes. One day when we were shooting I offered him a different line reading: he didn't want to do it differently, and I suggested that he just try it. And then I realised that his decision to read the line a certain way had been made months, maybe even *years* before. This whole thing had been gestating in his head for years. And in rehearsals he was more or less co-directing, because he had such a fix on the character, and he had this book he had made up that worked out Wade's relationship to every other character over the years. That level of intense commitment is not so unusual in stage actors, but most movie actors don't do it. When you've watched the film as many times as I have, you see all the little things Nick's doing, with his hands, his face – and how he's letting you see the character make decisions, see his thought process. It's a heavy piece, and it's Nick's performance that carries the film, because you have a situation where the character is predestined – he's doomed. You know from the first line of the film that he will fail, and

54 *Affliction* (1997): Nick Nolte as Wade Whitehouse.

disappear. Yet, throughout it all, Nick manages to keep you sort of rooting for him. 'Come on, Wade! Just get it together, you'll be all right . . . '

KJ: *I remember meeting you and your then-producer Linda Reisman about once a year or so throughout that period, and every time it was the same story – 'We will get* Affliction *made, but . . . '*

PS: At one point, after about four or five years, I did officially give up. In fact – this is a Pauline Kael story – I was speaking to Pauline on the phone, and she said, 'You really sound blue, what's wrong?' And I said, 'Well, I've been trying to make this film with Nick Nolte for years, and as of today I've officially given up.' She asked me to send her the script and I did, and she called back four days later and said, 'It's all for the best. You shouldn't make this movie, who'd want to see it? You're lucky you're out of it!' But while I was making *Touch*, Linda finally managed to put the whole thing together. A company called Largo, which subsequently became defunct after making a lot of bad business decisions, put up the money. They had given Martin Sheen five million to be in a movie that was never released. And I'm sure that outsiders thought that making *Affliction* was another one of their bad decisions. They were financed by JVC, and they didn't really make any money on *Affliction* – they sold it off in a kind of fire sale. Alliance bought it for a million bucks, and they went on to make money.

But anyhow, after I made the film there was then a whole year between the editing and the time it was released. And during this year, I sent Pauline a copy on videotape, saying, 'This is the film you told me not to make. I made it anyway.' I never heard from her, and then the film finally was released, and it got very good reviews, and started winning awards, and I got a call from Pauline saying how wonderful the film was. And I don't know whether she had ever seen the tape, but it was a cherished vindication.

KJ: *What made you so tenacious about the project, throughout all the difficulties?*

PS: I just knew how to make it. It was sort of fully formed in my head, I didn't have any kind of hesitation or insecurity or reservation about it. I remember that in rehearsal, and in pre-production, people were saying, 'How are you gonna pull this off?' And I thought, 'What do you mean? There's no problem, I can do this, it's easy.' I had very little creative frustration or soul-searching while making it, I came home from work every day feeling we were right on track – none of those dreadful evenings when you fall into a black pit and you think it's not going to work and you have to re-examine some basic premises. None of that.

KJ: *Was Banks's novel one that went easily into a screenplay? Is it conceived in strongly visual terms?*
PS: It was fairly easy – a little long for a film, so there were a couple of sub-plots I had to take out, but apart from that it's a very faithful adaptation. It's ironic; there's a tendency in this business to work a thing to death, to keep a thing in development for a long time, or to keep re-editing. In some cases, that really works – the script of *Jerry Maguire* was being developed by Jim Brooks and Cameron Crowe for three, maybe four years, and the final script is a polished gem. But more often than not, these projects that have been laboured to death lose their vitality. If you can write scripts fast, and make them fast, sometimes that's perfect. *Affliction* was written fast, and eventually it was made fast, it's just that there were six years between the two. But no re-writing in those six years.

Initially, my real attraction to it, the thing I loved, was that it was a story pretending to be something else: sort of meandering around, leading you to believe that a murder mystery was afoot. And then, in the book and in the film, about two-thirds of the way through, you realise that there was no murder, and that this is a character study, and this man has gone crazy. And I love that gimmick of disguising the character study in what seems to be a murder mystery. I'm still surprised – because I've read enough and seen enough that when I see something I know what's going on – that a lot of viewers are utterly flummoxed when they realise that there's not going to be a solution to the murder. They don't understand that it doesn't matter whether it was a murder or an accident.

KJ: *The business of deer-hunting is obviously sociologically accurate, but it seems to chime with the idea of male humans as predators.*
PS: The whole notion of the kill . . . My favourite cut in the film is where you have this flashback of Wade's father beating him up, and then you cut to a restaurant exterior, and to shots of deer that have been killed, and Skeeter Davis is singing this old country song: 'I forgot more than you'll ever know about him . . . '

KJ: *One of the clear themes of* Affliction *is the grim, maybe even tragic notion of generation inevitably handing on violence to generation.*

PS: Yeah, that whole issue of male violence, those anachronistic genes, where we have all this stuff in our DNA that we really don't know what to do with any more, the need to go out and kill, and eat what we kill. These things that don't seem very useful, and yet we still have them. There's a book called *Demonic Males*, and I gave a copy of it to everybody on the film. Finally somebody had baseball caps made up that said '*Affliction*: The *Demonic Males* Tour.' There's that theme, and then you have the complexity of the narrative, pretending to be about a murder when in fact it's not. Then, underneath that, there's the notion of the storyteller – the burden of memory, the elusiveness of memory, and the fact that there's a hidden main character, the younger brother, played by Dafoe, who's slowly revealed to you. Russell Banks said to me at one point that the main character *is* the narrator. 'Why is this man telling me this tale, why is he unburdening himself to me?'

KJ: *Like the Ancient Mariner, with a story he's compelled to tell.*

PS: And you know he'll be telling it his whole life. As it begins, he says, 'In telling the story of my brother I am telling my own story as well.' But you don't see that much of him or his life. And at the end of the movie, he says, 'Why can't I let it go? Why can't I sell the house?' At one level you're watching the disintegration of a man, Wade, and his problems with male violence and his father. At another level, you're watching a movie about the younger brother, who's observing this situation, and has withdrawn from the conflict, and in fact envies his older brother for being on the frontlines. What tends to happen in an abusive family is that there will be a chosen sibling, chosen for violence; and in some way they protect the other siblings. Now, the reaction of the siblings is very conflicted. On the one hand, the younger brother is very grateful for the protection, but on the other hand he's jealous, because the older brother got the love – because in that scenario, love means this violent attention. In a line I added, James Coburn says to Nolte, 'Still standing up for your little brother?' Even though he mocks his son, he thinks he's a worthy combatant. The other brother doesn't even figure. And the sister, fuck her . . .

KJ: *Dafoe brings a kind of feminine quality to the role of the brother, very different from the tough-guy persona he's sometimes adopted.*

55 *Affliction*: Wade confronts his father (James Coburn).

It's as though he's renounced all the masculinity that his brother has in excess.

PS: Yeah. He describes himself as someone who's interested in books, interested in history – he's got out of that situation. The thematic exchange in the piece is when he says, 'At least I wasn't afflicted by that man's violence', and his brother says, 'That's what *you* think.' Just because he's gone to Boston and become a professor doesn't mean that he's escaped.

KJ: *Are there any echoes or resonances in the script about the relationship with your own brother?*
PS: You know, looking back, I think there have to be. Obviously, I have an older brother; I had a very strong father, and a lot of very, very negative feelings about my father. At some level, that's certainly what attracted me. But at the time, it was a kind of secondary attraction, or an attraction that I was in denial about. I always saw it as Russell's story, not my story, though I figured that I would be in there somewhere – you can't write, direct and edit a movie and take yourself out of the equation, you're going to be there. I just felt that if I was as faithful as I could be to Russell in capturing his voice, I would be in there somewhere.

KJ: *Did you talk to Banks about the extent to which the book is autobiographical?*
PS: It's the most autobiographical of his books, although I'm not quite sure whether it's about him and his father, or about his father and his grandfather. He came up to the set quite a bit, because he was very interested in seeing this visualised, and he told me a story. When he was writing the novel, he didn't quite know where to go at the end, and he said that he kept getting pulled back to the barn – something *must* have happened in that barn. So he called up his older brother, who lived in Utah, and said, 'Did anything ever happen in Grampa's barn?' And his brother said, 'Funny you ask, because I've been discussing this with my psychiatrist for over a year now.' They decided that they must have seen something in that barn when they were up in the hayloft, some childhood thing, and he was never able to recover the memory, but he thinks he maybe saw his grandfather beat up his father, something like that. 'So then', he said, 'I knew how to finish the book. I knew that I had to go back to the barn, go back to this primal scene, and burn it down.' And he really wanted to see that barn burn down – he came up to the set to watch it.

KJ: *That particular sequence of the barn burning stuck me as quite a feat of logistics, the Nolte character coming into frame at just the right moment. Presumably it was all done just once?*

PS: Just once. We had two cameras, one in the kitchen looking out at the barn – and we built the barn so that it would be right there in that sight line – and then a second camera on a remote crane. No one knew for sure how fast that barn would burn. Even though the place was full of gasoline, they told me it might take six or seven minutes to get into full flame. So I'm on the megaphone, and the idea was that we would torch the barn, Nick would walk into shot, wait until the fire was started, then I would cue him, he would come up and wait in the kitchen doorway until the fire got nice and hot, and then he would come into the kitchen. Well, they torched the thing and it just went up. So I'm on the megaphone, shouting, 'Run into the shot, Nick! Don't wait in the doorway!' I wasn't so concerned about Nick fucking up, or the barn fucking up – the barn's not my problem, and if Nick trips or something, well, he's an actor, he can carry that off. He's not going to look at the camera and say, 'Sorry', he's going to soldier it through whatever happens. No, what I was afraid of was panicking myself and giving the wrong instruction – for no reason at all, shouting 'Cut!'

KJ: *It's your first film set wholly in a rural environment. How did that feel?*

PS: I was raised in that sort of environment: those people are all like my relatives, I know them. So I didn't feel at a loss. Visually, you have that white tableau, there's no green in the movie, not a piece of dirt, not a blade of grass, and I wanted a continuity of snow. That's why we ended up in Canada, because I was afraid we would have a mild winter in the United States, which in fact we did. But up in Montreal we had a nice, strong winter, I got all the snow I wanted, and it was a very cold shoot. What I hadn't quite realised when I wrote the script was exactly how much of it was set outdoors. One day we were out at the barn with Willem and Nick and we were freezing cold and I said, 'What was I thinking when I wrote this? They could have this conversation in the house, where it's warm!' But I liked the idea of a very hostile environment – and this is a story which would not take place in quite the same way in a Mediterranean environment – with people who have to struggle just to go about their day-to-day business, and the caves they live in: the hostile, white, frozen world. We worked to do a lot of the lighting, particularly at the farmhouse, from the outside in, so that you had dark interiors. Preparing the film, I looked at a lot of films that had snow scenes – to see how you deal with all that whiteness, all that bounce light.

KJ: *How did you shoot the flashback scenes with James Coburn as a young father, which look a little like a demented home movie? Different film stock?*
PS: No, same stock. It was shot in 16mm, over-exposed two stops, and then projected onto a screen, re-shot – again, over-exposing – and zooming in and out while you're re-shooting. You're trying to simulate a memory – it's not really a home movie, because there's sound, but you're trying to replicate a memory which may or may not be true.

KJ: *Because the brother is an unreliable narrator?*
PS: Even more so in the novel than the film, because you don't actually see events. Banks does things in the novel I couldn't do in the film. He describes quite literally Jack shooting the hunter. Later, you realise that it didn't happen. I had to reduce that to a kind of black and white conspiracy theory, otherwise the audience would be confused.

KJ: *Was that amazing scene when Nolte tears out his tooth in the book?*
PS: Yes. In the book, you think the tooth is the affliction, but it turns out that the affliction is the father.

KJ: *The film has an unusual opening: like a sequence of stills of the town, each with an aspect ratio contained inside the larger frame.*
PS: Yes, within an anamorphic aspect ratio. So many films open that way, and still don't create any tone. But by isolating the images, you get a sense of this frozen little world, and then you come out from the image, and the movie begins. They're not stills, but they look like they are, just because there are no cars or people in them.

KJ: *You chose Paul Sarossy as your cinematographer.*
PS: He also shot *The Sweet Hereafter* for Atom Egoyan, so he went straight from one Russell Banks movie to another. I said to him, 'Paul, is this going to look like *Sweet Hereafter*?' And he said, 'No.' I said, 'Okay, let's never mention *Sweet Hereafter* again, I don't want to get into any kind of pissing contest with Atom Egoyan about who has the best Russell Banks movie.' Actually, I like Atom's film and he likes

mine. His has the same kind of small-town world, only it's kind of an intellectual overview of the town and the social unit, how the town interacts; whereas *Affliction* just burrows into one family.

KJ: *James Coburn had been away from movies for quite a while when you cast him.*
PS: He'd had a lot of health problems – you can see those arthritic hands he had. He had the same thing in his knees, and he couldn't walk for a while. But I needed a tall, powerful American actor, someone physically larger than Nick, and Nick's a big guy. Also, an actor who would agree to be a bad guy. And what I found in Coburn that was so interesting was that, even though he and Nick are only fifteen years apart, they do represent two generations of Hollywood males. Coburn is of that fifties generation, where men were men and women were babes, and Nick is of that sixties generation, where men are partners, and they're asking themselves, 'What do I do with this woman?' Also they're different types of male movie icons. In Coburn, what you got was a sense of that earlier generation of Hollywood hero, someone who wasn't into sensitivity training. Nick is very into the whole idea of the 'feminine side'.

KJ: *Were you surprised by the two Oscar nominations for Nolte and Coburn?*
PS: I was, because one doesn't really expect justice in the world of awards. I felt that Nolte's nomination was completely earned, that he had given the best performance of the year. I didn't feel that so much about Coburn, I thought that was more a special pleading kind of thing. But I think that a lot of people in Hollywood woke up about a month after the Oscars and said, 'What did we do? We gave it to that Italian? What were we smoking. . . .?'

Forever Mine

KJ: *There was an even longer interval between the writing and the shooting of* Forever Mine *than* Affliction. *You wrote it in the late eighties, and almost got it going in about 1989?*
PS: Yes. I'd written it for Alan Ladd at MGM, but it didn't work out there, then it was sold to Columbia and I was going to make it with Patrick Swayze. This was right after *Ghost*. I had some doubts about

whether Patrick could pull off the double role, but he believed he could do it, Columbia wanted to do it with him, and I wanted to make a studio film. Then the studio production head called me in and said, 'Look, Patrick is having second thoughts about doing *Forever Mine*, but if you go up to his ranch, I think you can talk him back into it.' And I said, 'I think the reason he's having second thoughts is that he's realised he can't pull it off, and the only thing that made me think he could pull it off was that *he* thought he could. Now that he doesn't think he can, *I* don't think he can, and I'm not going up to try to convince him to do something that neither of us thinks he can do.' It was right at this time, when all this was collapsing, that I got the phone call from Jeff Berg at ICM saying, 'Do you want to make a film in Italy?' So I took off, and let it collapse.

Time went on, and I was in Montreal, making *Affliction*, and somebody said to me, 'Do you have anything you'd like to make?' So I said, 'Well, I wrote this real retro, melodramatic kind of love story, and I've always wanted to make an old-fashioned love story.' So this person introduced me to a young Sri Lankan man, Damita Nikopota, who read *Forever Mine* and said, 'I can raise the money.' Damita had been in the legal and distribution and promotional side of films in London, and at one time had a job at Dreamworks, but basically he was just one of those people who was into inventing himself, and had a lot of connections in London. Sure enough, over the next year and a half he got the film financed.

My thinking before making it was that everything had got so deconstructed and hip and referential that it would be fun to make a film that was completely old-fashioned, that harked back to the Douglas Sirk kind of sensibility. The initial reaction to the film was that that idea was better as a premise than a reality. We showed the film around, and we got two distribution offers which were very low. The company that financed it was fighting to survive, and they thought that if they accepted one of those low offers it would expose their situation to the bankers, so they refused. They preferred to keep it on the shelf, let it die, than have to make that sale. It was a situation very similar to the one I had with *Affliction*. Eventually the company couldn't maintain the deception any longer, the banks and insurers were on to the fact that something was wrong and so they moved in to protect their interests, and the movie was sold to a cable channel.

Obviously, I liked the film enormously when it was finished, but when other people fail to respond, you start to second-guess: maybe you miscalculated. Of course, I went through the same thing with *Affliction*. We showed it at Venice, where you'd think that it would have a good reception; but no, nothing. *Affliction* was on the shelf for a year before it took on a life of its own, and that's a very rare thing to happen.

KJ: *One of the things that surprises me about the lukewarm reception of* Forever Mine *is that it's such a handsome-looking film, incredibly lavish and glowing, right from the opening shot of an amazing building in St Petersburg, Florida.*
PS: The budget was $17 million, and I brought back John Bailey as cinematographer. John is now one of *the* Hollywood cinematographers, he gives your film that big Hollywood look. I hadn't worked with him since *Light of Day*, but I ran into him and he said that he'd be willing to work for less than his usual fee. But that's a two-edged thing: just because a cinematographer says he will work for less doesn't necessarily mean you should hire him, because if you don't have the budget to let him do what he does well, then you're worse off than if you have someone who works on lower budgets. It's a matter of time, and of equipment. Dante Spinotti, who is one of the world's great cinematographers, is also one of the most expensive cinematographers. He worked on *The Comfort of Strangers*, and he received an Oscar nomination for *The Insider*. Mary Beth, my wife, was in Los Angeles when Dante was shooting *The Family Man* with Nic Cage, and he came up and said, 'I would love to work with Paul again. Tell him it's not a matter of money.' But I said to Mary Beth, 'It *is* a matter of money. Because even if Dante worked for nothing, if I don't have the budget to support his machinery, why am I hiring him?' With the budget for *Forever Mine*, there wasn't a lot of money by John's standards, but it was just about enough.

KJ: *Why did you go for Joseph Fiennes as lead?*
PS: Well, it's a double role, very hard: two performances, one of which is very natural, the other very theatrical. So it's like being Leonardo DiCaprio in *Titanic* and Pacino in *Carlito's Way* in the same movie. When you start looking at actors in their twenties who not only are handsome but also can work in those two different styles, you end up with a very short list. I was after Johnny Depp for about a year – he could have done it. I had seen twenty minutes of Joe's work in *Shakespeare in Love* before it came out, and the film had a buzz already, so that helped.

56 *Forever Mine* (1999): Joseph Fiennes as Alan, Gretchen Mol as Ella.

KJ: *When we discussed the screenplay in the first edition of this book, we talked about the Dante and Beatrice theme, but watching the film it struck me that the idea of the hero coming back in a new form is a bit like a role-reversed version of* Vertigo.

PS: It's really more all that nineteenth-century schmaltz: the formerly-thought-dead lover comes back in altered form, that Count of Monte Cristo/Heathcliff thing. I was trying to tap into that old sense of melodrama, with very lush visuals, and make a retro movie.

KJ: *Why the particular time frame – 1973 for the original story, 1987 for the return?*

PS: Because this character, Esquema, has connections with the drug underworld and with the supplying of the Contras – Ollie North was working out the triangle of guns-for-drugs that would keep US fingerprints off the guns that were going to the Contras. That is the element of plausibility, to explain how he can have that kind of power, because that's not going on right now. I also thought that to set it in an identifiable past was a good idea, because otherwise it's such a fairy tale. But one of the problems I had in screening the film was that, even though it's a fairy tale, people were still full of questions, like 'How did he survive?' Even in a fairy tale, you have to fight all those credibility issues.

KJ: *The film has an epigraph from Walter Pater: 'It is the addition of strangeness to beauty that constitutes the Romantic character in Art.'*

PS: I don't know why I put that up. I'm so torn about this film, because in a way I want it to be brainless romantic entertainment, but I'm not a brainless romantic person, so it's not what comes naturally to me. *Affliction* is what comes naturally to me – that is the simplest thing in the world, to make that work. But to make a brainless romance . . . *that's* a challenge.

Auto Focus (2002)

KJ: *One of the most striking things about* Auto Focus *– a bio-pic about a minor actor called Bob Crane, who's remembered, if at all, as the lead in the sitcom* Hogan's Heroes *– is that it's about the sort of unreflective, shallow character who, if you met him in real life, would seem silly and boring. And yet watching him on screen is morbidly*

57 Schrader on the set of *Forever Mine*.

fascinating. How do you go about the process of making a schmuck interesting?

PS: This is a character not unlike characters I've done before, who have a disconnect in their lives, who want one thing but do another, see themselves as one thing but behave in a counter-productive way. And out of that disconnectedness comes an obsession, whether it is homicidal, or a conspiracy theory as in *Affliction*. Bob Crane had this very fundamental disconnectedness, which is that he saw himself as a very likeable, normal, one-woman, family kind of guy, but behaved in another fashion. The challenge in making the film is that, when I've done these characters before, they usually have some degree of introspection and a clouded sense of self-awareness, in that they're trying to figure out why it doesn't work, why they can't get what they want, why they can't be what they think they are. In *Auto Focus* I wanted to do a similar study about a superficial man, who was absolutely clueless from start to finish: but how do you do a film about a superficial man without making a superficial film? So the whole concept of the era and the times comes into play a little more prominently than it would in another character study, because we have to see him in the prism of that environment.

KJ: *The Bob Crane character is a completely uncritical participant in slightly corny, would-be cool notions of what the 'good life' might be.*
PS: Right. Incidentally, I feel I should have received credit for that script. When I first got it, it was a rather conventional biopic – Crane did this, then he did that, and the character of John Carpenter was much more minor. I introduced the device of the narration, so that I could just jump around more and do the stuff that interested me, and not worry too much about the connective tissue. And also to get inside the head of somebody who is clueless, so that you hear him think, and you know that the reason you're not getting a deep portrait is that there's no deep portrait *there* – there are no dark nights of the soul in the Crane household. It was suggested to me that I re-write the final narration, in such a way that you get some perspective on the subject. And when I did that in *Affliction*, of course, I had an outside narrator who could put some perspective on it, even though not necessarily the right perspective. But here, I said, 'Look, we have a guy who's clueless his whole fucking life, and just because he's dead doesn't mean that he gets it. He's still out there, saying, "Well, Bob Crane was a nice guy, a cool guy, in his way, and that's the way it is! Men gotta have fun!" '

KJ: *How did the project come to you?*

PS: A company called Propaganda, who specialised in music videos and advertisements, owned the project and approached me. Then Propaganda went bankrupt about four weeks before we started shooting. An announcement came over the intercom one day telling all of us that we had one hour to leave the office. Then we were allowed back in the next morning to get our stuff, and there were no security guards there. So at ten o' clock in the morning, the first computer walked out. By noon, the office was pretty much stripped clean of chairs, furniture, everything: because nobody had been paid for two weeks, and they hadn't had health insurance for four weeks, and they were pissed. But fortunately for me, Propaganda had been so broke that they hadn't paid anybody anything, not a single dollar had changed hands, so over that weekend we rewrote all the contracts, taking Propaganda's name out, and paid everybody something, even if it was only a dollar. So that the bank, when they assumed Propaganda's assets, was quite upset when they realised that *Auto Focus* was not among those assets. If they had paid, say, $100 for that script, the movie could never have been made, because all the profits would have gone straight to the bank, and there's no way that Sony Classics – who came forward next – would have financed the movie under those conditions. But Michael Barker and Tom Bernard, who I'd known for many, many years, came up, and they had some money in their pockets because of the success of *Crouching Tiger, Hidden Dragon*. This was the biggest film that they'd fully financed so far – $7.5 million. And Michael Barker said to me 'This is our *Lawrence of Arabia* and you're our David Lean!' On 32 days of shooting . . .

But it turned out very well, it had some great reviews, and everyone was pleased with it. There were a lot of problems behind the camera – eight producers, none of whom had ever produced a movie before, a lot of double-dealing and general inexperience in the making of it, and I was thrown into being a ghost production manager a lot of the time to get the thing going. But in front of the camera, I had two strong horses, cast right on the mark, and they got along terrifically. I brought in Willem Dafoe not only because he was right for the role and because he's my friend and because he agreed to work for a low salary, but also just to have somebody who would give Greg Kinnear the confidence to go into these waters.

Greg had been approached before I got the script, but he hadn't committed, and someone said to me, 'What do you think about Greg

Kinnear for this role?' I thought, 'That is a *great* idea, because he's very, very good at what I'm not good at, which is light comedy.' And that's not easy. An actor can't just decide to do that, you have to have those skills. I thought, 'Greg is real good in the shallow end, and I'm pretty good in the deep end, so we'll protect each other in our respective ends and this might just work.' Whereas if I'd cast an actor who was more experienced in the deep end, like John Cusack, you wouldn't have gotten this kind of totally, flip, glib, shallow protagonist. He had to be really charming, funny, personable on screen. Otherwise, why take this journey with him?

Greg began, like Bob Crane, as a disc jockey, and then he had a TV show called *Talk Soup* which was a kind of ironic, flip thing. Then he got his big break when Sidney Pollack cast him in the William Holden role in the remake of *Sabrina*. And then he got to playing light, romantic comedy, and was becoming more and more trapped into what I call the Ralph Bellamy role – the good guy who doesn't get the girl. So it was very important for him to try to smash that mould. And in his head he knew he had to do it, but in his heart he was very reluctant, so it was important for me and Willem to be able to give him confidence, to say to him, 'You can do this. Even though you have no real experience, no template for it, it will work.'

KJ: *At the level of style, the film is very sharp and witty, with lots of visual play, lots of inventiveness – dialogues shot in extreme close-up, lots of hand-held camera, fantasy sequences: very much a mixture of tones, very mongrel.*

PS: Well, it does work on a consistent curve. That idea came when the production designer said to me that he thought that, as the movie went along, there should be an accretion of clutter: moving from the clean 1950s all-American house to the jumble of video-cables in the 1970s. So I took that idea and spread it through the whole spectrum of the film – through film-stock, colour saturation, camera work, make-up, hair, wardrobe, music. It all slowly degrades. It starts as a very richly-coloured, static, conventional kind of movie, and then it moves into this really ugly area. My thought was that Crane was like any other addict: an addict wakes up one morning and says, 'I used to have a family, I used to have friends, I used to have a job, I used to have respect. And now all I've got is this bottle, or this needle. What happened to my former life? What happened to that big Technicolor movie that I used to be in? Now I'm in this grungy little low-budget movie.' The same thing happens to Bob Crane. He ends up in a

58 *Auto Focus* (2002): Willem Dafoe as John Carpenter,
Greg Kinnear as Bob Crane.

different movie. And at some point – it comes at different points for different viewers – but the audience start to realise that they're watching a different movie. It's very clear at the end that this is not the same movie you started watching an hour and a half ago.

KJ: *Where did the title come from?*
PS: It was on the original script, and I thought it was a good title. There is a pun in terms of the camera device, but auto-focus had not been developed before Bob Crane died. So it really refers to self-absorption, like 'auto-eroticism'. Because Crane's sin, if it's right to call it a sin, was not too much sex, but too much selfishness: just not understanding the consequences of his behaviour for others, thinking that he can do whatever he wants without paying for it.

KJ: *Self-deceit is one of the very oldest comic devices – the guy who doesn't know how pompous he is, or what a jerk he is. And in this case, someone who's persuaded that he's a clean-cut, regular guy –*
PS: 'I'm normal! Sex is normal! Don't be so square!'

KJ: *This is the first of your films since* American Gigolo *where you've contributed some song lyrics.*
PS: I'd originally wanted a Sammy Davis Jr. song for the opening credits, 'A Lot of Livin' to Do', but it was $65,000, and we couldn't afford it, so I said to Angelo Badelamenti, 'I know a writer who works cheap', and he said, 'I know a *composer* who works cheap.' So we did that song and got David Johansen – or Buster Poindexter as he's known – to sing it: 'A little rang-dang-doodle turns a pit-bull to a poodle / A little hanky-panky gives the boot (*boom!*) / To Mr. Cranky.'

KJ: *I haven't seen* Hogan's Heroes *for decades, but my memory is that it was pretty feeble comedy.*
PS: It ran in the late sixties, something like 1965 to 1971, and of course I was in college at that time and involved in the whole counter-culture thing. So I regarded the show as somewhere between offensive and unfunny, and I had no particular fond or nostalgic memories of it.

KJ: *You do have a couple of scenes which acknowledge that some people, especially those who'd heard the rumour that it was set in a concentration camp rather than a POW camp, were very strongly offended by the idea of a show about 'funny Nazis'.*

PS: That was an element that was much more played up in the original script. One of the things that I regret about the film, although it probably would have hurt its commercial life, was that, in the script I was given, there was a really strong narrative curve which basically said: Hollywood makes Good Bob go Bad. I don't believe Hollywood makes *anyone* go bad. I think bad people come to Hollywood in order to be bad. And I don't think people change that much, anyway. I think Crane was the same creepy guy at the beginning as he was at the end, and that the only thing that really changed in his life was the level of hypocrisy. When he was in TV, he really played the role of the hypocrite to the hilt, doing all sorts of *Photoplay* spreads of the all-American dad, and all that, and of course on *Hogan's Heroes* he had minders from CBS who made sure that his private life was kept private. Greg and I, when we were doing publicity, ran into an actress from the show, Shirley Jones, and Greg asked, 'Did you know what Crane's private life was really like?' And she said, 'Well, you know, you heard stories, but nobody really liked to talk about it back then.' It was like with Jack Kennedy – there were stories, but no one talked about it. Today, of course, it's just the opposite. People make up the stories. But the level of hypocrisy fell when the show ended, Crane's marriage ended, and the sexual revolution kicked in.

As I say, the original script had that whole element of 'he was a good guy who went bad'. Unfortunately, Greg had completely bought into that, and that was one of his motivations for playing the role, that was his character arc. And I toned it down as much as I could, but I still find that he's too good at the beginning. I just don't believe that he was ever like that.

KJ: *But what's curious, and gives the performance a richness, is that Kinnear himself does have a fairly likeable on-screen quality.*
PS: Oh, but Crane himself was likeable. That's what he was. I mean, he was a hip, flip, disc jockey, ironic, all that. He could be really charming, and obviously that's how, with a mixture of that charm and fame, he procured a whole cavalcade of women.

KJ: *Presumably you must have thought quite a bit about what makes a man be driven to want so much sex of a quasi-onanistic kind?*
PS: Any addiction is a displacement of some sort. Obviously, he's running from something. After researching into his background, I sort of figured out what it was, which is not really in the movie – there's only one brief reference to it. He had an older brother named

Albert, same name as his father, who was a real war hero. His ship was hit and he got burned, and all his life after that, Bob's older brother was a drunk and a layabout, but Bob's father still respected the older brother more. And Bob, who was the good son, who was the successful son, I don't think he ever felt he had respect from his father. I had a scene earlier in the film with him and his wife Anne where he refers to his brother being a drunk and how he has to help him out, but I cut that out because Good Bob was just so boring. I had to make a decision in rewriting it whether to get into that back-story, and two things kept me away from it. One, I had so many other things running – I had the Carpenter thing, I had the wives, I had the TV show, I had the whole sexual arc. And then to get into his family, his brother, his father – I didn't know how to squeeze all that in. Carpenter is really the co-star, it's really the story of Bob and John, the Lone Ranger and Tonto. Two, I've always liked characters that more or less present themselves, and you have to figure out the background for yourself. And that's frustrating for many people in the audience – they don't like to have to do that work for themselves, they like the answer put out there.

KJ: *It's curious that a film which ends in murder and is about degradation and downfall and loss is pretty light-hearted for much of the time, and fun to watch.*
PS: Oh yeah. I thought it was a hoot. There were a number of days when I was standing behind the camera biting my lips so I wouldn't start laughing. When the two of them, Crane and Carpenter are sitting there jerking off together, and complaining: 'What is it about women? Can't live with them, can't live without them . . . ' Both banal guys, talking American man-talk . . .

KJ: *How true to life is the film's portrait of a strong, obviously gay bond between Carpenter and Crane?*
PS: Well, Bob would have been very offended had anyone suggested he was gay. Carpenter, on the other hand, was openly bi. And they did get into swinging scenes. I remember Greg Kinnear said to me, 'I just don't think that Crane was homosexual.' And I said, 'Well, maybe he wasn't, Greg, but, you know, he hung around with Carpenter more or less for twelve years; his son said that Carpenter was his father's only friend; they filmed each other having sex; they watched each other having sex on screen; they went to swingers' parties together; they jerked off together . . . I mean, this may not exactly be gay, but tell

me, Greg, what *is* it?' But Greg really didn't feel that Bob was gay, and he was quite right to hold that position as an actor – he couldn't go there as an actor, it would be wrong.

KJ: *There are a lot of jokes in the film about the ways in which Crane and Carpenter are more erotically aroused by technological reproductions of sex than by sex itself. And if this were the 1970s, I'd probably have spent the whole interview asking you about that alone.*

PS: In Crane's case, it wasn't just Don Juanism, womanising – part of the addiction had to do with the cataloguing and the technology. As a young father, he would keep records of the scores of all the competitive games his children had played – he was a compulsive record-keeper. His sons told me that he felt that the collecting of sex was as much a turn-on as the sex itself. One interviewer said to me after the movie was released, 'The truest thing about your movie is that, for men, it's not the women, it's the gadgets.' That goes along with the whole *Playboy* mentality.

KJ: *And also with another strand of jokes in the film, about how technology has moved so swiftly that the cutting-edge gadget soon becomes a clunky dinosaur. I enjoyed the joke in the scene where you see really low-grade video footage of Crane getting a blow-job, but the explicit details are veiled by modern-day pixillation.*

PS: It was one of the things I had to do to get an R-certificate. Another was that . . . well, the ratings board in the US is very big on this concept of 'thrusting'. Apparently, about two and a half thrusts are all that you can expect to get. But it's kind of negotiable. So I said to the ratings board, 'What are the most thrusts there have ever been in a movie?' And they said, 'Thirteen, but that was in *End of the Affair*, and the woman was dying and they were Catholics and it was under the sheets.' So I had a scene where I had two taboos working at the same time: rear entry, which is another one of their taboos, and also thrusting. They originally wanted me to cut that out, and I didn't want to – it was so important in terms of the relationship between the two men. So I thought, 'What if I just do it as freeze-frames? Then there won't be any thrusting.' It took two months to pass through the ratings board, we went back five times until I brought in the freeze-frame version and they said that was okay. And it also lends itself to the whole cartoonish feeling. I also remember that when the ratings board told me that rear entry was taboo, I said, 'Well, I just saw two films where there's rear entry.' Two scenes in *Monster's Ball*, and another one in *Faithless*, and in those films it's about empty souls having perfunctory sex, and in my film it's about having a good time. So I said to the board, 'Is the problem that it's rear entry, or that he's enjoying it?' And they said, 'We're not even going to answer that question.'

Exorcist: The Beginning

PS: The *Exorcist* prequel had been in development with a company called Morgan Creek, which owned the rights to the *Exorcist* franchise. It had been a script that was just sitting there – the original writer was William Wisher, and Caleb Carr had re-written it. When the re-release of the original *Exorcist* was so successful, they decided to put this on the boards, and they signed up John Frankenheimer as director and Liam Neeson as lead. They were supposed to start shooting in September 2002, and then John got sick, and eventually died. There was a man from the production end of Morgan Creek who was a mentor to my agent, my agent suggested me as a replacement, and eventually they hired me.

KJ: *Did the positive critical buzz around* Auto Focus *play any part?*
PS: Well, that was happening right at the time, so it certainly helped. Another thing that helped was that I had done *Cat People*. This was my first so-called 'studio film' for twenty years, so it was a good thing that I was seen to have worked in the horror genre before. Morgan Creek films, even though they release through Warner Brothers, are solely financed, and prints and advertising are all paid for by one man, named Jim Robinson, so it's really his sandbox – he makes the decisions, and he hired me. I don't think Warner Brothers would have hired me to direct a $40-plus million film. Then Liam got cold feet, for a series of reasons. One is that he was always uncomfortable with what is essentially a passive character, because by instinct he always plays more active characters. Also he was thrown by Frankenheimer's death, and thrown by the commercial failure of a film he did called *K-19*, and I think he was just reassessing it all and decided to do a comedy in England instead. So we had to quickly decide to go forward and get another actor. I had met Stellan Skarsgard in Telluride several years ago when he was the honouree, and I was a big fan of his work. He also had all the same physical equipment that Liam has,

the kind of four-square, solid sort of guy, on top of which, he was Swedish, and would be playing the Max von Sydow character. But most importantly, he was very, very comfortable with going interior, in the same way that Liam is comfortable with going exterior. That's the kind of actor I like best anyway, so I was not at all displeased when that switch occurred.

The irony is that Warner Brothers will now be releasing, in a major way, a big-budget movie directed by me and starring Stellan, which I don't think that anyone would have approved of going in.

KJ: *But the original* Exorcist *wasn't really carried by a cast of big American stars, either. Ellen Burstyn was about the biggest box-office name they had.*

PS: That was a big argument that William Friedkin had, and won. Warner's wanted Jane Fonda, and Jane Fonda wanted the role, and she was a big star at the time. But Friedkin was very correct in insisting that, though the character of the mother was supposed to be a movie star herself, she had to be more like the woman who lives next door, and that the star of the movie had to be the subject, not the actors. It was a battle worth winning. In the same way here, Stellan is not a big international star, but I had the *Exorcist*, I didn't need any more names, and I think it would have been wrong to load the cast with names.

KJ: *Why do you think the first* Exorcist *film made the colossal impact that it did?*

PS: It created a new genre. The same thing was true of the book, which was a huge best-seller. That genre has spawned many, many imitations, as well as sequels, as well as parodies – and part of my challenge was to deal not only with the original but with all of those. I'm sure that there are many directors who wouldn't have done this simply for that reason – 'Why take it on?' But I felt that I could somehow make this my own.

KJ: *How much of the basic form of the film you're shooting was there in the script you were handed? The African setting, the* Sophie's Choice-*style prelude in Holland at the end of the Second World War, and so on?*

PS: That was all there. The only really major changes I made were to the end. The script ended up in almost ten pages of dialectic, a conversation between Farther Merrin and . . . well, in Caleb's script it was actually Satan himself, rather than a demon. And it was a long, and what I considered sophomoric and untenable, discussion about evil. There had been a movie called *End of Days*, where Gabriel Byrne plays the Devil, and he has a four-page scene with Schwarzenegger where he explains his position. Gabriel Byrne is a very good actor, and he gives a terrific performance, but half-way through, you're thinking, 'This is such a confusing and contradictory thicket, the more you try to explain it, the worse it gets.' So I said to myself, 'If Gabriel Byrne can't pull off that kind of thing, who can?' And I resorted to Merrin calling on all the forces that have ever been – all the angels, all the saints, this endless litany – and then spreading the evil all through the area, because the demon that he is exorcising is not a scared girl strapped to a bed, but a kind of glorified Presence. You don't have the simplicity of the original metaphor, which is, 'We've got to get the Devil out of this poor girl.' You've got to get the Devil out of this area.

KJ: *1947 was a very interesting moment for Africa in any case – the withdrawal of the British, the beginnings of nationalism.*
PS: And then Lake Takana is where the Leakeys found the remains of the earliest humans. I think that was Caleb's idea.

KJ: *There's something of a Zulu sub-plot in the film, too – the British army facing African warriors. Was that also part of Caleb Carr's draft?*
PS: Yes. There was actually a bit more of that, I toned it down – all the ugga-bugga stuff. And I added a scene where an African doctor comes in from Nairobi, because I thought we've got to have at least one educated black guy in a suit.

KJ: *There are some interesting casting choices. I'd never even heard of Billy Joe Crawford, who plays the outcast, disabled boy character, Che Che. He's some kind of pop star?*
PS: Primarily in France, where he's a big club star. Frankenheimer did an extensive casting search to find someone who had that unique kind of multi-ethnic look that you couldn't pin down, and Billy is half-Filipino, half-Anglo-American. I thought that he was a good choice, and they had already cast Gabriel Mann, whom I also thought was a good choice, as the younger priest, Father Francis. For the part of Rachel, the female doctor, Frankenheimer had wanted a French actress, Alexandra Martinez, who's Claude Chabrol's wife, but

59 *Exorcist: The Beginning* (2004): Stellan Skarsgard as Merrin,
Gabriel Mann as Francis.

Morgan Creek wasn't happy with that choice. But Frankenheimer was right in thinking that it shouldn't be an American actress: the role is a European woman who's been in the concentration camps, and it's better to have someone you haven't seen before, and who has that accent by nature, like Clara Bellar.

KJ: *Part of the logic of the film is that it has to take Christian theology and demonology seriously, or else there's no real story. And I wondered how far that connects, if at all, with your own deep background? Does it confront the kind of issues about supernatural evil that you might take seriously, or is it just part of the franchise machinery?*

PS: More the latter. Although, as I was working with Stellan, and getting more and more into this question of unresolved religious issues, that part of me was very much in there. The position that the film takes is essentially that, at the beginning, Merrin thought the church was a good strong building, and he was protected by it. Then the building collapsed, for him. And at the end he realises that it's more like a kind of leaky hut, but it's still better than the alternative, so he decides to go back inside the leaky hut.

One thing I knew I could bring to it is that I know how to make these passive characters interesting. The template for the movie is *Shane*. I mean, it's about the retired gunslinger who is trying to have another vocation, until things finally get so bad that only he can strap on the guns and save the town. That is essentially Merrin's situation here.

KJ: *At one point in the screenplay, Merrin is said to have a book of Auden's poems by his side – just as you do now as we talk. Your idea?*
PS: Yes. I thought, 'He can't have a Bible by his bedside, so where do you go? What's the next step down?' In 1947, Auden is about where Merrin is in terms of Christianity.

KJ: *One of the problems with any supernatural movie is that audiences are now so knowing that it's hard to spook them rather than make them laugh. It's a very long time in this script before anything definitely supernatural happens.*
PS: And the evil that occurs is predominantly just exaggerated forms of realistic evil – things that could happen, from a lion eating its own cubs to a man beating his wife. I had to stay away from the special effects of the first film: the head turning, the projectile vomit. And

then I had in mind four films which came out around the millenium, all of which focussed on demonic possession: *Lost Souls, End of Days, Stigmata* and *Fallen Angel*, none of which worked, all of which were directed by people from the visual side, either from cinematography or commercials or MTV, all of which relied very, very heavily on special effects/CGI gimmickry. And they all exuded a sense of panic, of not being secure in their own story. *Stigmata* in particular was just over the top, with all these very beautiful, very well-done, exaggerated images. But the characters got lost. Now, fortunately for me, M. Night Shyamalan had just made two very successful films – *The Sixth Sense* and *Signs* – that went back to the Hitchcock template of really building character, and then endangering people you have strongly identified with. And those films have a sense of confidence, the sense that a good story-teller exudes. 'Let me tell you a story . . . ' So it starts out, 'This man named John and his brother are going hunting . . . ' And you're already listening, because you trust that it's going to be a good story. The *Exorcist* script, in the time Frankenheimer was sick, had gotten all hyped-up and pumped-up by executives who were afraid there weren't enough shocks and enough scares in it. And when I re-wrote it, I had to back everything off, just in my belief that if you're going to make it work you have to make it work with the confidence of story-telling rather than the whiz-bang stuff.

KJ: *There's a nice set of ideas towards the end of the film, of murders being committed in allusion to hagiographies, the bloody deaths of saints: John the Baptist beheaded, St Sebastian pierced by arrows.*
PS: That was Caleb's idea, again, though instead of St Sebastian he had the Gabriel Mann character crucified upside down like St Peter. But I just took one look at Gabriel, who's such a handsome boy; and St Sebastian being such a homoerotic icon, I thought, 'Well . . . why not dance with the girl you brought?'

KJ: *Speaking of dancing with girls, was there ever a thought that this was a production with too low an oestrogen level? There's only one substantial woman character, and she's not a conventional 'love interest'.*
PS: Well, it's the first film I've done with more pretty boys than pretty girls. There was talk at one time of pushing the relationship between Merrin and the French doctor that way. But you know that Merrin is going to end up back in the Church, and I think audiences get very

pissed off when you start doing priest love stories, because they know you can't deliver and you're just jerking them around.

KJ: *When did Vittorio Storaro get involved as cinematographer?*
PS: Frankenheimer had already brought Vittorio on, and I was just thrilled. Vittorio has a rather punishing deal, and not many studios will make it any more. He has his own system called Univision, which is a three-perforation system. Most films use four perforations, so it means different cameras, different *everything*. You're committed to working on a system that only he works on, which can't be projected anywhere in the world except on his equipment. On top of which, he has to have all his own people, which is rather a large contingent of Italians. On top of which he doesn't like to work American hours. On top of which he has extremely stringent controls over the post-production: he can't be rushed, and he has all kinds of rights and clearances, control over the print. I think a lot of studios take one look at that contract and say, 'Well, there are a lot of great cinematographers out there . . . ' But again, you have a case where you have the one man, James Robinson, who can make the decision, and Frankenheimer, who sort of seduced him into taking Storaro. And I don't think that anyone realised until quite recently exactly what that contract means that they signed off on, and how much it ties their hands.

KJ: *Well, that's the bad side of the Storaro story. What's the good side?*
PS: It's completely unique. I was afraid that he would be slow, but it's completely the opposite. He puts all the lights on a dimmer board like for a stage production. The BBC did a wonderful documentary about him, which shows some of this, so I knew about it. And originally I thought, 'What's the big deal? A lot of cinematographers will put all the dimmers on one board instead of setting them up light by light.' Well, once we started shooting, I realised what's so revolutionary: he changes the lights during set-ups, while the camera's rolling. He moves the lights around during the shot, raises and lowers the levels. He has his monitor, and he moves the lights depending on how the characters are moving and how the cameras are moving in the scene. He watches the blocking while we're rehearsing, and he has it all planned out. And that allows him to work very, very fast. Plus, he works with two crews. He has two full camera crews, so he's already setting up the next shot while you're doing the previous shot. My big

concern was that I was going to be spending a lot of my time in the trailer on this film. In the low-budget world I've been operating in, it's been run-run, gun-gun, you never get in your trailer till lunch. And I thought, 'Oh fuck, it's just going to be like the old Hollywood days, I'll be sitting in my trailer for an hour while they light.' Well, that never happened once in the course of the shoot. And in that respect it was just like a low-budget film. Because the lighting's always there. The actors start to wander off, and suddenly they hear: 'Don't go too far! We'll be ready in five!'

KJ: *In a way, this film goes in almost the opposite direction from the first film: instead of an innocent child who is tortured and mutilated by an unclean spirit within, you have a mutilated, rejected child who is eventually transfigured into beauty.*
PS: Right. Also, I'm free of all those characters from Friedkin's original. You don't know much about Lankaster Merrin in that film. The sequels had their hands tied, because the characters were in place, and that's often what hurts or kills a sequel. But now I can create whole new characters.

KJ: *One of the riches of the first film is that it's not too explicit about Merrin's past, though you assume that it must have been full of hazardous experiences, both with this world and other worlds.*
PS: There is a Merrin flashback in John Boorman's film, *The Heretic*, which, again, is a younger Merrin in Africa – played by von Sydow, actually looking his real age instead of being made up as an old man. Stellan wears a hair-piece in this film, because von Sydow had quite a lot of hair, and even though they don't look alike, I don't want some reviewer to talk about how all his hair had obviously started to grow back. But nor did I want Stellan to think too much about trying to look or act like Max – though Stellan has done stage work with Max and, from time to time, just for fun, he'll start doing his Max imitation. But we discussed whether he wanted to make the character Swedish and he said 'No', so Merrin is now half-Dutch, half-English.

KJ: *Is there the hope for this film that it's going to appeal to a slightly older audience than the usual horror flick?*
PS: Well, no. I've got a fourteen-year-old son, and he's all excited because Dad's making a film that he and his friends will want to see. And *I* sure as hell want to make a movie that they want to see, too. But

that youth demographic is around a $12 to $15 million film. When you get up to $40 million-plus, you have to reach out.

KJ: *One is struck, though, by how much Carr's script touches on themes that wouldn't be out of place in a more self-consciously adult movie like, say,* The English Patient: *themes of racism, war, the end of Empire.*

PS: Also that whole argument between Francis and Merrin, the young and the old: 'Just because you've lost your faith doesn't mean that it may not be valid for others.'

KJ: *How does it feel to be working on a large-scale studio film again? A relief?*

PS: It's certainly kind of cool to see all those extras and to work on that big canvas. There are story demands of a $40-plus million film that don't exist for a $7 million film. Even *Auto Focus*, I couldn't have told that story for $12 or $14 million. You've got to tell it for $6 or $7 million, otherwise you can't have that ending or that character, you've got to have something more conventional. But this story kind of demands a conventional arc, and you know it has to have a positive ending, because Merrin's going to have to go on and be in *The Exorcist*. So our final shot is the final shot of *The Searchers* – Merrin walks out of the hospital, across the square, framed in the doorway, and he's obliterated by the dust-storm.

Coda: Stage Plays and Other Considerations II

KJ: *Is* Cleopatra Club *the only other stage play you've written apart from* Berlinale?

PS: Yup. It was based on something that happened to me in Egypt, at a film festival. My hotel room got robbed, and I fell into the hands of the Terrorism Police – because the anti-terrorism division is also in charge of security at five-star hotels. Once I had reported this robbery, they thought that I had a hooker in my room, and that I was hiding this fact; and they couldn't let me go out and spread this story, since I was a guest of the country. So I was interrogated for a long time, most of the night. There was a colonel who was very well-spoken, but the other three guys had leather jackets and guns and unfiltered Cleopatra cigarettes. I didn't take it too seriously, I thought it was kind of a hoot, but my guide was a Coptic Christian, and they interrogated her too, and really brought her to tears – a very frightening group. Anyway, they caught the robber, who turned out to be an Italian soccer hooligan – they were all very, very efficient, and then they found heroin on the guy and he ended up in jail for five years. At the end of it all, the colonel suddenly became my best friend, and he took me out and told me a lot of stories. About two weeks before I was there, a bomb had gone off and killed the Minister of Defence and some schoolchildren, and while I was there they announced that they had captured the terrorists. The colonel's brother had been in charge of interrogating the terrorists, and he said, 'We had them within an hour – it just took a couple of weeks to get them back into a condition where we could show them to the press . . . '

The colonel then invited us to his house, and they had so mistreated and terrified this Coptic Christian girl that they wanted to apologise to her, so the colonel asked me to make sure that she came, too. So I went and told her this, but she said, 'You don't understand this country. You cannot have anything to do with these people, nothing good comes of it.' I said, 'Okay', and went alone, and the colonel gave me an envelope to pass on to her. She opened it, and inside was a hand-written letter from him, apologising for her mistreatment. And she said, 'You know what this is? If I ever get in trouble, I can just hand this in. Basically, they owe me one.'

Anyway, my meetings with the colonel got me thinking, and I split myself up into the play's two main characters, the Director that I am, and the Critic I used to be. I threw them together, and then had the Colonel be the knife that cuts between them.

KJ: *How did you set about writing the play, and where did you eventually stage it?*
PS: I felt that what had happened was an interesting story, and when I told it to people it was sort of dramatic in and of itself. At that time, I was still somewhat under the spell of Pinter's writing, having worked on *The Comfort of Strangers*, and I wrote the play as a kind of self-entertainment, a chance to write that kind of dialogue, all that elliptic back-and-forth in the continuity of a stage production. It was produced by a group called New York Stage and Film. Every summer, at the Power House, which is a theatre at Vassar, they have three new productions. It ran for two and a half weeks but never went any further than that, and to make it go further I would have had to put a lot more work into it, because it wasn't quite long enough, and needed another level of complexity to be a real play. Plus the time had come for me to make some money and get on with my film-making career, because that whole episode must have eaten up eight months.

KJ: *The 'Critic' character is extremely disparaging about contemporary American cinema, and the 'Director' is far more, let's say, pragmatic: he recognises the quality of good craftsmanship even in otherwise poor films, and so on. Is this a kind of debate that comes out of what you yourself believe on a good day versus what you believe on a bad day?*
PS: Well . . . look, I don't think I can make a living doing the kind of films that I *really* want to do – you have to mingle with the commercial world. On top of that, we all have that part of us that enjoys the diversionary aspects of movies. I remember getting a letter from Bresson around 1970, he was about 65, and it was one of the most despairing letters I've ever received. He was trying to finance *L'Argent*, and he was writing to me, a film critic for the *LA Free Press*, trying to raise money. And he wrote of his despair, how impossible it

was for him to work, how he worked only on patronage. Well, that sort of patronage doesn't exist in America, or anyway it doesn't exist for me, so I have to find a way to sort of eke along.

One of the things that surprises me is when I hear people younger than me talking about the 'Golden Age of 1970s Cinema', which never struck me as particularly Golden at the time. And I think what they mean by that is that there were a higher percentage of movies that were serious. When you actually look through the release schedule from those years, you're sort of shocked to see how many idea-movies, theme-movies are coming up. That's all changed. I think movies are bad now, but I think they've always been bad. I'm more the pragmatist. I don't really buy that line of thought that movies are worse than ever, any more than I would buy the line that movies are better than ever. Most movies, like most art at any given time, are bad, and you can always make a case for times being better or worse, when usually all they are is different.

KJ: *But there are obvious periods when there's excitement, freshness, a buzz in a particular art or arts – the sixties for pop music, some would say the seventies for American cinema.*
PS: Yeah, but there is a buzz around again right now. The big old Hollywood factories have been dying off incrementally. Originally, they created stories, they created stars, they made movies, they distributed movies, they collected revenue. But now they don't create the movies any more, they don't create the stars, they only partially finance the movies – a smaller and smaller number of them – so all that's really left is the distribution and collection of revenues. And that's about to go by the board, too, because once we get into broadband internet and digital film-making, the traditional need for distribution will change. The reason why Time-Warner bought AOL was that AOL would be the next big distribution network. So everything's changing.

KJ: *Do you personally experience that as a liberation?*
PS: I'm a little too old to feel that it will be liberating. I remember when cable came in, I thought that would be liberating, and then realised it's not, it's just different. The culture is liberating in that it's so fragmented, and it's possible for every creative aspect to be served. Recently I was speaking to somebody representing Kenneth Anger, and they asked me if I thought that there was any experimental cinema left? And I said, 'No, society has changed, nothing is outré, and

there are no methods of distribution out there.' But now there are more and more of these short film channels . . .

I've been reading a book called *Non Zero* by Robert Wright, a cultural Darwinist, who believes that cultural evolution and biological evolution are of one piece, so that morality is evolved because it's in our best interests, biologically. Wright talks a lot about two impulses which are going on in world culture. One is 'McWorld': this whole idea of global economy, global entertainment, global commerce – and eventually, global government. The other tendency is Jihad – the Balkanization of the world at the same time. These can both co-exist – in whole cultures, and in the movie industry. There's a huge Balkanization, so that tiny little fragments, all of a sudden, can find a financial life – more and more of them, as the internet explodes. But at the same time, there's a bland, Hollywood, McWorld official culture. So, depending on who you are, and how you make your living, you can look at the situation and find justification for being either encouraged or discouraged. And I'm very suspicious of anyone who looks at the evidence and takes just one point of view.

I could not have come into Hollywood in the fifties. My sensibility and my way of working were a by-product of the counterculture, and the collapse of a lot of studio power in the sixties. And there are people who are now coming into the business who could not have come in in the sixties. I was speaking with Francis Coppola about his nephew, Spike Jonze, the director of *Being John Malkovich* and *Adaptation*. Francis and I are of that Film School generation, that college-driven generation, Spike is not. He's basically the high-school drop-out, MTV, commercials, video games.

So many of these jeremiads that you hear and read are really just the special interests of people. I can't really say whether it's better or worse. It's harder for me to make my movies these days, but is it objectively harder, or is it just because I'm older? Film is very much a young person's medium, commercially, all the demographics are there. So, all of a sudden, and unbelievable as this sounds, Michelle Pfeiffer reaches a certain age and she's no longer on top of everybody's lists. So it is, in fact, easier for someone right out of MTV to throw a movie together than it is for me. One, because he knows the audience better; two, because he's plugged into all the right cultural accoutrements; three, because he knows those actors – most of the actors I know are more or less my age; and four, he doesn't have any track record, and in some ways that's more appealing.

So I'm having a hard time getting *The Walker* off the ground, but is it really any harder than, say, *Blue Collar* was, or *Mishima* was? They were all difficult to make. But I did get them made.

KJ: *When we first started doing these interviews more than a decade ago, you told me that you preferred not to go into print with some of the more colourful and salacious back-stage stories from your early career – both those that took place around your own productions, and throughout the movie industry generally. Since then, Peter Biskind's book* Easy Riders, Raging Bulls *has spilled all the beans and then some. Would you like a right-of-reply to that book by way of a new finale?*

PS: Well, first, rather than being offended, I was disappointed for him, because a lot of that interview material was done under another pretext. He was editor of *American Film* and a contributor to *Premiere*. You would go out to dinner with him, and you would do your work on the record, promoting whatever you were promoting at the time; and then you would go off the record, and just talk about the state of Hollywood, who was doing what. A lot of the stuff in that book is off-the-record material, and much of it is hearsay, and malicious back-biting. Now, Biskind had an extraordinary opportunity to do something of value, because he had had the access, and he had a wonderful theme. And rather than address it, he succumbed to the temptations of doing a pop, gossip-driven book.

I know that in my own case because there was a particular story he told about Richard Pryor on *Blue Collar*, and he came to me to fact-check it, and I said, 'Well, Peter, that's an interesting story, but the reality is that it's a composite of two different stories that happened at two different times, and you've put them together.' He said, 'I got this from a reliable source.' And I said, 'Peter, there were two people in the room when this happened. One was me, and the other was Richard Pryor. I know you didn't get this from Richard Pryor, because he's not able to address those issues any more. So that makes me the only reliable source, and I'm telling you it didn't happen, it's a composite story.' And sure enough, it turned out that someone had heard two different stories that I had told, and put them together, and Peter had heard it second-hand. Now, I'm not particularly offended by that, but I use it as an example of the mentality that informs the entire book. From what I know, and from what I've heard from people like Coppola and Scorsese and Bob Towne, it's just one misrepresented anecdote after another.

One of the problems of these writers is that they get a thesis, and they try to fit everybody into it, and if you don't fit, you're manipulated. *His* thesis was that the film school generation had had their day, and crashed and burned, and he had to make sure that we all fit into that. So he was using some of my later work as an example of the fact that my career had fried. He was also using some particularly vindictive things that my brother had said – I haven't spoken to my brother in fifteen years, but he has a very vested interest in the notion that my only good work was done when he was involved. So I knew that Peter was drifting this way, and I told him, 'I really don't think this is true. If you're really going to do this, you should see *Affliction*.' I invited him to three screenings, and I couldn't get him to come, because his theory was pretty much locked in, and that if he saw it, he might have to back out.

My argument is more on the principle and the general thrust of the book, not on its sheer petty maliciousness. You really sense somebody who has spent many years kissing ass, and is now settling a whole litany of scores.

KJ: *It's also odd how many key players seem to be left out of the story: there's hardly anything of moment on Walter Hill, not much on De Palma, or John Carpenter.*
PS: Or James Toback. Yeah. So my response is, I'd rather be left in and mistreated than left out and ignored, because it's good company. I'd probably have been more offended if I hadn't made the short-list.

KJ: *But presumably you'd agree with the opening part of his thesis. You've more or less said it yourself: that there was a certain moment when the studio system weakened to the point that a bunch of wild young men, and a few wild women, could run in.*
PS: Yeah. And it's happening again right now – a new generation is running in.

KJ: *So in one sense, it's just the eternal story of a generation growing up?*
PS: Well art, for the most part, is a relatively young man's game. You can list all the exceptions to that rule throughout history, but you've often done your best work by 40. Then you work on a little bit, for the next two decades. People say what they have to say, they get older, they get richer: that's just the circle of creativity. Then technology turns around, and all of a sudden the social fabric has been ripped

and torn and you need new voices to address it. And what voices are those going to be? Usually, they're going to be the young voices.

KJ: *If there's a kid out there now who has a background similar to yours – harsh religious upbringing, intense reading, seeing some visionary films – do you think that kid would want to go into cinema today? Or has it lost its appeal as a medium for self-expression?*

PS: I don't know if it's really cinema that *I* went into. I went into storytelling. Some years earlier, it probably would have been traditional fiction. At the time I came in, it seemed like movies were the logical thing. Today? In terms of movies as we have known them for the last one hundred years, there are changes afoot, and it may well be that we are in for some rocky years where it all appears to be rather ridiculous. I believe that audio-visual entertainment is about to undergo a big change: it's falling apart both internally and externally, the distribution is changing, the technology is changing. And movies will come out in a different form. I won't predict what they will be, but it's safe to predict they will be different. Whether or not the existential hero of the twentieth century – which is where I have my investment – will be relevant any more, I can't say. He might be a much more deconstructed cyber-hero. Because deconstruction, which has been part of the other arts for the last 30 or 40 years, has now finally come, fully formed, into the movies. Movies used to be an irony-free zone: well, not any more. So you are getting deconstructed protagonists, and a movie like *Being John Malkovich* is now Oscar material. And it is kind of scary, particularly for those of us who were raised on the existential tradition and find these deconstructed characters very un-nourishing.

But you have to be careful not to rush to judgment, and just step back a little bit and see how the thing will evolve. This book *Non Zero* is all about, 'Take the long view, see how things are going to shape.' They're having an election in Iran today, and presumably Iran will loosen up, and twenty years of self-flagellation will start to change. But anyone who looked at Iran fifteen years ago would have said, 'Oh, it's all ruined.' If you just lean back, you know it's going to change and evolve. And there are a lot of people making a living by acting as if what's happening today is the definitive thing. It's not.

Coda: Pauline Kael, 1919–2001,
My Family Drama

I've always feared Pauline Kael's death, almost from the day I first met her. At first my reasons were simple and selfish; later they became more complex.

I met Pauline the summer of 1967 in New York City. As a college student I'd become interested in 'cinema', specifically the European films of the Sixties. I'm not sure if it was because of their extraordinary vitality or because my church (and consequently my college, Calvin) had proscribed motion picture attendance and other 'worldly amusements'. Probably the latter. Revolt was in the air, and advocating movies was a way to be simultaneously an artist and a rebel. Definitely more prestigious than drinking, vandalism, or shoplifting, my previous forms of rebellion.

The problem was, there was no way to see foreign films in Grand Rapids, Michigan. (The local soft-core theater had attempted a run of Bergman films; it petered out.) So I saved my money and applied for summer courses at Columbia's film school. I stayed at John Jay, worked in the cafeteria, and took introductory courses in film history.

One night, after a European film history course, I found myself sitting as usual at the West End bar (the New York drinking age was 18). Pauline's second book, *Kiss Kiss Bang Bang*, had just come out in paperback, and I was in a pitched discussion with the fellow beside me. We were both mad for the book. 'So,' he said after he returned from a bathroom break, 'let's go see her. You want to?' His name was Paul Warshow. His father, Robert Warshow, had been a film critic for *The Nation*, writing seminal articles on the Western and gangster films. Robert Warshow had died young, and Pauline had been a friend to Paul ever since. A day or two later I got a message from Paul; he had spoken with Pauline, and we were going to her apartment for dinner.

I remember that first evening as vividly as a first date. Sitting around an oak table, beneath a spider-patterned Tiffany lamp, we ate and drank and argued: the quintessential Kael experience. I had seen only a couple dozen films but had strong opinions. I couldn't understand how she could champion *L'Avventura* but not *La Notte*. She found my advocacy of Buñuel and Bergman quaint. I thought she was being harsh; later experience made me realize she was being kind. Pauline was then writing for *The New Republic*. She had recently reviewed *Masculin-Feminin* after it had lasted but a week at the New Yorker theater. Her review, blown up and mounted outside the movie house, brought Godard's film back for a successful run. Her bully pulpit techniques, the ones she'd honed at the Berkeley Cinema Guild, now worked in New York: she was on the cusp of exercising her clout. That headiness, that evangelical purpose, permeated the room.

The hour grew late. Paul Warshow left. Having drunk excessively, I ended up on the sofa. The following morning, after scrambled eggs and toast, she escorted me out. 'You don't want to be a minister,' she told me, 'you want to be a film critic. We are going to keep in touch.'

Thus I was ushered into the Paulettes. I saw her again that summer and corresponded after returning to Calvin College, sending her articles I'd written for the college paper. She had offered to help me get accepted at UCLA film school. UCLA was then, as now, very difficult to get into, the acme of film schools, but she was friends with its head, Colin Young. She assured me that her word would have weight.

Those were the days when I would go to bed at night and pray to God to keep Pauline alive. I dreaded picking up the paper and reading she'd died. She was my only way out of Calvin, the Christian Reformed Church, and Grand Rapids. If she died I'd be trapped there forever! Please God, just let her live another year. I won't ask anything else.

Well, she lived, I was accepted at UCLA, and my life changed. She helped me get a weekly reviewing gig at the *LA Free Press*. Like her other acolytes, I read her religiously, sent her everything I wrote, and waited for her call. The phone would ring. Pauline, in that passionate, bullying voice, would explain that such-and-such a film (*La Chinoise*, for example) needed our support and to the barricades we'd run.

Pauline was a complex mentor. On one hand, she infused your life like a whirlwind, dominating your thinking, affecting your personal relationships, demanding fealty; on the other, she could not respect anyone who would not stand up to her. Love her too little and she attacked you, love her too much and she disregarded you. It was a formula for heartbreak, a heartbreak I think the acolytes felt more deeply than the mentor. Mine came in two stages.

The first was Christmas 1971. I had flown to New York to visit her. Even though I was increasingly influenced by the structuralist criticism of *Screen* magazine in London, I still considered her my mentor. I had been writing criticism for several years, editing a film magazine and working on a book. I was ready for the next step. At that time, newspapers and magazines around the country would solicit Pauline's recommendations before hiring a film critic; she was the clearing house. She explained that she was thinking of me for a paper in either Chicago or Seattle; Seattle, she felt, would be best. It was an arts town – a movie town, a serious town. I could develop a readership. I was in doubt, I had never made a living as a writer. Yet I was torn. I explained to her that I'd been experiencing sorry personal turmoil and had been thinking about writing a screenplay. If I left Los Angeles, I said, I was afraid that possibility would be gone forever. If I didn't try now, I never would. She was unmoved: 'I need an answer.' I asked her if I could have a week to think about it (it was the holidays after all). She said no. She needed my answer now. I said something to the effect, 'If you need the answer now, the answer would have to be no.' Silence. Some cold chitchat. My time, I realized, was up. I excused myself, left, returned to my hotel room, and made a plane reservation for Los Angeles. On the plane home I thought to myself, 'Well, you fucked that up. You're no longer a film critic. You better try to be a screenwriter.'

The second break was in 1979. I was preparing *American Gigolo* at Paramount. Pauline also had an office on the lot, having been brought out by Warren Beatty to develop scripts. (Warren is the master of patient seduction. He is also the master of patient revenge. In manipulating Pauline, the critical bête noire of commercial Hollywood, he accomplished both.) I had seen her a couple of times in the intervening years. I'd sent her the script of *Taxi Driver* and had dinner with her and Brian DePalma at the Algonquin after the film's release. She'd seemingly forgiven me for forsaking criticism. Now I was hearing disturbing stories. She'd told David Chasen, a vice-president at Columbia, that I was a good writer but a terrible director. I asked her to lunch on the lot. I explained that she was free to say anything about me she wished in print, but when she badmouthed me at a cocktail party she was not acting as a critic but as a Hollywood insider. And was thus my enemy. The break was then complete. Communication ended. I used to look forward to her comments. Now I appreciated it when, for whatever reason, she chose not to review a film I was involved in.

I began to fear her death anew. My mother had died in 1978, and I blamed myself for not expressing my love for her until after it was too late. What if this ultimate family drama were to be re-enacted? What if Pauline, my second mother, the enabler of my creative life, were to die before I had a chance to express my gratitude?

Fortunately, an opportunity for rapprochement availed itself ten years later. Not all family dramas end in silence and darkness. Terry Rafferty, *New Yorker* film critic, moved near my country house in Chappaqua. He mentioned Pauline, and I asked if he would call her, speak to her on my behalf. Terry arranged for us to drive up to Great Barrington and visit Pauline. I got out of the car with trepidation, walked toward her rambling brown Victorian. Terry trailed thoughtfully behind. She appeared on the porch, smaller than I'd remembered, and opened her arms. After a sustained embrace she said to me, 'I saw your film, *Comfort of Strangers*. I liked it. You've become a good director.' I didn't care so much if she thought I was a good director; what mattered was that she cared for me.

Over the last decade I visited Pauline most summers. One occasion stands out. I was returning from Canyon Ranch in the Berkshires; I called and said I'd like to stop by. I knew she had just returned to Great Barrington after two operations in Boston. She said she wasn't fit for company. I said I would stop by nonetheless. Her daughter Gina ushered me up to Pauline's bedroom, and I was taken aback by her appearance. Always small, she now seemed skin and bones. I could encompass her wrist between my thumb and forefinger. I pulled up a chair and began time-honored bedside chatter: how are things, fall is early, blah, blah, blah. But she would have none of it. She wanted my opinions on movies. I spoke in gentle tones, clearly a mistake. Retorts shot from her mouth like spinning razor blades, adjectives zipping past my head, adverbs cutting my bare arms, clauses battering my torso. Ever formidable. I told her the thing I had never told my own mother on her deathbed. I told her that I loved her.

Two years ago, on her 80th birthday, there was a convocation of the tribes in Great Barrington. Pauline had always resisted attempts to honor her. (Once, Altman, Bertolucci and I attempted to manage a tribute at the Museum of Modem Art. Pauline firmly declined. 'I'm too small to put on a pedestal,' she told me by phone.) Now Gina had convinced her to have a birthday fest. Her sister came from Berkeley. As did three generations of acolytes, most, if not all, with emotions as conflicted as my own. From the first generation, there were David Denby, Joe Morgenstern and I; from the second, Terry Rafferty and

Meredith Brody; from the third, David Edelstein (and others I've neglected to mention).

James Hamilton took a group photo and mailed it to all the participants. It hangs in my office.

Film Comment, November/December 2001

Filmography

As director or writer/director

1970

For Us, Cinema is the Most Important of the Arts

Schrader describes his UCLA student project as 'a media game film, a puzzle film. It's hard to describe. What happens is that there's a student demonstration at UCLA which is reported in the media, and then the students take over the media, and then the media takes over the students. So there's a flip-flop point of view. The title is a quotation from Lenin.'

Production company: UCLA
Written, produced and directed: Paul Schrader
Cast: Jean-Marie Bernard and UCLA students
Super 8 mm
10 mins

1977

Blue Collar

Three friends working in a Detroit car factory – Zeke, Smokey (both black) and Jerry (white) – steal $600 of their union's funds. They are stunned when the local union president announces that the sum stolen could be as high as $10,000. The friends have also stolen a notebook which contains incriminating evidence about illegal loans. They are divided: Jerry advocates exposing the corruption, but Smokey proposes blackmail. Their plans are discovered. Smokey is 'accidentally' killed in the factory's paint shop; the ambitious Zeke is bought off with a job as shop steward. Increasingly terrified, Jerry turns to Burrows, an FBI agent, for help. When Jerry and his escort arrive at the factory to pick up his gear, he is spurned by the other workers and attacked by Zeke.

Production company: TAT Communications for Universal
Producers: Robin French, Don Guest, David Nicols
Screenplay: Paul Schrader, Leonard Schrader, based on source material by Sydney A. Glass
Cinematography (colour): Bobby Byrne
Editor: Tom Rolf
Music: Jack Nitzsche, Ry Cooder
Production designer: Lawrence G. Paull
Cast: Richard Pryor (*Zeke Brown*), Harvey Keitel (*Jerry Bartowski*), Yaphet Kotto (*Smokey*), Ed Begley Jr (*Bobby Joe*), Harry Bellaver (*Eddie Johnson*), George Memmoli (*Jenkins*), Lucy Saroyan (*Arlene Bartowski*), Lane Smith (*Clarence Hill*), Cliff De Young

(*John Burrows*), Borah Silver (*Dogshit Miller*), Chip Fields (*Caroline Brown*), Harry Northup (*Hank*), and others
114 mins

1978
Hardcore
(In UK, *The Hardcore Life*)
Jake VanDorn, a prosperous furniture manufacturer in Grand Rapids, Michigan, sees his daughter Kristen off to California for a Calvinist convention and is horrified when he hears that she has gone missing. He travels to Los Angeles and hires a private investigator, Andy Mast, who returns to Grand Rapids with a reel of pornographic film featuring Kristen. VanDorn takes up the search himself by posing as a pornographic film producer and, with the help of a prostitute, Niki, traces Kristen to San Francisco where she is in the hands of Ratan who makes snuff movies. When Mast and VanDorn finally find them, Ratan is shot by Mast and Kristen leaves with her father.

Production company: A-Team for Columbia
Producers: John Milius, Buzz Feitshans
Screenplay: Paul Schrader
Cinematography (colour): Michael Chapman
Editor: Tom Rolf
Music: Jack Nitzsche
Production designer: Paul Sylbert
Cast: George C. Scott (*Jake VanDorn*), Peter Boyle (*Andy Mast*), Season Hubley (*Niki*), Dick Sargent (*Wes De Jong*), Leonard Gaines (*Ramada*), David Nichols (*Kurt*), Gary Rand Graham (*Tod*), Larry Block (*Detective Burrows*), Marc Alaimo (*Ratan*), Leslie Ackerman (*Felice*), Charlotte McGinnis (*Beatrice*), Ilah Davis (*Kristen VanDorn*), Paul Marin (*Joe VanDorn*), and others
108 mins

1979
American Gigolo
Julian Kay is a highly paid gigolo in Los Angeles. As a favour to a friend, Leon Jaimes, he agrees to an assignment with a married couple, the Rymans, which takes a sado-masochistic turn. He also becomes involved with Michelle, the wife of a Californian senator. When Mrs Ryman is murdered, suspicion falls on Julian. The rich woman who could provide him with an alibi refuses to acknowledge him, and Julian realizes that he has been framed. He is imprisoned, and his position looks hopeless until Michelle defies her husband and commits herself to Julian's defence, finally convincing him of her love.

Production company: Pierre Associates for Paramount
Producers: Freddie Fields, Jerry Bruckheimer
Screenplay: Paul Schrader
Cinematography (colour): John Bailey
Editor: Richard Halsey
Music: Giorgio Moroder
Visual consultant: Ferdinando Scarfiotti
Cast: Richard Gere (*Julian Kay*), Lauren Hutton (*Michelle Stratton*), Hector Elizondo (*Detective Sunday*), Nina van Pallandt (*Anne*), Bill Duke (*Leon Jaimes*), Brian Davies (*Charles Stratton*), K. Callan (*Lisa Williams*), Tom Stewart (*Mr Ryman*), Patti Carr (*Judy*

Ryman), David Cryer (*Lieutenant Curtis*), Carole Cook (*Mrs Dobrun*), Carol Bruce (*Mrs Lucille Sloan*), and others
117 mins

1981

Cat People

Irena Gallier comes to New Orleans to live with her brother Paul, from whom she has been separated since childhood. Paul speaks of their strange family heritage and his belief that he and Irena belong together. Terrified, she rejects his advances. That night, transformed into a black leopard, Paul attacks a prostitute before being tranquillized and captured by Oliver, curator of the local zoo. Oliver subsequently meets Irena, is attracted to her and offers her a job. The captured leopard wounds a keeper, escapes and changes back into Paul, who explains to Irena that they can mate only with each other since sex with a human changes them into beasts. After committing further slaughter, Paul is shot dead. Oliver, now aware of the curse, makes love to Irena while she is bound. He has a new addition to the zoo . . .

Production company: RKO/Universal
Producers: Jerry Bruckheimer, Charles Fries
Screenplay: Alan Ormsby, based on the script for *Cat People* (1943) by DeWitt Bodeen
Cinematography (colour): John Bailey (New Orleans), Paul Vom Brack
Editors: Bud Smith, Jacqueline Cambas, Ned Humphreys, Jere Huggins
Music: Giorgio Moroder
Visual consultant: Ferdinando Scarfiotti
Cast: Nastassia Kinski (*Irena Gallier*), Malcolm McDowell (*Paul Gallier*), John Heard (*Oliver Yates*), Annette O'Toole (*Alice Perrin*), Ruby Dee (*Female*), Ed Begley Jr (*Joe Creigh*), Scott Paulin (*Bill Searle*), Frankie Faison (*Detective Brandt*), Ron Diamond (*Detective Ron Diamond*), Lynn Lowry (*Ruthie*), John Larroquette (*Bronte Judson*), Tessa Richarde (*Billie*), Patricia Perkins (*taxi driver*), Berry Berenson (*Sandra*), Fausto Barajas (*Otis*), and others
118 mins

1985

Mishima: A Life in Four Chapters

1. BEAUTY   On 25 November 1970, the novelist Yukio Mishima prepares to carry out a political provocation at the Japanese army headquarters in Tokyo. A flashback shows him as a frail, sheltered child living with his grandmother. As he grows into adolescence he is sexually aroused by a picture of St Sebastian and challenges a bully at school. He dreams of dying for the Emperor in the war but lies about his health to avoid conscription. (In Mishima's novel, *Temple of the Golden Pavilion*, a shy stuttering temple acolyte tries to make love to a girl but finds himself rendered powerless by the beauty of the golden pavilion. He finally makes love to a prostitute and loses his stutter but determines to destroy the pavilion by setting fire to it.)

2. ART   Mishima drives to the headquarters with his supporters. A flashback shows the beginnings of his career as a writer and his obsession with remaking his own body. He shows off his physique by posing for photographs, including one as St Sebastian. (In Mishima's novel, *Kyoko's House*, a young actor desires to improve himself through body-building. He meets a woman to whom his mother is indebted and she offers to cancel the debt if he will sign his body over to her. The affair becomes intensely sado-masochistic and there are hints of suicide.)

3. ACTION   Mishima and his followers approach the headquarters. (In Mishima's novel, *Runaway Horses*, a young cadet has formed a cell sworn to purge Japan of its modern

corruptions by assassinating leading figures. The cell is broken up by police.) A flashback shows Mishima engaging in paramilitary activities with his private army. (The cadet escapes, assassinates a businessman, and prepares to commit *seppuku*.)

4. HARMONY OF PEN AND SWORD   Mishima and his followers tie and gag the Japanese general and then Mishima addresses the assembled troops, exhorting them to return Japan to its old purity. Greeted with jeers, he sets about committing *seppuku* (in each of the three stories the protagonists reach their destructive or suicidal ends).

Production company: Zoetrope/Lucasfilm/Filmlink International
Producers: George Lucas, Francis Coppola, Mata Yamamoto, Tom Luddy
Screenplay: Paul Schrader, Leonard Schrader, Chieko Schrader. Sections based on the novels, *Temple of the Golden Pavilion*, *Kyoko's House* and *Runaway Horses* by Yukio Mishima
Cinematography (colour/black and white): John Bailey
Editor: Michael Chandler, Tomoyo Oshima
Music: Philip Glass
Production designer: Eiko Ishioka
Narrator: Roy Scheider
Cast: 25 NOVEMBER 1970: Ken Ogata (*Yukio Mishima*), Masayuki Shionoya (*Morita*), Junkichi Orimoto (*General Mashita*)

　　　FLASHBACKS: Naoko Otani (*Mother*), Go Rijo (*Mishima, age 18–19*), Masato Aizawa (*Mishima, age 9–14*), Yuki Nagahara (*Mishima, age 5*)

　　　TEMPLE OF THE GOLDEN PAVILION: Yasosuke Bando (*Mizoguchi*), Hisako Manda (*Mariko*), Naomi Oki (*girl*), Miki Takakura (*girl*)

　　　KYOKO'S HOUSE: Kenji Sawada (*Osamu*), Sachiko Hidari (*Ozamu's mother*), Reisen Lee (*Kiyomi*), Setsuko Karasuma (*Mitsuko*)

　　　RUNAWAY HORSES: Toshiyuki Nagashima (*Isao*), Hiroshi Katsuno (*Lieutenant Hori*), Naoya Makoto (*kendo instructor*)

120 mins

1985

Tight Connection
A promotional video for the Bob Dylan song.

Producer: Alan Poul
Screenplay: Paul Schrader
Cinematography (colour): Makoto Hishida
Cast: Bob Dylan, Mitsuko Baisho, Mary Jane Adams
6 mins

1987

Light of Day
Cleveland, Ohio. Joe Rasnick and his sister Patti are lead performers in a group called The Barbusters. Joe works in a local factory, Patti has an illegitimate four-year-old son and is at loggerheads with her religious mother. When Patti steals some electrical equipment Joe is confronted at work by the victim's brother-in-law and has to borrow money from their mother. After being laid off at work, Joe takes The Barbusters on a tour of the Midwest in winter but the tour ends when Joe is shocked at Patti's shoplifting. The Barbusters break up and Patti goes on the road with a heavy-metal band instead. Their mother is taken ill and proves to have incurable cancer. Patti returns from a concert and has an emotional reunion with her mother. At the funeral it seems that Patti will not put in an appearance until she is

confronted by Joe. After paying respects to her mother, Patti joins Joe and the re-formed Barbusters on stage.

Production company: Taft Entertainment Pictures/Keith Barish Productions. In association with HBO
Producers: Doug Claybourne, Rob Cohen, Keith Barish, Alan Mark Poul
Screenplay: Paul Schrader
Cinematography (colour): John Bailey
Editor: Jacqueline Cambas, Jill Savitt
Music: Thomas Newman, Bruce Springsteen and others
Production designer: Jeannine Caudia Oppewall
Cast: Michael J. Fox (*Joe Rasnick*), Gena Rowlands (*Jeanette Rasnick*), Joan Jett (*Patti Rasnick*), Michael McKean (*Bu Montgomery*), Thomas G. Waites (*Smittie*), Cherry Joens (*Cindy Montgomery*), Michael Dolan (*Gene Bodine*), Paul J. Harkins (*Billy Tettore*), Billy Sullivan (*Benji Rasnick*), Jason Miller (*Benjamin Rasnick*), and others
107 mins

1988

Patty Hearst

4 February 1974. Patricia Hearst, nineteen-year-old granddaughter of William Randolph Hearst, is kidnapped by the Symbionese Liberation Army. The SLA first try to use her as a bargaining counter for the release of two comrades, then demand a food-distribution scheme for the poor. Patty is kept blindfolded and subjected to sexual and other kinds of abuse by her captors. After fifty-seven days of captivity she is offered the choice of going home or joining the SLA; doubtful that her captors will really let her leave alive, she opts to stay. Renamed Tania, she joins them in a bank raid and becomes notorious. The SLA decamps to Los Angeles. During a shopping expedition, Patty, Teko and Yolanda are almost caught by security guards. They flee to a motel and are horrified to see TV coverage of the SLA's safe house being stormed. The trio go on the run to Pennsylvania and San Francisco. In September 1975 they are caught. Patty maintains that her actions were carried out under duress but is convicted and sentenced to a prison term. Visited by her father, she tells him that she believes her greatest crime was in becoming a living inconvenience to the world's assumptions about her.

Production company: Atlantic Entertainment/Zenith
Producers: Thomas Coleman, Michael Rosenblatt, Marvin Worth, James Baubaker, Linda Reisman
Screenplay Nicholas Kazan, based on the book *Every Secret Thing* by Patricia Campbell Hearst with Alvin Moscow
Cinematography (colour): Bojan Bazelli
Editor: Michael R. Miller
Music: Scott Johnson
Production designer: Jane Musky
Cast: Natasha Richardson (*Patricia Campbell Hearst*), William Forsythe (*Teko*), Ving Rhames (*Cinque*), Frances Fisher (*Yolanda*), Jodi Long (*Wendy Yoshimura*), Olivia Barash (*Fahizah*), Dana Delany (*Gelina*), Marek Johnson (*Zoya*), Kitty Swink (*Gabi*), Peter Kowanko (*Cujo*), Tom O'Rourke (*Jim Browning*), Scott Kraft (*Steven Weed*), Jeff Imada (*neighbour*), Ermal Williamson (*Randolph A. Hearst*), Elaine Revard (*Catherine Hearst*), and others
108 mins

The Comfort of Strangers

A young English couple, Mary and Colin, go on holiday to Venice to try to patch up their failing relationship. They meet Robert, a rich Venetian gentleman who runs a bar as a hobby, and his wife, Caroline, who is disabled. Despite finding the older couple disagreeable, Mary and Colin gradually fall under their influence. In a final meeting, Mary is drugged and Colin killed. The police capture and interrogate Robert.

Production company: Erre Productions
Producers: Angelo Rizzoli, Mario Cotone, Linda Reisman, John Thompson
Screenplay: Harold Pinter, from the novel by Ian McEwan
Cinematography: Dante Spinotti
Editor: Bill Pankow
Music: Angelo Badalamenti
Production designer: Gianni Quaranta
Cast: Christopher Walken (*Robert*), Natasha Richardson (*Mary*), Rupert Everett (*Colin*), Helen Mirren (*Caroline*)
107 mins

1992

Light Sleeper

John LeTour works as a drug deliverer to a range of clients in Manhattan, but his boss Ann hopes to move into a legitimate cosmetics business. He re-encounters Marianne, whom he loved and lost because of past drug use; but she shuns his company, claiming to be clean and sober. Anxious, with plainclothes cop Guidone on his tail, LeTour consults psychic Teresa who sees an aura of death around him. Visiting a hospital to deliver valium to Tis, Ann's Swiss 'ecstasy connection', LeTour again runs into Marianne, visiting her dying mother; they make love in a hotel, but she deserts him. Delivering to Tis's apartment, LeTour finds Marianne, the worse for drugs. As he leaves the hotel, she falls to her death. LeTour fingers Tis to Guidone. Ann tells LeTour Tis has asked to see him: LeTour is wary, so Ann accompanies him to Tis's hotel, where they find him flanked by armed goons. Ann stages a distraction and LeTour shoots Tis dead. Ann visits LeTour in prison and they acknowledge their love for one another.

Production company: Grain of Sand Productions
Producer: Linda Reisman
Co-producer: G. Mac Brown
Screenplay: Paul Schrader
Cinematography (colour): Ed Lachman
Editor: Kristina Boden
Music: Michael Been
Production designer: Richard Hornung
Cast: Willem Dafoe (*LeTour*), Susan Sarandon (*Ann*), Dana Delaney (*Marianne*), David Clennon (*Robert*), Mary Beth Hurt (*Teresa*), Victor Garber (*Tis*), Jane Adams (*Randi*), Sam Rockwell (*Jealous*), and others
103 mins

1994

Witch Hunt

Los Angeles, the 1950s. U.S. Senator Larson Crockett is holding hearings on the influence of magic in Hollywood, which he decries as Un-American. Private detective Philip Lovecraft is considered unique in his profession for his refusal to use magic in his work. Actress Kim Hudson hires Lovecraft to find out if her husband, movie producer N.J. Gottlieb, is cheating, but the job takes a twist when Gottlieb is killed in circumstances that suggest the nefarious use of magic. Kim is accused of the murder of her husband, and Lovecraft uses the talents of a local witch, Hypolyta Kropotkin, to explain what is happening only to see her accused of the murder and sentenced to be burnt at the stake.

Production company: Home Box Office / Pacific Western
Producers: Gale Ann Hurd, Michael R. Joyce
Co-producers: David Gale, Betsy Beers
Screenplay: Joseph Dougherty
Cinematography (colour): Jean-Yves Escoffier
Editor: Kristina Boden
Music: Angelo Badalamenti
Production designer: Curtis A. Schnell
Cast: Dennis Hopper (*H. Philip Lovecraft*), Penelope Ann Miller (*Kim Hudson*), Eric Bogosian (*Senator Larson Crockett*), Sheryl Lee Ralph (*Hypolyta Kropotkin*), Julian Sands (*Finn Macha*), Alan Rosenberg (*N.J. Gottlieb*), Valerie Mahaffey (*Trudy*), John Epperson/Lypsinka (*Vivian Dart*), Debi Mazar (*The Manicurist*), Gregory Bell (*Shakespeare*), and others
100 mins

1995

New Blue

A short appreciation of the painting *New Blue* by artist and film critic Manny Farber, made for the seven-part Arts Council/BBC series *Picture House*.
Produced and photographed by Mitch Gross
Edited by Adrienne Berofsky
Music by Philip Grass
5 mins

1997

Touch

Juvenal, nee Charles Lawson, is a lapsed Franciscan monk who winds up in Los Angeles, counselling alcoholics at the Sacred Heart Rehabilitation Centre. He has stigmatic powers and can heal people with his touch. When word of Juvenal's gift gets out, everyone wants a piece of him: fanatical right-wing Catholic leader August Murray, who sees Juvenal as the key to taking his movement national; Bill Hill, a smooth-talking former evangelist who now sells RVs for a living and hopes to sell Juvenal; and Debra Lusanne, a TV talk show host who wants to expose Juvenal as a fraud on live television. Hill manages to snare Juvenal with the help of a former associate, Lynn Faulkner, but Lynn falls for Juvenal and has second thoughts about exploiting him. Murray sees Lynn as a corrupting influence on Juvenal and is determined to free him of her.

Production company: Initial Productions / Lumiere International
Producers: Lila Cazes, Fida Attieh
Co-producers: Llewellyn Wells
Screenplay: Paul Schrader, based on the novel by Elmore Leonard
Cinematography (colour): Ed Lachman
Editor: Cara Silverman
Music: David Grohl
Production designer: David Wasco

Cast: Skeet Ulrich (*Juvenal*), Bridget Fonda (*Lynn Marie Faulkner*), Christopher Walken (*Bill Hill*), Tom Arnold (*August Murray*), Paul Mazursky (*Artie*), Gina Gershon (*Debra Lusanne*), Janeane Garafolo (*Kathy Worthington*), Lolita Davidovich (*Antoinette Baker*), Anthony Zerbe (*Father Donahue*), Richard Schiff (*Jerry*), L.L. Cool J (*Himself*), and others
96 mins

1997
Affliction

Lawford, New Hampshire, a harsh winter. Wade Whitehouse, Lawford's only policeman, is divorced and lives alone in a trailer, beset by toothache, drinking heavily and forced to work menial jobs. He is unloved by his young daughter Jill and burdened by his elderly father Glen, an alcoholic who used to beat him. But he maintains a relationship with Margie and phone friendship with his younger brother Rolfe, a history professor in Boston. When a wealthy weekend visitor dies in a deer-hunting accident, Wade suspects first murder, then a conspiracy. But he is distracted from his ham-fisted attempts at investigation by the death of his mother (which brings Rolfe back to town for the first time in years), by his anguished steps to regain custody of Jill from his ex-wife Lillian, and by excruciating toothache. He abducts Jill and when she fearfully resists him, he hits her. Chastened, he allows Margie, who is leaving him for good, to take Jill back to her mother. Glen taunts him, and father and son launch into a brawl which ends with Wade killing the old man and burning his corpse. Rolfe, who has been the film's narrator, explains that the supposed conspiracy was all in Wade's imagination, and that Wade's circumstances are now unknown.

Production company: JVC Entertainment Inc. / Kingsgate Productions / Largo Entertainment
Producer: Linda Reisman
Co-producers: Eric Berg, Frank K. Isaacs
Screenplay: Paul Schrader, based on the novel by Russell Banks
Cinematography (colour): Paul Sarossy
Editor: Jay Rabinowitz
Music: Michael Brook
Production designer: Anne Pritchard
Cast: Nick Nolte (*Wade Whitehouse*), Sissy Spacek (*Marge Fogg*), James Coburn (*Glenn Whitehouse*), Willem Dafoe (*Rolfe Whitehouse*), Mary Beth Hurt (*Lillian*), Jim True-Frost (*Jack Hewitt*), Marian Seldes (*Alma Pittman*), Holmes Osborne (*Gordon LaRiviere*), Brigid Tierney (*Jill*), Sean McCann (*Evan Twombley*), Wayne Robson (*Nick Wickham*), Eugene Lipinski (*J. Battle Hand*), and others
114 mins

1999
Forever Mine

1987: Manuel Esquema, an international financier whose face is badly scarred, sits aboard a flight from Miami to New York. 1973: Alan Riply is a student working as a cabaña boy at a Miami Beach resort. He falls deeply in love with Ella Brice, a young honeymooner vacationing with her husband Mark, an aspiring politician. They begin a passionate affair, but when Mark learns what has gone on, he has Alan arrested on trumped-up charges, then shot in the face and left for dead. But Alan escapes back to Miami and enters the drug trade with his friend Javier. 1987: Esquema is Alan, his face reconstructed. Mark has worked his way up from crooked construction deals to a seat on the city council. But Manuel and Javier meet him as he is about to be indicted for fraud, and faces a long Federal prison sentence. Mark doesn't recognize Esquema as Alan, nor does Ella. But when they get together again, he reveals who he is and the romantic sparks start over.

Production company: J&M Entertainment / Moonstar Entertainment
Producer: Damita Nikopota, Kathleen Haase, Amy J. Kaufman
Screenplay: Paul Schrader
Cinematography (colour): John Bailey
Editor: Kristina Boden
Music: Angelo Badalamenti
Production designer: Francois Seguin
Cast: Joseph Fiennes (*Manuel Esquema/Alan Riply*), Ray Liotta (*Mark Brice*), Gretchen Mol (*Ella Brice*), Vincent Laresca (*Javier Cesti*), Myk Watford (*Rick Martino*), Lindsey Connell (*Stewardess*), Sean C W Johnson (*Randy*), Shawn Proctor (*Cabana Boy*), and others
115 mins

2002
Auto Focus

Los Angeles, 1964. Radio host Bob Crane wins the lead role in the TV show *Hogan's Heroes*, set in a World War II prison camp. The show becomes a hit, but Crane's home life suffers when his wife Anne discovers girlie magazines in their garage. On the *Hogan's* set, Crane meets hi-fi installer John Carpenter, who turns Crane on to his passions for video tape recorders and strip clubs. Soon the two are pairing up for after-show sex with the strippers. Crane begins an affair with *Hogan's* cast member Patti Olson, and breaks with Carpenter over the latter's apparent bisexuality, but the two make up. Crane marries Patti, but *Hogan's Heroes* is cancelled, and with two families to support, Crane begins playing dinner theatres around the country, Carpenter joining him for their usual exploits. Crane's agent Lenny warns him to be careful of his off-screen image, and after Patti decides to divorce him, his popularity slumps. Trying to go straight, Crane breaks conclusively with Carpenter. Later that night, someone slips into Crane's hotel room. . .

Production company: Propaganda Films / Good Machine / Focus Puller Inc.
Producer: Scott Alexander, Larry Karaszewski, Todd Rosken, Pat Dollard, Alicia Allain
Co-producers: Eric Berg, Frank K. Isaacs
Screenplay: Michael Gerbosi, based on the book The Killing of Bob Crane by Michael Graysmith
Cinematography (colour): Fred Murphy
Editor: Kristina Boden
Music: Angelo Badalamenti
Production designer: James Chinlund
Cast: Greg Kinnear (*Bob Crane*), Willem Dafoe (*John Carpenter*), Rita Wilson (*Ann Crane*), Maria Bello (*Patricia Crane*), Ron Leibman (*Lenny*), Bruce Solomon (*Feldman*), Michael Rodgers (*Richard Dawson*), Kurt Fuller (*Werner Klemperer*)
105 mins

2004
Exorcist: The Beginning

Production company: Morgan's Creek Productions / Dominion Productions
Producer: James G. Robinson
Co-producers: Wayne Morris, David C. Robinson, Art Schaeffer
Screenplay: William Wisher Jr. & Caleb Carr

Cinematography (colour): Vittorio Storaro
Editor: Tom Rolf
Music: Christopher Young
Production designer: John Graysmark, Norris Spencer
Cast: Stellan Skarsgaard (*Father Lankester Merrin*), Gabriel Mann (*Father William Francis*), Clara Bellar (*Rachel*), Ilario Bisi-Pedro (*Sebituana*), Billy Crawford (*Che Che*), Antonie Kamerling (*Kessler*), Nick Komornicki (*Private Parts*), Julian Wadham (*Captain Granville*), Rick Warden (*Corporal Williams*), and others

As writer

1974

The Yakuza

Harry Kilmer is an ex-GI who stayed in Japan after the war to live with his mistress, Tanaka Eiko, until her brother, Ken, returned from the Philippines. When the daughter of an American shipping magnate, George Tanner, is kidnapped by a yakuza gangster, Tono, Kilmer agrees reluctantly to travel back to Japan and rescue her, knowing that he will have to rely on Tanaka Ken for help. Acknowledging his debt to Kilmer for saving Eiko after the war, Tanaka helps to rescue the girl. Kilmer is warned that the underworld will seek revenge on Tanaka; meanwhile Tanner makes a deal with Tono, agreeing to co-operate with him in a plan to murder Kilmer. Kilmer's host and Eiko's daughter are killed in an attempt on his life. In response, Kilmer persuades Tanaka to allow him to join in an attack on Tono, spurred on by the revelation that Eiko is in fact Tanaka's wife. The attack is successful, but Tanaka kills his nephew, Spider, and cuts off his own finger as a penance in accordance with the yakuza code. As he prepares to leave Japan, Kilmer realizes that he must do the same for Tanaka to atone for the wrong he did him by living with his wife.

Director: Sydney Pollack
Production company: Warner Brothers
Producers: Shundo Koji, Sydney Pollack, Michael Hamilburg
Screenplay: Paul Schrader, Leonard Schrader, Robert Towne
Cinematography (colour): Okazaki Kozo, Duke Callaghan
Editors: Fredric Steinkamp, Thomas Standford, Don Guidice
Music: Dave Grusin
Production designer: Stephen Grimes
Cast: Robert Mitchum (*Harry Kilmer*), Takakura Ken (*Tanaka Ken*), Brian Keith (*George Tanner*), Kishi Keiko (*Tanaka Eiko*), Okada Eiji (*Tono Toshiro*), James Shigeta (*Goro*), Herb Edelman (*Oliver Wheat*), and others
112 mins

1975

Taxi Driver

Travis Bickle takes up driving a taxi in New York in search of an escape from his sleeplessness and disgust with the corruption he finds around him. After failing to begin a romance with the beautiful Betsy, who is working on the election campaign of presidential candidate Charles Palantine, Bickle's pent-up rage leads him to buy a set of guns. While training himself to use them, he meets a teenage prostitute, Iris, and becomes determined to rescue her from her sordid profession. Foiled in his attempt to assassinate Palantine, he goes to Iris's room and kills the men who 'own' her. Failing to commit suicide after this ritual act, Bickle becomes a hero in the press, and returns to driving a taxi.

Director: Martin Scorsese
Production company: Columbia Pictures
Producers: Michael Phillips, Julia Phillips
Screenplay: Paul Schrader
Cinematography (colour): Michael Chapman
Editors: Marcia Lucas, Tom Rolf, Melvin Shapiro
Music: Bernard Herrmann
Visual consultant: David Nicols
Cast: Robert De Niro (*Travis Bickle*), Jodie Foster (*Iris*), Cybill Shepherd (*Besty*), Harvey Keitel (*Sport/Matthew*), Steven Prince (*Andy, the gun salesman*), Albert Brooks (*Tom*), Peter Boyle (*Wizard*), Leonard Harris (*Charles Palantine*), Diahnne Abbott (*woman at concession stand*), Frank Adu (*angry black man*), Martin Scorsese (*man watching silhouette*), and others
113 mins

1976

Obsession

New Orleans, 1959. Michael Courtland's wife, Elizabeth, and daughter, Amy, are kidnapped and held to ransom. Michael is persuaded by the police to trace the kidnappers through a scheme involving fake money but the plan appears to backfire and Amy and Elizabeth are killed. 1975: Michael joins his partner, Robert, on a business trip to Florence where he meets a woman, Sandra, who looks exactly like the late Elizabeth. She accompanies him home and agrees to marry him. On the eve of the wedding she disappears and he receives a replica of the original ransom note. Trying to pay the demands, he contacts Robert to sell out his interest in their partnership, only to find that he is carrying fake bills again. Sandra is in fact Amy, who was sent to Italy by Robert in 1959 and has joined Robert in swindling Michael as an act of revenge, believing that he had knowingly condemned her and her mother to death. But Michael kills Robert when the latter boasts of his triumph, and is joyfully reunited with his daughter.

Director: Brian De Palma
Production company: Yellow Bird Films
Producers: Robert S. Bremson, George Litto, Harry N. Blum
Screenplay: Paul Schrader, Brian De Palma
Cinematography (colour): Vilmos Zsigmond
Editor: Paul Hirsch
Music: Bernard Herrmann
Visual consultant: Anne Pritchard
Cast: Cliff Robertson (*Michael Courtland*), Genevieve Bujold (*Elizabeth Courtland/Sandra Portinari*), John Lithgow (*Robert LaSalle*), Sylvia 'Kuumba' Williams (*Judy*), Wanda Blackman (*Amy Courtland*), Patrick McNamara (*third kidnapper*), Stanley J. Reyes (*Inspector Brie*), and others
98 mins

1977

Rolling Thunder

San Antonio, Texas. Major Charles Rane returns home after seven years in a Vietnamese prison camp to find that his wife wants to divorce him. Still mentally disturbed, he is attacked in his home by four men in search of the money he has been given as a civic award. Rane withstands torture, including the mutilation of his hand, but when his wife and son return home, the son gives away the money's whereabouts. The men then kill his wife and son. After being discharged from hospital, Rane tracks the men down to Mexico and wipes them out in a combat attack.

Director: John Flynn
Production company: American International Pictures
Producers: Lawrence Gordon, Norman T. Herman
Screenplay: Paul Schrader, Heywood Gould
Cinematography (colour): Jordan Cronenweth
Editor: Frank P. Keller
Music: Barry De Vorzon
Cast: William Devane (*Major Charles Rane*), Tommy Lee Jones (*Johnny Vohden*), Linda Haynes (*Linda Forchet*), Lisa Richards (*Janet*), Dabney Coleman (*Maxwell*), James Best (*Texan*), Cassie Yates (*Candy*), Luke Askew (*Automatic Slim*), Lawrason Driscoll (*Cliff*), Jordan Gerler (*Mark*), James Victor (*Lopez*), and others
99 mins

1978

Old Boyfriends

After the break-up of her marriage, psychologist Dianne Cruise sets off on a journey into the past to rediscover old boyfriends. In Colorado she finds Jeff, the man she almost married after college, who is now a film-maker. Just as they seem to be falling in love again, Dianne leaves for Minneapolis to find her high-school sweetheart, Eric, and seek revenge for the way he humiliated her by claiming her as a sexual trophy. Meanwhile Jeff sets out to trace her through a private investigator. Dianne moves on to Michigan, where she finds that the boy she loved in childhood, Lewis, had died in Vietnam. She strikes up a friendship with his disturbed younger brother, Wayne, who has been frozen in childhood by feelings of guilt over Lewis's death. Dianne's attempt to recreate her first love causes Wayne to have another breakdown. She flees in confusion, is eventually found by Jeff, and moves in with him and his daughter.

Director: Joan Tewkesbury
Production company: Edward R. Pressman Productions
Producers: Paul Schrader, Edward R. Pressman, Michele Rappaport
Screenplay: Paul Schrader, Leonard Schrader
Cinematography (colour): William A. Fraker
Editor: William Reynolds
Music: David Shire
Cast: Talia Shire (*Dianne Cruise*), Richard Jordan (*Jeff Turin*), John Belushi (*Eric Katz*), Keith Carradine (*Wayne Vantil*), John Houseman (*Dr Hoffman*), Buck Henry (*Art Kopple*), Bethel Leslie (*Mrs Vantil*), Joan Hotchkis (*Pamela Shaw*), and others
103 mins

1980

Raging Bull

New York, 1941. Middleweight boxer Jake La Motta, managed by his brother Joey, forsakes his wife when he falls for teenager Vickie, whom he marries but treats with constant jealous suspicion. By following underworld advice, La Motta becomes world champion when he beats Marcel Cerdan in 1949. La Motta's increasing weight problem and obsessional rages lead him to beat up his wife and Joey, believing both to have been unfaithful. After a brutal defeat by 'Sugar' Ray Robinson, La Motta opens a night club in 1956. Vickie finally leaves him, and he is arrested for soliciting minors and sent to jail. Back in New York in 1958, he unsuccessfully attempts to make up with his brother, and six years later is found giving recitations in a club.

Director: Martin Scorsese
Production company: United Artists
Producers: Irwin Winkler, Robert Chartoff in association with Peter Savage
Screenplay: Paul Schrader, Mardik Martin, from the book *Raging Bull* by Jake La Motta with Joseph Carter and Peter Savage
Cinematography (black and white/colour): Michael Chapman
Editor: Thelma Schoonmaker
Production designer: Gene Rudolf
Cast: Robert De Niro (*Jake La Motta*), Cathy Moriarty (*Vickie La Motta*), Joe Pesci (*Joey La Motta*), Frank Vincent (*Salvy*), Nicholas Colasanto (*Tommy Como*), Theresa Saldana (*Lenore*), Mario Gallo (*Mario*), Frank Adonis (*Patsy*), Joseph Bono (*Guido*), Frank Topham (*Toppy*), Lori Anne Flax (*Irma*), Charles Scorsese (*Charlie*), Don Dunphy (*himself*), Mardik Martin (*Copa waiter*), Martin Scorsese (*Barbizon stagehand*), and others
129 mins

1986

The Mosquito Coast

Disgusted with modern civilization, Allie Fox, handyman and obsessive genius, sets off to the Mosquito Coast of Central America to found his own society. Despite finding that the village he has bought is no more than a few broken-down shacks, Allie soon clears the jungle and constructs a gigantic ice-making machine, 'Fat Boy'. In a nearby village he finds three men, apparently prisoners, and shows them how to escape to his town. They prove to be armed mercenaries and, when he fails to persuade them to leave, Allie traps them inside Fat Boy. They try to shoot their way out but the machine explodes, causing widespread devastation. Fox's shattered family set off towards a village on the coast, but as they proceed upriver his sons increasingly resent their father's tyrannical and eccentric behaviour. When they come upon a mission, the boys rebel. Allie is shot while setting fire to the church and dies on the raft as his family head back to the sea and so to America.

Director: Peter Weir
Production company: The Saul Zaentz Company
Producers: Saul Zaentz, Jerome Hellman
Screenplay: Paul Schrader, based on the novel by Paul Theroux
Cinematography (colour): John Seale
Editor: Thom Noble, Richard Francis-Bruce
Music: Maurice Jarre
Production designer: John Stoddart

Cast: Harrison Ford (*Allie Fox*), Helen Mirren (*Mother*), River Phoenix (*Charlie Fox*), Jadrien Steele (*Jerry Fox*), Hilary Gordon (*April Fox*), Rebecca Gordon (*Clover Fox*), Jason Alexander (*clerk*), Dick O'Neill (*Mr Polski*), André Gregory (*Reverend Spellgood*)
119 mins

1988

The Last Temptation of Christ

Jesus of Nazareth, whose carpentry skills are put to making crosses for the occupying Roman force, is tormented by visions of a special purpose in His life. Reviled for His weakness by Judas, a Zealot, and Mary Magdalene, a prostitute who was a childhood friend, Jesus sees manifestations of Satan and is convinced He should now preach God's message. Joined by Judas, then Mary, and then more disciples, He delivers the Sermon on the Mount, but John the Baptist tells Him He must go into the desert to speak with God. After resisting temptation, Jesus returns with a new anger, performs miracles, raises Lazarus from the dead, and leads an assault on the Temple in Jerusalem. Telling Judas he must betray Him, Jesus is arrested by the Romans and crucified. On the cross, an angel appears, tells Him God has spared Him, and apparently offers Jesus a normal life as a family man. But when Paul tells Him about the crucifixion and resurrection, and Judas accuses Him of failing the cause, Jesus accepts His destiny and crawls back on to the cross.

Director: Martin Scorsese
Production company: Universal Pictures
Producer: Barbara De Fina
Screenplay: Paul Schrader, based on the novel by Nikos Kazantzakis
Cinematography (colour): Michael Ballhaus
Editor: Thelma Schoonmaker
Music: Peter Gabriel
Production designer: John Beard
Cast: Willem Dafoe (*Jesus*), Harvey Keitel (*Judas*), Paul Greco (*Zealot*), Steven Shill (*Centurion*), Verna Bloom (*Mary, Mother of Jesus*), Barbara Hershey (*Mary Magdalene*), Roberts Blossom (*Aged Master*), Barry Miller (*Jeroboam*), Gary Basaraba (*Andrew Apostle*), Irvin Kershner (*Zebedee*), Victor Argo (*Peter Apostle*), Michael Been (*John Apostle*), Paul Herman (*Philip Apostle*), John Lurie (*James Apostle*), Leo Burmeister (*Nathaniel Apostle*), André Gregory (*John the Baptist*), Harry Dean Stanton (*Saul/Paul*), David Bowie (*Pontius Pilate*), and others
163 mins

1996
City Hall

Kevin Calhoun is right-hand man to charismatic New York city Mayor John Pappas. Six-year-old James Bone is killed by a stray bullet during a street shootout between Eddie Santos, an undercover narcotics cop, and Tino Zapatti, a small-time drug dealer. Pappas speaks at the boy's funeral and defuses a potential race riot. But Calhoun learns that Tino Zapatti was the son of mafioso Paul Zapatti and had been granted five years' probation under suspicious circumstances. Digging deeper, he uncovers collusion between the Mafia, Judge Walter Stern, and Frank Anselmo, head of the South Brooklyn Democratic Club. Assisting Calhoun is Marybeth Cogan, an attorney representing Santos's widow, who wants to find out why the cop's pension is being withheld. Cogan draws Calhoun deeper into a scandal that undermines his belief in all that he has previously worked for.

Director: Harold Becker
Production company: Castle Rock Entertainment / Columbia Pictures Corporation
Producers: Edward R. Pressman, Charles Mulvehill, Harold Becker, Ken Lipper
Screenplay: Ken Lipper and Paul Schrader & Nicholas Pileggi and Bo Goldman
Cinematography (colour): Michael Seresin, Jamie Silverstein
Editor: David Bretherton, Robert C. Jones
Music: Jerry Goldsmith
Production designer: Jane Musky
Cast: Al Pacino (*Mayor John Pappas*), John Cusack (*Deputy Mayor Kevin Calhoun*), Bridget Fonda (*Marybeth Cogan*), Danny Aiello (*Frank Anselmo*), Martin Landau (*Judge Walter Stern*), David Paymer (*Abe Goodman*), Tony Franciosa (*Paul Zapatti*), Richard Schiff (*Larry Schwartz*), Lindsay Duncan (*Sydney Pappas*), Nestor Serrano (*Det. Eddie Santos*), Mel Winkler (*Det. Albert Holly*), and others
111 mins

1999
Bringing Out The Dead

Frank Pierce, a New York ambulance driver who works the graveyard shift, is close to cracking up. We see him over three successive nights with fellow drivers Larry, Marcus and Tom. Frank revives Mr Burke from a heart attack and rushes him to Our Lady of Mercy hospital where he is put on life support. Frank still feels guilt about the death of Rose, a young woman whose ghostly face he sees everywhere. He begins to fall for former drug-user Mary, Mr Burke's daughter, and tries unsuccessfully to get himself fired. With Mary he visits drug dealer Cy: they both take powerful drugs, and Frank experiences macabre hallucinations. Back at the ER, Frank hears the voice of Mr Burke, begging to be allowed to die. Frank is called to help Cy, who has been impaled on a railing by a gang. Frank almost allows Tom to beat up local drug casualty Noel, but repents at the last minute. He returns to the ER and allows Mr Burke to die peacefully. He goes to tell Mary the news; she invites him in and cradles him as he drifts towards sleep.

Director: Martin Scorsese
Production company: De Fina-Cappa / Paramount Pictures / Touchstone Pictures
Producers: Barbara De Fina, Scott Rudin
Co-producers: Eric Steel, Joseph Reidy
Screenplay: Paul Schrader, from the novel by Joe Connelly
Cinematography (colour): Robert Richardson
Editor: Thelma Schoonmaker
Music: Elmer Bernstein
Production designer: Dante Ferretti
Cast: Nicolas Cage (*Frank Pierce*), Patricia Arquette (*Mary Burke*), John Goodman (*Larry Verber*), Ving Rhames (*Marcus*), Tom Sizemore (*Tom Wall*), Marc Anthony (*Noel*), Mary Beth Hurt (*Nurse Constance*), Cliff Curtis (*Cy Coates*), Nestor Serrano (*Dr Hazmat*), Aida Turturro (*Nurse Crupp*), Sonja Sohn (*Kanita*), Cynthia Roman (*Rose*), Afemo Omilami (*Griss*), Cullen Oliver Johnson (*Mr Burke*), Arthur J. Nascarella (*Captain Barney*), and others
121 mins

Index

References to illustrations are in bold. Films directed by Paul Schrader are entered in upper case.